LIFE'S
CHALLENGES
YOUR
OPPORTUNITIES

LIFE'S CHALLENGES YOUR OPPORTUNITIES

JOHN HAGEE

Charisma
HOUSE
A STRANG COMPANY

Most Strang Communications/Charisma House/Christian Life/Excel Books/FrontLine/
Realms/Siloam products are available at special quantity discounts for bulk purchase for sales promo-
tions, premiums, fund-raising, and educational needs. For details, write Strang Communications Book
Group, 600 Rinehart Road, Lake Mary, Florida 32746, or telephone (407) 333-0600.

Life's Challenges—Your Opportunities by John Hagee
Published by Charisma House
A Strang Company
600 Rinehart Road
Lake Mary, Florida 32746
www.strangdirect.com

Unless otherwise noted, all Scripture quotations are from the New King James Version of the Bible.
Copyright © 1979, 1980, 1982 by Thomas Nelson, Inc., publishers. Used by permission.

Scripture quotations marked AMP are from the Amplified Bible. Old Testament copyright © 1965,
1987 by the Zondervan Corporation. The Amplified New Testament copyright © 1954, 1958, 1987 by
the Lockman Foundation. Used by permission.

Scripture quotations marked KJV are from the King James Version of the Bible.

Scripture quotations marked NAS are from the New American Standard Bible. Copyright © 1960, 1962,
1963, 1968, 1971, 1972, 1973, 1975, 1977, 1995 by the Lockman Foundation. Used by permission.
(www.Lockman.org)

Scripture quotations marked NIV are from the Holy Bible, New International Version. Copyright ©
1973, 1978, 1984, International Bible Society. Used by permission.

Scripture quotations marked NLT are from the Holy Bible, New Living Translation, copyright © 1996,
2004. Used by permission of Tyndale House Publishers, Inc., Wheaton, IL 60189. All rights reserved.

Scripture quotations marked TLB are from The Living Bible. Copyright © 1971. Used by permission of
Tyndale House Publishers, Inc., Wheaton, IL 60189. All rights reserved.

Design Director: Bill Johnson
Cover design by Karen Grindley

Library of Congress Cataloging-in-Publication Data

Hagee, John.
  Life challenges-- your opportunities / John Hagee. -- 1st ed.
    p. cm.
  Includes bibliographical references.
  ISBN 978-1-59979-269-9
  1. Problem solving--Religious aspects--Christianity. I. Title.
  BV4599.5.P75H34 2009
  248.8'6--dc22
                                        2008045315

First Edition

09 10 11 12 13 — 987654321

Printed in the United States of America

Contents

Introduction

TRUE CONFESSIONS OF
A PASTOR

T HIS IS A VERY PERSONAL CONFESSION OF A PASTOR WHO HAS survived and prospered in the ministry for more than fifty years. The truths found in this book are the results of the life lessons I have learned in those years. No one wants to hear from a prophet who has no scars.

I have endured many problems in my life. Some have been self-imposed, while other problems have been spiritual or physical attacks from the depths of hell. No matter what the source, God has used these problems to help build character, endurance, and understanding. I have sometimes received God's supernatural promises swiftly, and other promises have taken me months or years to receive because of how I have conducted myself while in the problem.

I believe there is an all-knowing and all-powerful God who created the heavens and the earth and controls the affairs of men.

I believe that every person has a divine destiny, one known only to God since before the world was created…before we breathed our first breath. That divine destiny or purpose is our only path to love, joy, and peace.

I also believe there is a divine principle found in sacred Scripture called "promise, problem, and provision." Simply stated, God begins leading us to our divine destiny by giving us a scriptural promise. The promise is followed by a problem or series of problems, meant to bring us to the level of spiritual maturity whereby we can receive His miracle provision. If we reject His provision, we will miss our divine destiny, and we will live our life without meaning or purpose.

A classic biblical illustration that helps us understand the absolute truth of promise, problem, and provision is found in the example of the children of Israel.

God promised Abraham, Isaac, and Jacob that He would give to them and their descendants a nation whose boundaries are forever specified in Scripture. This Promised Land, a land flowing with milk and honey, would be God's miracle provision.

The Jewish people became a nation in Egypt. God sent Moses as their deliverer and brought about the first Passover, which led them to their exodus out of Pharaoh's bondage.

Then came the problems—at the Red Sea, with the idol crafted by Aaron at Mount Sinai, and at the tent of meeting where two hundred fifty Israelites who rebelled against Moses were buried alive by God in an earthquake. The children of Israel were stuck in the wilderness—their problem—for forty years, when it could have taken only forty days to arrive at their promise. It is while in the problem that God exposes the inner weaknesses preventing His children from reaching their destiny.

Eventually God allowed them to reach the Promised Land, His provision and their divine destiny.

As you explore the spiritual principles in this book, you will discover that it is written simply to help you understand why you have problems and to reveal to you that every problem has a promise that will lead you to God's supernatural provision—your promised land.

The promised land is your land, one flowing with milk and honey, a land of unspeakable abundance. It is a land filled with the favor of God, a land of love, joy, and everlasting peace.

Chapter 1

WHY DO I HAVE ALL THESE PROBLEMS?

Life's Challenges—Your Opportunities will change you and the way you think about problems for the rest of your life. Problems not only happen to bad people; bad problems also happen to good people. Adversity is God's university!

God has given to us more than three thousand precious promises in His Word. Every promise is custom designed in heaven to help us journey through the problems of life and receive the supernatural provision available for each problem we encounter.

Throughout this life-changing book, I will include encouraging testimonies of people just like you and me who encountered major problems, stood upon God's supernatural promises, and received God's perfect provision for their lives. If sorrow makes us shed tears, faith in the promises of God helps us dry them.

I share these real-life stories to bring hope to you as you strive to break through the heartache and crisis you or those you love now face. This is your day to experience God's favor!

It is imperative for God's children to discover the principle for transforming the problems of our lives into the provisions of God. Promise, problem, and provision is a supernatural principle based on the Word of God that will give you wells you did not dig, houses you did not build, and vineyards you didn't plant. It will turn your darkest night to golden day; it will fill your driest desert into streams of living water.

This biblical principle will dramatically improve your marriage and your mental health, expand your business potential, and give you peace beyond measure. *Life's Challenges—Your Opportunities* will light a rocket in your soul and give you the tools to live victoriously forever.

We all detest problems, but problems are the reason for every improvement we make. Problems quicken your wit. Problems stiffen your spine. Problems force you to think outside the box.

A problem is an opportunity to step into a new dimension of accomplishment.

REMEMBER THIS TRUTH...

A problem is not merely an obstacle that makes it difficult to achieve a desired goal; it is a grain of sand in an oyster whose irritation creates a priceless pearl.

EXPECT PROBLEMS!

Problems happen to every member of the human race. Albert Einstein once said, "The only reason for time is so that everything doesn't happen at once." Thank God! Most of us can handle only one problem at a time. However, problems usually do come in pairs; they make no appointments; they do not respect age, nationality, or levels of income; and they usually stay in your life much longer than you want them to.

We must discipline ourselves to anticipate problems because they have a way of showing up when you least expect them.

A small-town prosecuting attorney called his first witness to the stand. Mrs. Ogden, a grandmotherly white-haired woman, sat patiently as the young attorney approached her and asked, "Mrs. Ogden, do you know me?"

His witness confidently responded, "Of course I know you, Mr. Thompson. I have known you since you were a little boy, and quite frankly, you have been a great disappointment to me. You lie at every opportunity, you are disloyal to your wife, you are controlling, and you speak badly of your friends behind their backs. You think you're a bigwig when you haven't the brains to realize that you will never amount to anything more than an insignificant paper-pusher. Yes, I certainly do know you, Mr. Thompson."

The lawyer was both stunned and embarrassed. Not knowing what to do next, he quickly turned and pointed to the defense attorney, who sat wide-eyed in his chair. The prosecutor asked his second question: "Mrs. Ogden, do you know Mr. Stevens?"

Once again, she assertively replied. "Why, yes, I do. I have known Mr. Stevens since he was a young boy as well. I know him to be lazy, bigoted, and a man with a severe drinking problem. He has the worst law practice in the state and has also cheated on his wife with three different women, one of them being your wife. Yes, I know Mr. Stevens quite well indeed."

The defense attorney nearly fainted.

The judge summoned both lawyers to his bench and sternly whispered this harsh warning: "If either one of you imbeciles asks Mrs. Ogden if she knows me, I will send both of you to prison for life!"

Some of the problems we have are self-induced. We don't understand why we are constantly bombarded with troubles, yet we are not walking in obedience to God's Word. Are you faced with a financial setback? Does your money run out before your month does? Are you faced with a health crisis? Is your bad health keeping you from successfully living your life? Is your marriage failing? Have the hopes and dreams of yesterday vaporized under the overwhelming burden of your unhappiness?

REMEMBER THIS TRUTH...

Every problem puts us to this test:
Do we trust God or don't we?

Do you wonder why you seem to go in circles with no end in sight? Have you called upon the Lord and asked Him why you are still in the problem? Have you listened to His voice and obeyed His commandments? You cannot have the peace *of* God until you are at peace *with* God!

Why were the children of Israel in the wilderness for so long?

One reason was murmuring. Murmuring separates us from the peace of God.

The Israelites were in oppression while in Egypt. There came a pharaoh who "knew not Joseph" who became fearful of the children of Israel because of their growing numbers and put "taskmasters over them to afflict them with their burdens." God protected His children during their time of suffering and increased their numbers even greater.

He heard their cry and began His plan of deliverance. He could have redeemed them from their oppression with one mighty blow, but He chose to deliver them through the life and deeds of a man named Moses. God chose the natural to perform the supernatural.

God spoke to Moses and said to him:

> I am the LORD. I appeared to Abraham, to Isaac, and to Jacob, as God Almighty, but by My name LORD I was not known to them. I have also established My covenant with them, to give them the land of Canaan, the land of their pilgrimage, in which they were strangers. And I have also heard the groaning of the children of Israel whom the Egyptians keep in bondage, and I have remembered My covenant. Therefore say to the children of Israel: "I am the LORD; I will bring you out from under the burdens of the Egyptians, I will rescue you from their bondage, and I will redeem you with an outstretched arm and with great judgments. I will take you as My people, and I will be your God. Then you shall know that I am the LORD your God who brings you out from under the burdens of the Egyptians. And I will bring you into the land which I swore to give to Abraham, Isaac, and Jacob; and I will give it to you as a heritage: I am the LORD."
>
> —EXODUS 6:2–8

Now *that*, my friends, is a *promise*! God sent His children a redeemer named Moses and confirmed His promise with Israel. What more could anyone want! Yet there was more. Much more!

The children of Israel witnessed the ten plagues brought by God to the Egyptians. They experienced firsthand His supernatural power as He mercifully led them out of bondage. God knew the character of His people, and He purposely did not send them by way of the shortest route to the Promised Land because they would encounter more opposition. God said, "Lest perhaps the people change their minds when they see war, and return to Egypt" (Exod. 13:17).

Instead, God sent them by way of the Red Sea. When they saw Pharaoh approaching, they lost sight of God's promise, became terrified, and began to murmur and complain, verbally assaulting Moses, the man God sent to them in answer to their prayers: "Because there were no graves in Egypt, have you taken us away to die in the wilderness? Why have you so dealt with us, to bring us up out of Egypt? Is this not the word that we told you in Egypt, saying, 'Let us alone that we may serve the Egyptians'? For it would have been better for us to serve the Egyptians than that we should die in the wilderness" (Exod. 14:11–12).

REMEMBER THIS TRUTH…

Sometimes the quickest way out
of the problem is the toughest.

God, in His faithfulness and true to His promise, parted the Red Sea and led the Israelites through to safety on dry ground on the other side. He then drowned Pharaoh and his mighty army. Imagine it! A man so powerful that he was worshiped as a god on Earth was reduced to fish food!

God personally gave the Jewish people directions through the "pillar of cloud" by day and the "pillar of fire" by night, yet how did they respond when they encountered their next problem?

When the children of Israel came to Marah, the place of bitter waters, they complained against Moses once again: "What shall we drink?" (Exod. 15:24). God heard their cry and used Moses to make the bitter water sweet. But with the provision came His decree: "There He made a statute and an ordinance for them, and there He tested them" (v. 25).

> If you diligently heed the voice of the Lord your God and do what is right in His sight, give ear to His commandments and keep all His statutes, I will put none of the diseases on you which I have brought on the Egyptians. For I am the Lord who heals you.
> —Exodus 15:26

What a promise! He would heal *all* of their diseases! All they had to do was to listen to His voice and obey His statutes, but when they continued their journey in the wilderness and became hungry, they complained all the more. "Oh, that we had died by the hand of the Lord in the land of Egypt, when we sat by the pots of meat and when we ate bread to the full! For you have brought us out into this wilderness to kill this whole assembly with hunger" (Exod. 16:3).

God heard their cry once again and sent quail at twilight and bread from heaven for their daily food supply. The psalmist records that "while their food was still in their mouths," He killed them (Ps. 78:30–31)! The message? Don't complain about God's provision; it may not be what you want, but it's exactly what you need.

Even though the children of Israel were ungrateful, God remained faithful, "for He remembered His holy promise" (Ps. 105:42). He continued to test them to see if they would obey His statutes, but they failed the test. They continued to complain, murmur, and whine.

Do you murmur? Does a problem come your way and instead of asking God to show you why you might be in the problem, do you complain for having one? This is usually what I hear when a church member comes to me with a problem: "Pastor, I don't know why I have this problem. I can't seem to find the answer. I don't feel God has heard my prayer. Where is He when I need Him? Why would God let this happen to me?"

This is what I call the "pity pot" syndrome. I begin to ask questions. Questions like: "Are you reading your Bible?" "Are you refusing to forgive someone in your past?" "Have you allowed the root of bitterness to take hold of your mind and your emotions?" "Are you tithing?" "Are you murmuring, or are you praising God for the problem?"

This is where the air gets thick. We all want answers to our problems, but we are not willing to obey the conditions that bring God's provision. We quickly beg for solutions without using the problem as an opportunity to draw closer to Christ.

We quote the prayer of Jabez: "Oh, that You would bless me indeed, and enlarge my territory..." (1 Chron. 4:10). But we don't bother to read the verse before the prayer: "Now Jabez was more honorable than his brothers" (v. 9). Are you honorable? Do you "diligently obey the voice of the LORD your God, to observe carefully all His commandments" (Deut. 28:1)?

GOD'S CONDITIONS

We readily quote: "My God shall supply all your need according to His riches in glory" (Phil. 4:19). But we seldom acknowledge the circumstances surrounding the promise of which Paul speaks. Paul was speaking to those who had financially supported his work while he was on the mission field. There are conditions to qualifying for God's provision.

God placed two conditions on the children of Israel when He gave them the promise of His continuous healing presence. Those conditions have not changed, and they still apply to us.

First, He asks us to listen for His voice. God speaks to us every day, but we must be willing to hear Him when He speaks. "He speaks in many ways: through His Word, through His anointed servants, and through direct revelation in your inner man (Eph. 1:17, 18)."[1]

Listening is the other half of talking. Listening is a simple task. By inherent nature we are not good listeners. We usually talk more than we listen. Our competitive culture puts value in speaking even when the speaker has nothing to say. God is speaking to us all the time with something important to impart, but His children have a tendency to use the gift of *selective hearing* when listening. In other words, we hear what we want to hear.

A mother can be in a room filled with a hundred people all speaking at the same time, but the moment she hears the voice of her child crying from across the room, she instinctively turns and walks in the direction of the sound of that voice. Why? Because that child is hers, because that mother loves that child, because she is used to the sound of its voice, because of her daily relationship with that child, and because of her desire to please those she loves.

So it is with our relationship with the Lord. He asks us to "heed" His voice, but if we don't have enough of a connection to Him, we won't be able to discern it among the hundreds of voices we hear every day. *Heed* means to, "pay attention to, to listen to, to regard and take notice." It is impossible to do any of these things, much less obey His commands, without first being familiar with the sound of God's voice when He speaks.

God's second condition is He asks us "to do what is right in His sight." He wants us not only to hear His voice but also to obey His commands.

Two young women working in a community hospital decided to quit their jobs. They were tired of dealing with ungrateful, complaining patients, backbiting between employees, and an apathetic administration. Just before quitting, the two friends decided to try an experiment. They had nothing to lose.

They decided to bend over backward for everyone they encountered. So, no matter how someone looked at them or treated them, they overwhelmed people with encouragement, courtesy, and appreciation. Before long, an amazing transformation took place. Patients didn't seem so miserable, staff began to smile at each other, and the administration seemed surprisingly interested in their affairs.

The two women did what was right in God's sight. They loved those who did not love them. They looked through the eyes of God and responded to their problems with supernatural principles that led them out of their wilderness.

The second reason why the children of Israel were in the wilderness for forty years was their rebellion against God.

When the children of Israel "saw that Moses delayed coming down from the mountain, the people gathered together to Aaron, and said to him, 'Come, make us gods that shall go before us; for as for this Moses, the man who brought us up out of the land of Egypt, we do not know what has become of him'" (Exod. 32:1).

They could not see God's appointed leader, so they rejected God's spiritual authority and went their own way. When you reject the man sent from God…you are in fact rejecting God. Bottom line, the Israelites were tired of Pharaoh but refused to follow Moses, God's delegated authority.

This rejection led them into the sin of idolatry. God rules through delegated spiritual authority. All spiritual authority is from your Father in heaven, and to distrust those He has anointed and put in authority is to distrust God. (See Luke 10:16.)

Do you respect the spiritual authority God has put over you? If you don't, severe spiritual and temporal problems will come your way, and they will stay longer than you want them to stay, for God will not send His provision until you follow the lines of spiritual authority He has set in place.

My father, who was a pastor for more than forty years, experienced open rebellion against the kingdom of God and its delegated authority, which brought both swift and severe judgment.

A man and his wife donated a plot of land to my father's church during the Great Depression as the site for a new church. Unfortunately, my trusting father did not contact a lawyer to formally transfer the title of the land into the church's name.

After months of raising funds from his newly formed congregation, and with the huge investment of volunteer labor, a simple white clapboard church was erected. The congregation was thrilled with their new sanctuary.

Within two weeks of the completion of the building, the donors of the real estate demanded the property back and decided to use the building as their new home. My father reminded the deceitful couple that they had given their word to God and to God's delegated authority and warned them that God would deal with them far more severely than a court of law.

Two weeks later an electrical fire burned the new building to the ground, tragically killing the couple as they lay sleeping. That night the two accounted to God for their spiritual rebellion.

A third reason the children of Israel wandered aimlessly in search of the Promised Land was their idolatry.

Once Israel rejected Moses and rebelled against God's mandates, they were open to idol worship. They sought spiritual direction from something other than God. They crafted the statue of the golden calf and began to worship *it* instead of the One True God who had delivered them.

When you reject the promises of the Lord and embrace rebellion, you will soon find yourself worshiping the pleasures of this world instead of desiring God's blessing over your life. Even your own opinions will become your idols. You fear being wrong, so you will not budge from your point of view. This stubborn inflexibility will prevent you from attaining God's provision for your life.

Who is a stubborn person? A stubborn person is one who will not change his or her opinion in the presence of truth even when that truth is the Word of God. Therefore that person's opinions become his or her idols.

Saul is a classic biblical example of idolatry. The prophet Samuel asked Saul, "Why then did you not obey the voice of the LORD?" Saul reveals his tragic character flaws as he attempts to explain away his rebellion. (See 1 Samuel 15:14–21.)

First he claims to have obeyed God's voice: "Blessed are you of the LORD! I have performed the commandment of the LORD" (v. 13). Then Saul blames Israel: "The soldiers brought them from the Amalekites; they spared the best of the sheep and cattle to sacrifice to the LORD your God…" (v. 15, NIV). And in a final attempt to justify himself he once again blames the Israelites: "But I did obey the LORD….I went on the mission the LORD

assigned me....The soldiers took sheep and cattle from the plunder..."
(vv. 20–21, NIV).

When God gave him the opportunity to repent of his rebellion, he tried
to justify it, and Samuel knew it:

> Does the LORD delight in burnt offerings and sacrifices as much
> as in obeying the voice of the LORD? To obey is better than sac-
> rifice, and to heed is better than the fat of rams. For rebellion is
> like the sin of divination, and arrogance like the evil of idolatry.
> Because you have rejected the word of the LORD, he has rejected
> you as king.
> —1 SAMUEL 15:22–23, NIV

Once his impure motives were exposed, Saul wanted to repent (v. 24),
but it was too late (v. 29). In my opinion, two of the worst possible judgments came upon Saul's life. First, God had no use for him (1 Sam. 28:17),
and second, the Spirit of God departed from him (1 Sam. 28:15). I could
not imagine living under either one of those consequences. Saul became a
weak and ineffective king.

REMEMBER THIS TRUTH...

*It is never wrong to do the right thing! The Lord
knows it all—He knows our sins and our motives.
When He asks you why you did not obey Him, He is
looking for a repentant heart, not an excuse for your
rebellion. If you refuse to acknowledge your mistake
at the appointed time, you will go from problem to
problem, never reaching your divine destiny.*

What of the person who *is* obedient? Even after his sin with Bathsheba
and the murder of Uriah, David repented and pleaded with God not to
take away His presence: "Do not cast me away from Your presence, and
do not take Your Holy Spirit from me" (Ps. 51:11). David describes the
promises that come to the person who stays connected to God's delegated authority.

Blessed is the man who walks not in the counsel of the ungodly, nor stands in the path of sinners, nor sits in the seat of the scornful; but his delight is in the law of the LORD, and in His law he meditates day and night. He shall be like a tree planted by the rivers of water, that brings forth its fruit in its season, whose leaf also shall not wither; and whatever he does shall prosper.

—PSALM 1:1–3

The children of Israel could have shortened their time in the wilderness, but they chose the long and difficult path—the path of murmuring, rebellion, and idol worship. The visual teaching tool I use to describe the aimless wandering of the children of Israel is the phrase, "Take another lap around the mountain." It emphasizes the path that makes no progress—a rut that is a grave with both ends kicked out; it is the path that leads to nowhere.

The children of Israel continued to wander in the desert. God was so close to them while they were on their wilderness walk, yet they were far enough away from Him that they failed to recognize His voice. Their conduct in the problem produced murmuring, disobedience, and rebellion. Their conduct prolonged their time in the desert.

REMEMBER THIS TRUTH...

How you conduct yourself in the problem
determines how long you stay in the problem.

WHY SOME PROBLEMS COME

God customizes some of our problems so that we can fulfill the purpose for which we were created. They are stepping-stones to our divine destiny. God knows our very being and potential; it is we who don't recognize the miraculous power we have living within us to accomplish great things. Never forget that the cross you carry was tailor-made by the carpenter's Son.

Moses was driven from the royalty of Egypt by an unexpected problem. In the fires of adversity, the mallet of God transformed him into a divine force that toppled Pharaoh's kingdom and liberated the Jewish people.

It was an unforeseen problem with his brother, Esau, that drove Jacob to Bethel, where God revealed his destiny to him.

It was a frightening problem that confronted Esther when she went before the king and interceded on behalf of the Jewish people living in Persia. Had she ignored the problem, she and her people would have been annihilated off the face of the earth.

It was an overwhelming problem that launched David from an insignificant young shepherd to the mighty king of Israel. All of Israel's forty thousand soldiers heard Goliath's taunting roar demanding a fight, yet only one answered—David. When his brothers saw him running toward Goliath, they thought he was running to his impending death. Instead, he was running to his divine destiny, the throne of Israel.

It is regrettable when we fail to recognize our flaws and weaknesses, but it is tragic to be unaware of our strengths and potentials. Our successes are not measured by the lack of problems. General George Patton believed, "Success is measured by how high you bounce when you've hit bottom."

Hitting bottom is a problem, but staying down is a missed opportunity for greatness. Joseph did not plan to be in the bottom of a pit after he recounted his God-given dream to his loved ones, but he was. Joseph did not foresee his brothers selling him into slavery, but they did. God had destined him for great things, but people and problems got in the way. What did Joseph do?

Joseph was faithful in the problem. He maintained his character and integrity while enduring the problem. He was patient throughout the duration of the problem. He did not complain while facing ridicule, rejection, envy, and jealousy. He held to his dream in the midst of lies, false accusations, and prison. Through it all, God showed favor to Joseph until the provision came.

Joseph had the vision to see the purpose of his problem.

> But now, do not therefore be grieved or angry with yourselves because you sold me here; for God sent me before you to preserve life....And God sent me before you to preserve a posterity for you in the earth, and to save your lives by a great deliverance. So now it was not you who sent me here, but God....But as for you, you

meant evil against me; but God meant it for good, in order to bring
it about as it is this day, to save many people alive.

—GENESIS 45:5, 7–8; 50:20

Even though Joseph spent years in the problem, he never stopped listening to the voice of God. He remained faithful to God, and God remained faithful to Joseph, leading him to the divine purpose for which he was created.

Are you in the middle of a severe problem? Have you gone through your spiritual checklist to make sure that you are not the cause of the problem? Do you find it difficult to find the purpose of the predicament you are in? Look for the promise in God's Word. Hold on to that promise. It is given to you by your Father in heaven, who is faithful to fulfill it. All of the provisions God offers in the pantry of heaven are available to the child of God who faithfully stands on His promises.

By which have been given to us exceedingly great and precious
promises, that through these you may be partakers of the divine nature, having escaped the corruption that is in the world
through lust.

—2 PETER 1:4

Sing praises to Lord while in the bleak times of your life, for He promises to inhabit the praises of His people. Remember the teakettle—it sings its sweetest song when it is up to its neck in hot water. When there is no reason to smile, put a smile on your face, and God will give you every reason to smile.[2] God will never let you walk alone in your darkest hour; He will journey with you until you see the light of your provision.

Have you had setbacks and disappointments as a result of the problems you have experienced? There is life after failure. Your endurance of the problem breeds success. Winston Churchill said, "Success is the ability to go from failure to failure without losing your enthusiasm."

Success is a path…often the path less traveled…a path perpetually under construction, frequently filled with detours and obstacles.

The famous basketball player Michael Jordan, when asked about his success, put it in perspective when he answered, "I've missed more than nine thousand shots in my career....I've lost almost three hundred games. Twenty-six times I've been trusted to take the winning shot and missed. I've failed over and over and over again in my life. And that is why I succeed."[3]

REMEMBER THIS TRUTH...

Trouble does not develop character; trouble reveals character.

You must see your problems as merely obstacles on the path to victory.

Some problems happen to us that seem to have no purpose whatsoever. Trouble comes not because of something we have done or not done; sometimes trouble simply comes: "I am not at ease, nor am I quiet; I have no rest, for trouble comes" (Job 3:26).

When these kinds of problems befall us, the natural eye cannot comprehend any valuable meaning to them. Think of Paul and his "thorn in the flesh":

> And lest I should be exalted above measure by the abundance of the revelations, a thorn in the flesh was given to me, a messenger of Satan to buffet me, lest I be exalted above measure.
> —2 CORINTHIANS 12:7

No one knows what Paul's "thorn" was, but scholars are certain it was an affliction. Paul identifies the source as Satan, and even though he pleads with God three times to remove it, God sees fit not to. What does Paul do?

He thanks God for his affliction. He takes pleasure in "infirmities, in reproaches, in needs, in persecution, in distresses for Christ's sake" (v. 10).

Not many bat in that league; I certainly don't! Charles Haddon Spurgeon describes these kinds of individuals as "masterworks of God."

> They stand in the midst of difficulties steadfast and immovable. Those that glorify God must be prepared to meet with many trials. No one can be illustrious before the Lord unless their conflicts are many. If yours is a much tried path then rejoice in it, because you will be better able to display the all-sufficient grace of

God. As for His failing you, never dream of it—hate the thought. The God that has been sufficient until now should be trusted to the end.[4]

The Holocaust was an enormous transgression against the Jewish people. Its horrors are beyond description, yet there were survivors who, in the midst of atrocious conditions, saw the light of God in their darkest hour. Imre Kertesz was one such person.

I experienced my most radical moments of happiness in the concentration camp. You cannot imagine what it's like to be allowed to lie in the camp's hospital, or to have a 10-minute break from indescribable labor. To be very close to death is also a kind of happiness. Just surviving becomes the greatest freedom of all.[5]

Another found hope in the midst of his problem. When Tristan Bernard was arrested with his wife by the Gestapo, he told her, "The time of fear is over. Now comes the time of hope."[6]

To the end that my glory may sing praise to You and not be silent. O LORD my God, I will give thanks to You forever.

—PSALM 30:12

One of my dear friends in the ministry is David Ring. I have known David for more than fifteen years, and never have I heard this man of God, who is stricken with cerebral palsy, complain about living his life against all odds. Allow me to share his heart-compelling testimony.

David Ring was born on October 28, 1953, in Jonesboro, Arkansas. Due to complications at birth, David was deprived of oxygen to the brain for the first eighteen minutes of his life. Believing him stillborn, the nurses laid his lifeless body on a table against the wall and attended to David's mother who was fighting for her life.

"The baby is dead anyway. We have to save the mom!" they thought. Even though they believed the newborn was lost, God had other plans. Eighteen minutes after birth God breathed life into David's body. It isn't over until God says that it's over! God had other plans for David Ring!

The lack of oxygen to the brain left David with cerebral palsy. This birth defect permanently affected his fine and gross motor skills as well as his speech.

David's dad, Oscar Newton Ring, had been a Baptist preacher throughout Northeast Arkansas for more than forty years. In order to provide for his family, Oscar also had a second profession as a farmer. In 1945, he was involved in an accident at the cotton gin, which severed his right arm below the elbow. Tragedy was not uncommon within the Ring family. Oscar and his wife, Leron, lost three babies at birth or within days of their birth. Four daughters and four sons lived to adulthood.

Their daughters were healthy, but the boys were all health impaired. David's three brothers were born with hemophilia. They had to receive frequent blood transfusions; as a result, all three died in their fifties of AIDS.

Making life worse, because of the overwhelming pressure on their marriage, Oscar and Leron divorced in 1962 when David was only nine years old. In November 1964, David's dad died of liver cancer.

Because of the cerebral palsy, David depended on his mother for everything. As he frequently shares in his testimony with a boyish grin:

> I was the baby of the family and when I came along they spoiled me rotten. I'm a spoiled rotten brat and I love every minute of it. My momma gave me everything that I wanted and she even gave me things that I didn't want! And I'm not only the baby of the family but I am a number one momma's baby boy. You can tell that I am a momma's baby boy because I have a momma baby face.

David loved his mother very deeply. He often refers to his momma as his "cheerleader" in life. In fact, she served as much more than David's cheerleader in those early years. She was his beloved mother, his helper, his spokeswoman, and his protector. She did everything for him and was honored to do so!

Then, when he was fourteen years old, his "cheerleader" got sick. She went into the hospital for surgery the day before Mother's Day in 1968. Shortly thereafter, the doctor told David's family that their mom would never come home again because she had cancer throughout her body and only a short time to live.

The news devastated David because he couldn't fathom that his mom would abandon him like that. She was the only one who loved him just as he was, and it was hard for David to comprehend living even one day without her.

He began to pray, "God, please don't take my momma, please don't take my momma. God, don't take momma, please." He watched her go from 185 pounds to 57 pounds, and in October 1968, the strongest force in this fragile little boy's life took her last breath. It was a very lonely day in the life of David Ring.

When David lost his mother, he lost all hope and trust in everything. He was so lonely that he wanted to die. Over the next two years, he was cast about from family member to family member with nowhere to call home. He endured physical pain, humiliating public ridicule, and constant discouragement.

David, to this day, remembers so vividly everyone laughing at his speech and the limp in his walk. He has told audiences hundreds of times as he is delivering his life's story, "It isn't any fun to be made fun of. Can you imagine every time that you open your mouth to speak, someone calls you every name other than your own?" Life was almost impossible for him to bear.

David continued losing hope in everyone and everything—especially God. He believed that God had let him down and had forgotten about him. Out of absolute desperation, David went to a church revival on a Thursday evening in April 1970.

He went into the church that night expecting one thing and left experiencing something entirely different. It was then that David found the joy and hope he had been searching for by accepting Christ into his heart. God was no longer *a religion* to David; he now had a personal *relationship* with Him.

In the face of seemingly insurmountable obstacles, David miraculously emerged that night not victimized but victorious! Life was worse than hopeless to him until his relationship began with Jesus Christ, who taught him self-respect and acceptance of his condition.

To most, physical challenges of this magnitude would prove to be a tombstone. For David Ring, this spiritual coming of age was and remains a supernatural milestone. God had great plans for David Ring!

After David accepted Christ into his heart, there was a tremendous transformation in David's attitude, and he reaped the positive results of that incredible change. The student body of his high school voted him the most popular student, Mr. School Spirit, and vice president of his class. He was manager of the year in football, basketball, and track during his senior year! After graduation, David attended college and received a bachelor of arts degree in religion and sociology from William Jewell College in Liberty, Missouri.

In 1971, before his freshman year of college, David answered the call to preach. He preached every weekend while attending school, and two years later he dedicated himself to full-time evangelism.

David began to minister with his life's story. Although difficult to understand at first, his audience was captured by his quick wit, warm personality, and genuine sincerity. Whether giving his inspirational testimony in churches or presenting a motivational speech at sales conventions, David always focuses on an individual's need to conquer the personal challenges and adversities of life.

Whoever his audience may be, they find themselves either laughing or crying while listening to David's life story. They are amazed at his triumph over insurmountable odds. They are also confronted to consider their own lives. To anyone who has not been hindered by physical limitations, David clearly asks this thought-provoking question: "I have cerebral palsy.... What's *your* problem?"

During those early days, nearly everyone tried to discourage David. He was even rejected by an esteemed seminary because of his cerebral palsy. He was disappointed at first. However, he soon realized the faithfulness of God to a degree he had never experienced before. God had great plans for David Ring.

A nationally known speaker since 1973, David shares his story with over a hundred thousand people each year at churches, conventions, schools, and corporate events. He has spoken in more than six thousand venues since he entered evangelism.

David was even dispirited by his siblings who told him daily that he would never find a wife. They reminded him that no woman in her right mind could love him the way a woman should love a man. However, God had a wonderful provision in store for him!

While conducting a revival in St. Charles, Missouri, he met a beautiful eighteen-year-old girl who would become his wife. David and Karen were united in marriage two years later on September 5, 1981. The faithfulness of God is so real to them. They have been married for over twenty-six years. It isn't over until God says it's over. God had a powerful plan for David's life from the very beginning.

David was also informed by his doctors that he would never have children. However, Karen got pregnant just three weeks after they got married. David will never forget receiving a phone call from Karen on that beautiful fall October afternoon. She told him that day she had gone to the doctor, and he confirmed that she was pregnant. God had miraculously provided once again! They are now the proud parents of four happy and healthy children: April, Ashley, Nathan, and Amy Joy. April is married, and David and Karen will soon be first-time grandparents.

There were many preachers who told him he wouldn't succeed in evangelism. It has been thirty-five years since then, and he is going stronger than ever. The absolute truth is that all things are possible with God. Today, David speaks about two hundred times each year, but receives over three hundred invitations to preach. He has also been featured on several nationally televised programs.

Most recently, he was a guest on Dr. Dobson's *Focus on the Family* daily radio broadcast. Dr. Dobson shared with David that when they broadcast those particular programs, there were around two hundred twenty million listeners who heard his life's story each day.

More than ever, David believes he may have died for eighteen minutes; however, he was reborn to serve his Lord. What the devil meant for evil, God meant for good. Cerebral palsy isn't at all a handicap or a disability to David; it is an opportunity to win souls for Christ.

He could have allowed his affliction to deter or hinder him in some way if he chose to. Instead, he chooses every morning to use cerebral palsy as his platform to share with his audiences that there is hope for everyone, no matter how hopeless the situation.

David believes as Paul the apostle did in Philippians 1:12: "The things which happened unto me have fallen out rather unto furtherance of the gospel" (KJV). It doesn't matter what an individual is going through in their life, there is always hope in Christ.

He challenges people throughout this country to quit going to a self-pity party, because no one shows up but them. David believes that it is time to get out of the stands and start serving God in their churches and communities. David often states that if God can use him, then He can use anyone.

God had other plans for David Ring!

I am reminded of Paul's words in Romans 8:35, 37:

> Who can separate us from the love of Christ? Shall tribulation, or distress, or persecution, or famine, or nakedness, or peril, or sword?...Yet in all these things we are more than conquerors through Him who loved us.

Expect problems, but don't allow these obstacles to separate you from God's promises on the road to His supernatural plans and provision for your life.

On November 8, 1970, there was a hard-fought game between the New Orleans Saints and the Detroit Lions. The game was nip and tuck, and it came down to the game's last final seconds to see who would win.

The crowd gasped as they realized that the Saints were going to try a field goal of sixty-three yards. To try something that had never been done in the history of man would take a Goliath of a person. The crowd looked for a man with a size 45 shoe and a chest as big as the back of a Mack truck.

REMEMBER THIS TRUTH...

Not all adversity will produce defeat.

But instead they saw a man run out onto the field who had no fingers on his right hand, no toes on his right foot, and only half of his kicking foot.

When Tom Dempsey kicked that ball and made that field goal, he made history for professional football and set a new world record!

The beautiful thought about Tom Dempsey is not that he won a football game in the last seconds of the game, but that he saw an obstacle and refused to be handicapped by it![7]

Some of the world's greatest men and women have encountered disabilities and adversities, yet they have overcome these obstacles and used them as stepping-stones to their divine destiny.

Cripple a woman, and you have Joni Eareckson Tada. Lock a man in prison, and you have Joseph, Daniel, or the apostle Paul. Bury him in the snows of Valley Forge, and you have George Washington. Deafen a genius composer, and you have Ludwig van Beethoven. Have them born black in a society filled with racial discrimination, and you have Booker T. Washington, George Washington Carver, and Martin Luther King Jr. Have him born of parents who survived a Nazi concentration camp, paralyze him from the waist down when he is four, and you have Yitzhak Perlman, the incomparable concert violinist. Call him a slow learner and write him off as mentally disabled, and you have Albert Einstein.[8]

Christ did not come to do away with suffering:

> Though He was a Son, yet He learned obedience by the things which He suffered. And having been perfected, He became the author of eternal salvation to all who obey Him.
>
> —Hebrews 5:8–9

He did not come to explain difficulty:

> Remember now your Creator in the days of your youth, before the difficult days come.
>
> —Ecclesiastes 12:1

He came to fill agony with His presence:

> And being in agony, He prayed more earnestly.
>
> —Luke 22:44

> Now to Him who is able to keep you from stumbling, and to present you faultless before the presence of His glory with exceeding joy.
>
> —Jude 24

Chapter 2

EVERY PROBLEM HAS
A PURPOSE

No one ever gets beyond the reach of problems. God even promises us problems: "Many are the afflictions of the righteous..." The good news is that He also promises His provision: "...but the Lord delivers him out of them all" (Ps. 34:19).

Every problem you face has a purpose. Problems have made you what you are. They are the reason for every improvement you've ever made. Problems either force you to go to the next level of spiritual or personal accomplishment, or they cause you to choose to stay in the squalor of Egypt or the land of Lodebar. The choice is *yours*!

A problem is like a nagging toothache. It is a warning sign that something is not right, and, like a toothache, it should force you to take action. Sadly, however, I have seen many toothless Christians trying to get by in life. They refuse to attack the problem. In order to get beyond the problem to the provision, you must recognize the purpose of the problem, take action to solve it, and take possession of your provision.

I am sure that some of the children of Israel were satisfied with the status quo of Egypt. Their complacency led them to believe they could exist with the status quo.

God had other plans. He wanted them to go to the Promised Land, their inheritance—the place of His provision. Yet while some were complacent, others were listening to God's voice, waiting for a sign that would lead them out of their misery and to their divine destiny.

Are you less than happy? Are you listening for the voice of God? Are you asking Him to reveal His purpose for your problem? Are you ready to take action on what He asks of you and to claim and proclaim your provision? Or are you complacent and satisfied to live in the oppression of your crisis for the rest of your life?

God refers to *hearing* and *obeying* throughout the Bible. In Jeremiah 7:23, the Lord says, "Obey My voice, and I will be your God, and you shall be My people." In John 10:27, Jesus teaches, "My sheep hear My voice, and I know them, and they follow Me."

The question now arises, How do I hear His voice? Mark 4:23 speaks of *what we hear* when Jesus says, "If anyone has ears to hear, let him hear."

For every divine sound, Satan has a deceptive counter-sound designed to destroy you. A baby loves to shake a plastic toy rattle in his tiny hand. Yet the sound of that harmless rattle is virtually identical to the rattling of a vicious and poisonous snake, coiled and ready to strike. One brings joy, and the other brings certain death.

It is possible for the spirit man to hear from three different sources:

1. The Holy Spirit
2. Your carnal flesh
3. A demon spirit

It's critical to be certain that what you hear can be verified by the Word of God while you are working your way through the problem.

REMEMBER THIS TRUTH...

Do not go by your feelings, your emotions, or the majority vote of your prayer group. Go by the yea and amen of the Word of God.

We are not born with the ability to hear God's voice. We learn to hear God's voice through the aid of the Holy Spirit, who lives within the believer.

Jesus reinforces our need to be careful to discern what we hear by saying:

> Take heed what you hear. With the same measure you use, it will
> be measured to you; and to you who hear, more will be given. For

whoever has, to him more will be given; but whoever does not have,
even what he has will be taken away from him.

—MARK 4:24–25

There are three major principles in these verses.

1. We need the ability to hear God's voice: "If anyone has ears,
   let him hear."
2. We must hear the right things: "…to you who hear, more
   will be given."
3. We see the result of hearing incorrectly: "…whoever does
   not have [or hear], even what he has will be taken away."

The basic message of Jesus's teaching is that believers will become spiritually bankrupt if they refuse to hear God's voice and listen instead to
evil, or to gossip and negative speech. The more we listen to these negative
forces, the more we become separated from the provision of God.

The Word of God contains specific *hearing tests*. Job 12:11 states, "Does
not the ear test words and the mouth taste its food?" If you put something
in your mouth that tastes bitter or rancid, you spit it out for fear it will
bring you harm. Are you as careful to reject words you hear that do not
glorify God or that hurt other people or bring destruction to your faith?
You should be, for God wants you to hear only good things.

Another important *hearing principle* is found in Romans 10:17: "So then
faith comes by hearing, and hearing by the word of God."

Faith comes. If faith comes, it also goes. Have you ever felt that you just
did not have enough faith to fill even a tenth of a mustard seed? I have. In fact,
most believers have. What do you do in those moments? You reconnect to the
faith source, which is the Word of God. A Chassidic master by the name of
Rabbi Moshe of Sambur said, "The Torah [the Word of God] is what God
gave to man. It is the God-given method whereby we can bond with Him."[1]

One way I reconnect with my faith is to listen to the Scriptures in my
home, my office, and my car. I allow my ears to hear God's encouraging
promises over and over again. It is impossible for Satan, the father of lies
and the great accuser, to penetrate the sacred atmosphere that is created by
the Word of God. He is forced to flee from my mind and thoughts.

When I need peace in my life, I listen to the words of Isaiah: "You will keep him in perfect peace, whose mind is stayed on You, because he trusts in You" (Isa. 26:3). If I am fearful, I go to the words of David in Psalm 27:14, which says: "Wait on the LORD; be of good courage, and He shall strengthen your heart." When I need healing, I hearken to the words of Jeremiah 17:14: "Heal me, O LORD, and I shall be healed; save me, and I shall be saved, for You are my praise."

When you hear the words of the Lord, you must learn to believe in them. He expects us to believe them, for His Word is truth: "As for God, His way is perfect; the word of the LORD is proven; He is a shield to all who trust in Him" (Ps. 18:30).

PROBLEMS CAUSE US TO TRUST IN GOD

Esther was in a problem. There was a major plot in the Persian Empire to annihilate the Jewish people, and she was chosen by God to intervene on their behalf. Easy enough, she was the queen of Persia. Not so!

If she chose to go before the king unannounced, she could be killed immediately. If she chose to remain silent, death would soon come, for she was Jewish. She had to trust God. She took action and called for fasting and prayer to set her plan in motion, knowing full well the possible consequences: "And so I will go to the king, which is against the law; and if I perish, I perish!" (Esther 4:16).

God prevailed. He places people in high positions to advance His purposes, and He rewards acts of righteousness openly in due time.[2]

Do you trust God through the problem? You must do all in your power to get through the problem, and then you leave the rest to God.

REMEMBER THIS TRUTH...

It is distrust of God to be troubled with what is to come.
Impatience against God, to be troubled with what is present,
and anger with God, to be troubled with what is past.[3]

You may find yourself in a major financial problem during the present mortgage crisis. Economic times are tough. Food and gas prices are soaring, but your income may not be. You may be having difficulty meeting your monthly bills. You are in a problem. So were Sandy and Scott at one time.

Sandy and Scott married while Scott was still in medical school. Soon after graduation, Scott was accepted into a residency program in Denver, Colorado. Disappointed to leave family, friends, and Cornerstone Church, they were determined to make their stay in Colorado a good one.

Between rotations and study, Scott was away for long hours at the hospital, and Sandy worked as a dental hygienist to supplement the small income of a resident. Shortly after their arrival in the city, they decided to buy a home in a quaint Denver suburb near the hospital and to start a family.

Soon after their purchase, they were expecting their first child. Sandy continued working after their daughter's birth. They found a great church, and Scott continued his strenuous hospital schedule. They were living a good life, and within a short time, their lives were in countdown mode as Scott's residency program neared a close. Sandy and Scott began to prepare for their move back to San Antonio, so they put their home on the market.

The economy in Denver was in a recession, and many of the lovely, historical homes in their neighborhood were in foreclosure. Sandy and Scott had no choice but to leave their home with a "For Sale" sign in the front lawn. They returned to San Antonio and prayed they would not fall into the same financial pit their neighbors were in.

After returning to San Antonio, Scott found a great position with a well-established medical firm, and Sandy was able to stay home with her little girl. Soon a son was added to the family.

They were forced to lease a home in San Antonio because their home in Denver was still on the market after nearly thirty months. The Denver economy was still in a lurch, and nothing was moving in the market other than foreclosures. Even though Scott had a good income, they were desperately trying to make ends meet due to two house payments, his medical school loans, and the everyday expenditures of family life. They waited on God to provide an answer to their problem.

I constantly marvel to see the way the Lord works in all of our lives. Every Monday morning after a demanding Sunday, I kneel at my prayer chair with the same request: "Father, what would You have me prepare for Your sheep for next Sunday?" Sometimes He answers me immediately, and other times not. Sometimes I have my hearing ears on, and other times not. But somehow, because of His faithfulness, He leads me through His Word, and a sermon is born.

Every Sunday morning, before I deliver my sermon, I pray with the elders of the church that my sheep will receive what they need for their lives. And every Sunday morning I do my best, and I leave the rest to God who promises that His Word will never return void. Then I step back and witness His miraculous work.

The Sunday came when Scott and Sandy would hear from God about the problem they were experiencing. This was the Sunday they would cling to God's promises, go through their spiritual checklist, and wait in wonder for their provision.

Scott and Sandy had tried everything. On this particular Sunday, they sat in church as they had done all the others, waiting to hear from God as to how to solve their problem. As they heard part one of my series titled "Promise, Problem, Provision," they identified with its precept—they were in a problem, all right—that part was easy...now what?

Later they accused me of what many of my church members accuse me of: "You were preaching right to me! It was as if you were in our living room! How did you know?" Little did they realize that I didn't know! I only listened and obeyed, something I try to do as often as possible. They wanted me to tell them what the second part of the series would teach, and I smiled, thinking to myself, "I don't know yet."

The second part of the series taught of the promises of God's Word and how we all benefit from these promises. The next part spoke of "going around the mountain" like the children of Israel. They were close to the Promised Land in distance, but miles away in their hearts and way of thinking.

Scott and Sandy looked at each other and simultaneously agreed, "We've been going around the mountain for thirty months." Enough was enough. They longed for God's provision.

They went home and began going through their spiritual checklist. "We serve in the choir...we volunteer with various ministries...we are in church every Sunday...and we give." They thought for a moment and then looked at each other as they realized that although they had continued to give—they were not tithing due to their lack of finances. They had rationalized that they could not make ends meet if they tithed on the whole of their income, yet they realized that by withholding the tithe, they had not trusted God to supply their needs.

The Lord has a promise in His Word regarding tithing:

> "Bring all the tithes into the storehouse, that there may be food in My house, and try Me now in this," says the LORD of hosts, "if I will not open for you the windows of heaven and pour out for you such blessing that there will not be room enough to receive it. And I will rebuke the devourer for your sakes, so that he will not destroy the fruit of your ground, nor shall the vine fail to bear fruit for you in the field."
> —MALACHI 3:10–11

Deuteronomy 28:2 promises that if we obey God's commandments, then "all these blessings shall come upon you and overtake you, because you obey the voice of the LORD your God." What an electrifying promise!

REMEMBER THIS TRUTH…

The God who created heaven and Earth… the God who breathed life into man… the God who parted the Red Sea for Moses and killed the giant for David… will cause His blessings to overtake us! This means that as long as you listen to His voice and do what He commands, you can't help but be blessed.

Scott and Sandy repented of their lack of trust in God and vowed to begin tithing on all their income, awaiting His sure provision. They went to the Scriptures and began to list God's promises over their problem:

> [Most] blessed is the man who believes in, trusts in, and relies on the Lord, and whose hope and confidence the Lord is.
> —JEREMIAH 17:7, AMP

> Delight yourself also in the Lord, and He will give you the desires and secret petitions of your heart.
> —PSALM 37:4, AMP

For the Lord God is a Sun and Shield; the Lord bestows [present] grace and favor and [future] glory (honor, splendor, and heavenly bliss)! No good thing will He withhold from those who walk uprightly.

—PSALM 84:11, AMP

Your Father knows what you need before you ask Him.

—MATTHEW 6:8, AMP

And my God will liberally supply (fill to the full) your every need according to His riches in glory in Christ Jesus.

—PHILIPPIANS 4:19, AMP

Beloved, I pray that you may prosper in every way and [that your body] may keep well, even as [I know] your soul keeps well and prospers.

—3 JOHN 2, AMP

Bring all the tithes (the whole tenth of your income) into the storehouse, that there may be food in My house, and prove Me now by it, says the Lord of hosts, if I will not open the windows of heaven for you and pour you out a blessing, that there shall not be room enough to receive it.

—MALACHI 3:10, AMP

The plan was set. They stood on God's promises daily. They began to tithe on their gross income and waited faithfully for God to provide.

Soon after they implemented their plan, Sandy and Scott received an offer on their home, but it was $25,000 less than what they owed, and they did not have the money to pay the balance on their note. They knew that foreclosure was not the answer, so they continued to wait on God.

Early one morning, Sandy received a phone call from a close friend and prayer partner. She suggested that Scott and Sandy write a letter to the bank that held their note and explain their situation to see if the bank could find a solution for their problem. They wrote the letter and waited. They were soon contacted by the bank's financial review board with a request to examine all their finances.

They submitted their expenditures to the last dime and waited for the head of the review board to contact them. He met with Scott and Sandy and informed them that he had a major question about their finances—related to their tithe. He told them that if they did not tithe they would be in better financial shape. Therefore he could not understand why it was part of their budgeted expenditures.

Sandy and Scott informed the examiner that their tithe was an investment and not an expenditure. Their giving was part of their commitment to the Lord in obedience to His Word, and that would not change.

Unhappy with their response, the bank official told them that he would not vote favorably on their request. Regardless, Sandy and Scott knew they had made the right choice and waited for the official evaluation.

On the day of the review, they prayed and stood on the promises of God. They asked for God's supernatural favor just as they had prayed many times before. But this time was different. This time they believed in His promises and knew He would provide an answer to their problem. They waited in anticipation of God's miracle provision.

The phone call came. A new voice was at the end of the phone. He introduced himself as the interim chair of the review board. The man they had been dealing with had suddenly become ill and was not able to attend the meeting. The interim chairman presented the decision of the review board. The bank offered to accept the purchase offer and would forgive $15,000 of their payoff to the bank, due to the devaluation of their home's value. In addition, the bank would allow them to pay the remainder of the $10,000 in the form of a five-year/no-interest note. Scott remained silent as he heard the question, "Would that be acceptable to you and your wife?"

Yes! Of course, they would accept the offer! They were on their way out of the problem. God had provided. His promises were manifested. They stayed faithful, and so did He. He "caused His blessings to overtake them."

Scott and Sandy have never looked back. The promises of God have given them hope, and His provisions have always prevailed.

PROBLEMS FORCE US TO PRAY

Another purpose for our problems is to force us to pray. We cannot solve all of our problems alone, but with God nothing is impossible.

Solomon acknowledged the importance of God's help when dealing with the challenges of life:

> Now, O Lord my God, You have made Your servant king instead of David my father, and I am but a lad [in wisdom and experience]; I know not how to go out (begin) or come in (finish). Your servant is in the midst of Your people whom You have chosen, a great people who cannot be counted for multitude. So give Your servant an understanding mind and a hearing heart to judge Your people, that I may discern between good and bad. For who is able to judge and rule this Your great people?
>
> —1 KINGS 3:7–9, AMP

If God's Word is the God-given method for man to bond with Him, then prayer is what man gives to God. It is the means whereby we can bind Him to us.[4]

In Hebrew, the term "to pray" is *l'hitpallel'*, which literally means, "to judge one's self." Therefore, when we pray, we are giving an accounting for our lives.[5]

REMEMBER THIS TRUTH...

A man on his knees can see more and further into the future than a man on a mountaintop. Problems force us to pray with an intensity that causes God to incline His ear toward our cry.

The challenge is that when we are in the problem, we usually try to paint ourselves in the best light possible. We conform to the world and hide behind the *no-blame* philosophy of our society. So we talk to God as if we are guiltless, a victim of some offense that provoked us to do what we did to cause our problem.

It's time to fess up! God knows the truth. We can't explain away our character flaws—He is familiar with every single one of them.

Some believe that the purpose of prayer is to ask God to run our errands and fix our mistakes, while secretly hoping that two plus two won't equal four. God is not your getaway car!

One person felt that prayer was asking "God to grant our wishes—sort of like downloading miracles and blessings."[6] Miracles and blessings are a by-product of prayer but not the reason for it.

REMEMBER THIS TRUTH...

It is far better to desire God because of who He is than to want God for what He can do.

When God answers prayer, it is not because He believes our side of the story or because He is manipulated by our whining, desperation, and pleading. He answers because we are transformed through prayer into a higher and more intimate relationship with Him.

Prayer is a miracle; it is the ability to talk to God! Yet so many people believe that they don't know how to pray.

My hope is that the following truths about prayer will help you learn to live in the rarified air of the supernatural on a daily basis and become so acquainted with the voice of God that you miss Him when He is silent.

Prayer Truths

1. *Pray simply and directly*, for He takes pleasure in our sincerity (Isa. 33:15, nas).
2. *Pray audibly and in alignment with His Word.* The utterance of God's Word helps to activate your faith. The Word of God is your blueprint for life, the architectural plan for your divine destiny (Deut. 5:5).
3. *Be honest.* Don't ask for something you really don't want or promise to do something you can't or won't do. Don't keep anything back! Remember, God knows your heart (1 Sam. 1:10–18).
4. *Pray passionately.* Your supplication need not be loud, but your desire should be intense. It is the "effective, fervent prayer of a righteous man" that "avails much" (James 5:16).
5. *Don't mock God.* Do not ask God to do for you what He has

already mandated for you to do for yourself. Continuing to pray about what God has already told you to do is rebellion against the known will of God (James 1:7–8).

6.   *Pray believing.* Know that God is never far from the person who seeks Him. Have faith that His promises are true and that they apply to you (Mark 11:24).

7.   *Pray without ceasing.* The door to prayer is always open; you should take full advantage of walking through that sacred gate often (Luke 6:12).

8.   *Pray with thanksgiving.* It is the spirit of thanksgiving that makes your prayer supernatural. Saint Paul said, "In everything by prayer and supplication, with thanksgiving, let your requests be made known to God" (Phil. 4:6).

Paul continues to teach us about the commands of Scripture, which includes thanksgiving:

> See that no one renders evil for evil for anyone, but always pursue what is good both for yourselves and for all. Rejoice always, pray without ceasing, in everything give thanks; for this is the will of God in Christ Jesus for you.
> —1 THESSALONIANS 5:15–18

When Jesus prayed for God to raise Lazarus from the dead, He prayed saying, "Father, I thank You that You have heard Me....Lazarus, come forth!" (John 11:41, 43).

REMEMBER THIS TRUTH...

Prayer is not demanding, "Listen, Lord, for Your child speaketh." It should be, "Speak, Lord, for your servant heareth."

When Jonah was delivered from the belly of the great fish, it was the spirit of thanksgiving in prayer that released him from certain death.

God promises to be where thanksgiving and praise to Him are offered:

But You are holy, O You Who dwell in [the holy place where] the
praises of Israel [are offered].

—PSALM 22:3, AMP

PROBLEMS ARE TESTS

God also uses problems to test our character. Within the pages of the Word
of God we find a purpose for everything under the sun, even tests. When
God spoke to His children in Deuteronomy 30:19, He presented them with
a multiple-choice test: "I have set before you life and death, blessing and
cursing; therefore choose life, that both you and your descendants may live."

He tested them in the wilderness. Why? The answer is in verses 19
and 20:

> ...that both you and your descendants may live; that you may love
> the LORD your God, that you may obey His voice, and that you
> may cling to Him, for He is your life and the length of your days;
> and that you may dwell in the land which the LORD swore to your
> fathers, to Abraham, Isaac, and Jacob, to give them.

He tests us so that as we hear His voice and obey His commandments,
we will be blessed beyond measure.

It is easy to obey God when everything is going grand—when the bills
are paid, the kids are healthy, and your marriage is great. But what about
obeying God's voice when you are in the middle of the most severe problem
of your life?

When I get into a problem I want to do something. I want to fix it! I
want to take action *now*! But God knows me, and because He wants to
build my character, He usually asks me to wait. I hate to wait! He wants
me to be still and listen for His voice and have patience. I don't *do* patience.
It is not one of my virtues.

I want to charge through the problem and blow it to smithereens! As
you can well imagine, sometimes I pass the test, and sometimes I fail.

You, on the other hand, may be of the temperament that does not like to
take action. You prefer to wait. Guess what? God wants you to get off your
blessed assurance and do something! He wants to build your character in a
different way than He chooses to build mine.

Every one of us has our own instruction manual, we all have unique personalities, *and* we all have our own tests. We may not like the way we are tested, but God chooses the test, and He is the one who issues the final grade.

No one likes to be tested, and no one likes to take the same test over and over again.

Delia and Andy fell in love soon after they met, and following a short courtship, they married in 1953. Within a year of their marriage, they were expecting their first child, and the next three children followed within six years.

REMEMBER THIS TRUTH...

The only way we can avoid taking a test the second time is to pass it the first time around.

Andy and Delia were devoted parents. Delia was a dedicated mother and supportive wife, and Andy a loving father and diligent provider. Even though Andy worked twelve hours a day, the money always seemed to run out by Wednesday. Delia and Andy persuaded the local grocer to allow them to buy the necessary provisions for their family on credit, and every Saturday morning Andy would faithfully take his weekly earnings and pay his account in full.

The couple believed they could not give their entire tithe and still have sufficiency for their needs. Yet every week they somehow managed to give at least $5 of their $7.50 tithe. No matter how hard they worked, they still needed more income to provide for their growing family, so Andy and Delia knew they had to step out in faith in order to get out of their problem.

I remember Delia's testimony. "Pastor, Andy and I knew that the Lord promised to 'supply all our needs according to His riches in glory,' and we knew we were giving all we could to His work and still feed our children. Somehow, we had peace that He would see us through our problem."

One day, Delia and Andy knew they had to take action with a huge leap of faith to work through their problem. They decided to save $15 and invest it into a barbecue barrel so that Andy could begin making *barbacoa*, a Mexican breakfast delicacy, in their home on the weekends to supplement their income. Their investment into the risky business venture was 20 percent of their weekly income! Where was it to come from? Delia stretched their budget even tighter, and soon they had their seed money.

Apprehensively, Andy and Delia purchased the barrel and the beef needed to make their first batch of barbecue. They prayed that the Lord would bless the work of their hands and that He would provide the additional income to raise their family.

Andy stayed up late Friday evening in preparation for the big day. Very early the next morning he prepared the barbecue and took it to local restaurants for purchase. Delia remained at home and cleaned the equipment, anxiously awaiting her husband's return. Andy came home with a smile on his face and $30 in his pocket! Their $15 investment had doubled in their first weekend!

Conditions only improved. Andy and Delia began to pay their full tithe on their gross income. They no longer needed to buy food on credit. They were providing for the needs of their family. Barbecue orders flourished, and before long Andy was faced with another huge decision. In order to go into their new weekend business—Garcia Foods—full-time, Andy would need to quit his job. Building on the initial faith that began their business, they took their next step of faith, and Andy submitted his resignation.

By now, Andy and Delia had six children, and Andy worked harder than ever. Their business outgrew their garage, and soon they invested in a small building near the restaurants they supplied. Andy and Delia took one leap of faith after another. They soon began to hire workers to add to the original one-man staff, and within a short time the new shop was also too small and a larger building was purchased.

Always looking to improve the business, Andy decided to expand his product inventory by including Mexican sausage (*chorizo*). He tested recipes on friends and family, including yours truly, and soon he began selling sausage to local restaurants along with the barbecue. The response was so good that he decided to sell to local grocery stores. Success breeds success, and Andy and Delia's prayers were answered above what they could ask or imagine.

After succeeding with the sausage endeavor, Andy expanded his product line to include *tamales*, another well-known Mexican food. The new addition was even more successful than the other two put together, and an even larger plant was needed for their expanding business.

Their company now services supermarkets nationwide in addition to exporting to Mexico. They are constantly trying new ideas and soon will be introducing *taquitos* to their Garcia Foods inventory.

During their journey, Delia and Andy remained faithful to the Lord, and He remained faithful to His Word. They passed their tests. They fulfilled their dream of providing for their children's upbringing, including sending them to the best universities, which produced six diplomas including a dentist, a physician, and a doctor of divinity.

What began as a problem of lack became a multimillion-dollar provision.

SPIRITUAL CHECKLIST

You have heard me refer to the term *spiritual checklist*; now allow me to explain its meaning. When Diana and I are in a problem, we have trained ourselves to go through our checklist to make sure we have not become an obstacle to our provision.

If you call a repairman to your home to analyze a problem with your air conditioner, he usually brings a series of tools and a thick owner's manual and begins to go through a manufacturer's checklist, making sure that the unit is in mechanical order before he can discern the problem.

If there is something amiss within the unit, he aligns what is off and thereby solves the problem. If all is in order within the unit, he then checks outside sources for the cause of the problem so he can repair the air conditioner.

This same principle applies to the believer. Father God is our Creator— our Manufacturer, so to say. He knows how we were made and with what potentials. He knows what He put into each one of us to solve the problems that life brings. If He created us, then shouldn't there be a book of instructions that guides us through life and its obstacles? Yes, and that guidebook is called the Bible. Take note of what the Manufacturer's Guide has to say about you:

> O LORD, you have examined my heart and know everything about
> me.... You made all the delicate, inner parts of my body and knit

me together in my mother's womb. Thank you for making me so wonderfully complex! Your workmanship is marvelous—how well I know it. You watched me as I was being formed in utter seclusion, as I was woven together in the dark of the womb. You saw me before I was born. Every day of my life was recorded in your book. Every moment was laid out before a single day had passed....

Search me, O God, and know my heart; test me and know my anxious thoughts. Point out anything in me that offends you, and lead me along the path of everlasting life.... Though I am surrounded by troubles, you will protect me from the anger of my enemies. You reach out your hand, and the power of your right hand saves me. The Lord will work out his plans for my life—for your faithful love, O Lord, endures forever. Don't abandon me, for you made me.

—Psalms 139:1, 13–16, 23–24; 138:7–8, nlt

When you are in the midst of the problem, it is vital to go through your spiritual checklist within the Manufacturer's Operating Manual to make sure you are not the source of the problem.

God presented Joshua a checklist as he was about to lead the children of Israel into their inheritance. It came down to three simple items: think, speak, and act on God's Word:

This Book of the Law shall not depart from your mouth, but you shall meditate in it day and night, that you may observe to do according to all that is written in it. For then you will make your way prosperous, and then you will have good success.

—Joshua 1:8

Diana and I begin our checklist by asking these questions of ourselves, and we encourage you to do the same.

1. Are you reading the Word of God (Josh. 1:8)?
2. Are you standing in obedience on the promises (Josh. 1:8)?
3. Are you proclaiming God's promises in faith (Josh. 1:8)?
4. Have you repented of all known sin in your life (Isa. 55:7)?

5.   Have you forgiven everyone who may have offended you (Matt. 6:14–15)?

6.   Are you tithing on your first fruits (Prov. 3:9)?

7.   Have you asked God for what you need (1 Tim. 5:5)?

8.   Do you trust God to take you through the problem and into your provision (Ps. 78:7)?

9.   Are you praising Him while you are in the problem (Exod. 15:2)?

10.   Are you ready to let God choose what His best is for you (Ps. 47:2–4)?

When you answer these questions, you can usually determine whether you are part of the problem. If so, God, through His Word or His delegated authority will direct you back on the right path. If you find that you're in alignment to God's Word, then you will know that the source of the problem is not *within* but comes from *outside sources*. Therefore, put your trust in God, and wait on Him, knowing that He will deliver you from your problem and take you into your provision.

There is only one catch to your "spiritual checklist"—you must be honest and true before the Lord no matter what the cause or purpose.

REMEMBER THIS TRUTH …

The person going through the problem is the person next in line for the promotion. Joseph was in prison one day, and the next day he was prime minister of Egypt, living in the palace! He went from the pit to the palace!

After Diana and I answer the questions on our spiritual checklist, we take a sheet of paper and draw a vertical line down the center. We list the positive positions of a specific choice in one column and the negative results on the other. Immediately we can analyze the consequences or rewards of the respective choices. Seeing the real problem clearly is the first step in solving the problem.

When things go wrong, don't go with them! Problems are inevitable, but suffering is optional.

God uses problems to help us reach our divine destiny. Pharaoh was a problem, and God used him to promote the children of Israel to their inheritance. (See Exodus 32:13.) Satan was a problem in Job's life, and God used Satan to produce in Job a repentant spirit and restore all the enemy had taken from him...and more. (See Job 42:10–12.) Judas was a problem, and God used him to produce the greatest act of redemption known to mankind—the cross. (See Ephesians 1:7.)

Problems don't prevent you from reaching your destiny—you do. God has painted a portrait of your life. He knows every detail of your future. The tests, trials, and tribulations of your life are purposed by God so that you may achieve your divine potential.

This man went through his problems and into his divine destiny: When he was seven years old, his family was forced out of their home on a legal technicality, and he had to work to help support them. At age nine, his mother died. At twenty-two, he lost his job as a store clerk. He wanted to go to law school, but his education wasn't good enough. At twenty-three, he went into debt to become a partner in a small store. At twenty-six, his partner died, leaving him a huge debt that took years to repay. At twenty-eight, after courting a girl four years, he asked her to marry him, and she said no. At thirty-seven, on his third try, he was elected to Congress, but two years later, he failed to get reelected. At forty-one, his four-year-old son died. At forty-nine, he ran for the Senate again, and lost. At fifty-one, he was elected president of the United States. His name was Abraham Lincoln, a man many consider to be the greatest leader the country ever had.[7]

REMEMBER THIS TRUTH...

Your future is just as bright as the promises of God!

We will discover in the next chapter that every problem has a promise. Let's find that special promise for you and stand on it until God leads you into your promised land!

Chapter 3

Every Problem
Has a Promise

THE CHILDREN OF ISRAEL LEFT THE BONDAGE OF EGYPT, MADE their miraculous crossing of the Red Sea on dry ground, and stepped onto the hot sands of their wilderness pathway to the Promised Land. Yet, before they had traveled more than three short days, they received a promise from God:

> If you diligently heed the voice of the LORD your God and do what is right in His sight, give ear to His commandments and keep all His statutes, I will put none of the diseases on you which I have brought on the Egyptians. For I am the LORD who heals you.
> —EXODUS 15:26

Although it took them forty years to walk out of their problem, there was not one sick or feeble among them during their wilderness journey. God kept His promise.

This important chapter establishes the principle that everything in Scripture comes in the form of a promise.

There are more than three thousand promises from God in His Word, and they all apply to His children! Every provision in heaven's pantry comes to you FedEx through God's promises.

Salvation is a promise. Psalm 37:39 promises, "But the salvation of the righteous is from the LORD; He is their strength in the time of trouble."

The Holy Spirit is called the Spirit of promise, for Galatians 3:13–14 says, "Christ has redeemed us from the curse of the law, having become a curse for us...that we might receive the promise of the Spirit through faith."

Healing is a promise. Psalm 103:2–3 declares, "Praise the LORD, O my soul, and forget not all his benefits—who forgives all your sins and heals all your diseases" (NIV).

Prosperity is a promise. Joshua 1:8 gives the conditions for prosperity: "This Book of the Law shall not depart from your mouth, but you shall meditate in it day and night, that you may observe to do according to all that is written in it. For then you will make your way prosperous, and then you will have good success."

REMEMBER THIS TRUTH...

Every problem is preceded by a promise from God.
Our God is the ultimate promise keeper. The greater
the promise, the greater the problem. If God gives you a
million-dollar promise, He is going to send you a
million-dollar problem. Generals are not made by
dress parades and marching bands. They are made by
combat. When God gives you a promise, put on the
whole armor of God and get ready. The battle is about
to begin! With God on your side, the victory is yours.

Most of us are familiar with economic concepts. Consider God's promises as spiritual certificates of deposit, and we are spiritual heirs to these deposits. Christ has paid the price for us at the cross for our sins, our diseases, and our suffering. He allows us to present our drafts—His promises—to claim that which He has pledged to provide. In return, we receive the great blessings God has guaranteed to us by, through, and on account of His Son, Jesus Christ.

As with most economic transactions, God's promises come with conditions. God's promises belong to His children through faith; we are heirs according to His Word. They belong to those who have surrendered their lives to Christ and have been cleansed by His blood. They belong to those who have joined into a spiritual union with Christ and have clothed themselves with His robe of righteousness.

For you are all sons of God through faith in Christ Jesus. For as many of you as were baptized into Christ have put on Christ. There is neither Jew nor Greek, there is neither slave nor free, there is neither male nor female; for you are all one in Christ Jesus. And if you are Christ's, then you are Abraham's seed, and heirs according to the promise.

—GALATIANS 3:26–29

OBEDIENCE IS A REQUIREMENT

God's promises are given to His children on the condition of our willingness to listen to His voice and obey His commands.

If you diligently obey the voice of the LORD your God, to observe carefully all His commandments which I command you today, that the LORD your God will set you high above all nations of the earth. And all these blessings shall come upon you and overtake you, because you obey the voice of the LORD your God.

—DEUTERONOMY 28:1–2

If you walk in My statutes and keep My commandments, and perform them, then I will give you rain in its season, the land shall yield its produce, and the trees of the field shall yield their fruit. Your threshing shall last till the time of vintage, and the vintage shall last till the time of sowing; you shall eat your bread to the full, and dwell in your land safely. I will give peace in the land, and you shall lie down, and none will make you afraid; I will rid the land of evil beasts, and the sword will not go through your land. You will chase your enemies, and they shall fall by the sword before you.

Five of you shall chase a hundred, and a hundred of you shall put ten thousand to flight; your enemies shall fall by the sword before you. For I will look on you favorably and make you fruitful, multiply you and confirm My covenant with you.

—LEVITICUS 26:3–9

God's promises are reserved for His children, and we must keep His commands in order to receive His provision. This truth is once again confirmed in the teaching of 1 John:

> Now by this we know that we know Him, if we keep His commandments. He who says, "I know Him," and does not keep His commandments, is a liar, and the truth is not in him. But whoever keeps His word, truly the love of God is perfected in him. By this we know that we are in Him.
>
> —1 JOHN 2:3–5

When you obey God, you lift Him up, and when you lift Him up, then men will be drawn to Him for their day of salvation.

God commands those He intends to bless. If you obey Him, you will experience His blessings. If you disobey Him, you will reap the consequences.

God had only unlimited blessings planned for Adam and Eve, yet they deliberately disobeyed Him. Their unrepentant conduct caused them to be driven from the garden by angels with flaming swords. It was the fall of man that, in fact, affected every person who would ever live on Earth from that day forward. Man's fall made the cross necessary for redemption.

Mary obeyed God, and she was chosen to bring the Redeemer of mankind into this world. God will command those He intends to bless.

Moses was commanded to "stretch out his hand over the sea," and the Red Sea parted, guiding the children of Israel across the dry seabed and to safety on the other side. They watched in awe as God Almighty turned Pharaoh into fish food and the chariots of Egypt into a rusty pile of junk.

Elijah and the widow were both commanded of God. Elijah was commanded to go to Zarephath, and God would provide for him *there* (1 Kings 17:9). God has an exact *there* for you. The place of His purpose is the place of His power. God will meet you when you get to the place called *there*! And *there* is where your miracle will happen.

The widow was commanded to feed Elijah. The widow "did according to the word…" and she received her supernatural blessing (v. 15). She received exactly what she gave. She gave food and received food that lasted the duration of the drought in Israel.

As soon as she gave Elijah the last taco in the house, the bin of flour began to fill up by an unseen hand and was never used up. Nor did the jar of oil run dry, "according to the word of the LORD which He spoke by

Elijah" (v. 16). Both Elijah and the widow could have missed their promised blessing had they disobeyed God's direction.

GET RID OF YOUR WORRY

Many of God's promises are based on other specific conditions; for example, God's promise of peace.

REMEMBER THIS TRUTH...

If you want the peace of God, you must first be at peace with God. If you are at war with God, you will be tormented day and night. "The wicked are like the troubled sea, when it cannot rest, whose waters cast up mire and dirt" (Isa. 57:20).

Is this you? Peace cannot be found in a prescription or in a whiskey bottle. Peace is the gift of God, and He gives it only to those who are obedient to Him. Peace and worry cannot coexist. The Word of God says:

> Be anxious for nothing, but in everything by prayer and supplication, with thanksgiving, let your requests be made known to God; and the peace of God, which surpasses all understanding, will guard your hearts and minds through Christ Jesus.
>
> —PHILIPPIANS 4:6–7

Worry is having faith in fear; it is the high interest we pay on tomorrow's troubles. Most of the problems we worry about never happen. The Lord says that worry gains us nothing. Worry enables fear to take hold of our minds in such a way that hope can find no home.

I often remind my congregation of a story Clovis Chappell recounts in *Questions Jesus Asked.*[1]

Years ago, in the pioneer days of aviation, a pilot was making a flight around the world. After he had been gone for some two hours from his last landing field, he heard a noise in his plane. After listening intently, he recognized the sound as the gnawing of a rat. He surmised that while his plane was on the ground, a rat had gotten into the engine well. Worry and fear took their grip like a tight, choking vise around his throat. For all he knew, the rat could be gnawing through a vital cable or control panel of the plane.

The pilot was in a very serious problem. He became more and more worried. As the noise continued, his worry turned to panic! It was more than two hours to the next landing field! He began to pray in search for God's answers to his problem.

Then suddenly he remembered; a rat is a rodent. It is not made for the heights; it is made to live near and under the ground. The pilot began to climb the plane. He went up a thousand feet, then another thousand, and then another until he was more than twenty thousand feet in the air. He climbed the plane until he no longer heard the gnawing of the rat. More than two hours later, the pilot brought the plane safely down on the next landing field, opened the engine compartment, and found the dead rat and a partially gnawed cable. The rat had not survived in the high atmosphere.

Worry is a rodent. It cannot live in the secret places of the Most High. It cannot breathe in the atmosphere made vital by prayer and knowledge of the Word of God. Worry dies when we ascend to the Lord through prayer, offer praise in His holy name, and have faith in His Word.

When a problem presents itself, the worst thing you can do is worry about it. Worry robs the mind of its creative powers to analyze the problem. Worry is a dark cloud that blocks the sunshine of your confidence needed to solve even the simplest problems of your life.

If your life's course is being tormented by worry, climb…climb…climb into the atmosphere of faith. Climb until you sense the presence of the living God! Climb until you feel His peace that surpasses all understanding and His joy that is unspeakable and full of glory. Climb until you feel His love and know beyond a shadow of a doubt that worry cannot live in the atmosphere of faith. You will then conquer the problem and enter the promised land of God's favor and abundance!

When faced with a problem, don't deny that it exists. Acknowledge it, but don't embrace it, for it doesn't belong in your life. Obtain all the facts surrounding your difficult circumstances. Next, analyze the facts; go through your spiritual checklist to make sure you meet God's conditions for your provision. Pray for wisdom and discernment.

Develop a plan based on what the Word of God counsels you to do. Write the plan down. Next, act boldly and immediately on your plan. And finally, act in faith on this plan, for the Bible says, "Without faith it is impossible to please God."

COME CLOSER TO GOD

Consider the promise of God's presence in your life. The condition applied to us is that we must come closer to Him. "Draw near to God and He will draw near to you" (James 4:8).

A twelve-year-old boy became a Christian during a revival. The next week at school, his friends questioned him about the experience. "Did you see a vision?" asked one friend. "Did you hear God speak?" asked another. The young convert answered no to all the questions. "Well, how do you know you were saved?" they asked.

The boy scratched his head and looked up to heaven and finally said, "It's like when you catch a fish. You can't see the fish or hear the fish; you just feel him tugging at your line. I just felt God tugging on my heart."[2]

God desires to be close to you, for He created you.

> ## REMEMBER THIS TRUTH...
> *When you make one small step toward Him, He makes great steps toward you, so great that He sent His Son to die for you. It is only in forgetting ourselves that we can draw near to Him.*

THE PROVISION IS IN THE PROMISE

God's promises are activated by our faith and our choice to believe in them.

> But let him ask in faith, with no doubting, for he who doubts is like a wave of the sea driven and tossed by the wind. For let not that man suppose that he will receive anything from the Lord.
> —JAMES 1:6–7

Therefore I say to you, whatever things you ask when you pray, believe that you receive them, and you will have them.

—Mark 11:24

God calls us to His promises. He instructs us to study the Scriptures diligently to know and understand His will and purpose for our lives.

Be diligent to present yourself approved to God, a worker who does not need to be ashamed, rightly dividing the word of truth.

—2 Timothy 2:15

God's promises are made to be taken, and claimed, by His children. They are not made to lie concealed in gilt-edged Bibles, but are meant to be read, understood, and activated.

The fact is, the Bible is like a checkbook given to the needy, and we are to use it when we want to make a withdrawal from our promise account. God has given promises to every kind and description of persons. They are not given to be hoarded up but to be used—we are to draw liberally and freely upon the divine bounty for all the blessings that we need.[3]

How to Build Your Faith

Francis Bacon said, "It's not what men eat, but what they digest that makes them strong; not what we gain, but what we save that makes us rich; not what we read, but what we remember that makes us learned; not what we preach or pray, but what we practice and believe that makes us Christians."[4]

The Bible says, "Faith comes by hearing, and hearing by the word of God" (Rom. 10:17). Your ability to receive the promises of God is a direct relationship of your belief and faith in God.

Now faith is the substance of things hoped for, the evidence of things not seen.... By faith we understand that the worlds were framed by the word of God, so that the things which are seen were not made of things which are visible.... But without faith it is impossible to please Him, for he who comes to God must believe that He is, and that He is a rewarder of those who diligently seek

Him....By faith he forsook Egypt, not fearing the wrath of the king; for he endured as seeing Him who is invisible.

—Hebrews 11:1, 3, 6, 27

That the genuineness of your faith, being much more precious than gold that perishes, though it is tested by fire, may be found to praise, honor, and glory at the revelation of Jesus Christ, whom having not seen you love. Though now you do not see Him, yet believing, you rejoice with joy inexpressible and full of glory, receiving the end of your faith—the salvation of your souls.

—1 Peter 1:7–9

Set your mind on the essential truths about faith found in God's Word, and your faith will begin to grow.

1. Faith is substance (Heb. 11:1).
2. Faith is invisible (Heb. 11:1).
3. Faith pleases God (Heb. 11:6).
4. God rewards your faith (Matt. 8:10–13).
5. Faith endures (Matt. 24:13).
6. Faith is tested (Heb. 11:17).
7. Faith brings eternal salvation (2 Tim. 2:10).

Let me tell you the story of Howard, a dedicated church member for more than twenty years. He was married and had four children and needed income to provide for his family. One day he walked into my office, asking me to pray with him that God would provide a better job.

I asked, "Howard, do you have the faith to believe that God will give you a better job?"

He responded quickly, "I do."

I said, "Howard, when we pray in faith, believing to receive the promises of God for your provision, God will immediately take action. Are you ready for God's invasion of your life?"

Howard nodded eagerly and said, "I am ready. I must have an answer from God to be able to provide for my family."

We prayed, we agreed, and Howard left my office. Two days later, Howard reentered my office in fury. He had been fired. He looked at me and said, "Preacher, we prayed that God would improve my financial situation, and then in two days, I got fired!"

I asked, "How do you expect to get a better job until you lose the one you've got?" Howard was not happy with my response. I looked into his eyes and tried to comfort him. "Howard, some things have to be believed before they can be seen. Do you still believe that God will provide a new and better job for you?" He nodded. "Do you believe that God is working on your behalf?" He nodded once again. "Then claim the promise, endure the problem, and by faith, wait on God's provision." Howard quickly repented of his attitude and proclaimed in faith that God would soon provide.

REMEMBER THIS TRUTH...

Faith is like the bird that feels the light and sings to greet the dawn while it is still dark. You will feel God's presence while in the midst of the problem. Sing praises to Him, and "joy will come in the morning."

Five days later, Howard was hired by one of the finest firms in the city, doing the same thing he had done for the past twenty years at three times the pay. He was back in my office for the third time in two weeks, this time grinning from ear to ear with joy that was beyond description. We held hands in prayer, giving God the praise for His miraculous answer. He had now, by faith, endured the problem and had received the provision. You can do the same.

THE POWER OF THE SPOKEN PROMISE

God created man in His image, and it is the responsibility of the believer to strive to become like the example that was set before us. The tool that best helps us—or hurts us—in mirroring that perfect image is our tongue. Scripture emphasizes the vital importance of our speech.

> Come, you children, listen to me; I will teach you the fear of the
> LORD. Who is the man who desires life, and loves many days, that

he may see good? Keep your tongue from evil, and your lips from speaking deceit.

—PSALM 34:11–13

This scripture teaches that if you keep your tongue from speaking evil, deception, and lies, then you can move into the "fear of the LORD." The fear of the Lord produces fullness, good days, and blessings. It is impossible to experience God's blessings and provision without controlling your tongue.

He who guards his mouth preserves his life, but he who opens wide his lips shall have destruction.

—PROVERBS 13:3

Death and life are in the power of the tongue, and those who love it will eat its fruit.

—PROVERBS 18:21

Let no corrupt word proceed out of your mouth, but what is good for necessary edification, that it may impart grace to the hearers.... Let all bitterness, wrath, anger, clamor, and evil speaking be put away from you, with all malice. And be kind to one another, tenderhearted, forgiving one another, just as God in Christ forgave you.

—EPHESIANS 4:29–32

Pleasant words are like a honeycomb, sweetness to the soul and health to the bones.

—PROVERBS 16:24

Whoever guards his mouth and tongue keeps his soul from troubles.

—PROVERBS 21:23

Scripture presents two effects of the spoken word. The positive effects are:

1. Your words bring rewards (Ps. 37:30–33).
2. Your words edify (2 Cor. 12:19).
3. Your words heal (Prov. 12:18).
4. Your words preserve life (Prov. 18:21).

The negative effects are:

1. Your words have consequences (James 3:5–8).
2. Your words breed malice and contempt (Prov. 17:20).
3. Your words embitter your spirit (Ps. 10:7).
4. Your words bring ultimate destruction (Ps. 5:9).

Every time you open your mouth, you invite blessings or curses into your life. The choice is yours.

God promises that the person who controls his or her tongue will have a life that is as sweet as a honeycomb. He also declares that the person who does not control his or her tongue will come to destruction. The Bible clearly teaches that the power of life and death comes out of your mouth with the words that you speak. There is power in the spoken word!

It may not always be prudent to speak the words that come from your carnal mind, but it is always fruitful to speak the promises of God. When God makes a promise, faith believes it, hope anticipates it, and patience quietly awaits it.

There is power in your proclamation of God's Word. The meaning of the word *proclaim* is "to make known publicly your opinions, and to extol or praise an action or individual." To "make a proclamation" is to "announce or declare, in an official manner; as in proclaiming war."

> It is good to give thanks to the LORD, and to sing praises to Your name, O Most High; to declare Your lovingkindness in the morning, and Your faithfulness every night.
> —PSALM 92:1–2

> But I trusted in, relied on, and was confident in You, O Lord; I said, You are my God.
> —PSALM 31:14, AMP

Contend, O Lord, with those who contend with me; fight against those who fight against me! Take hold of shield and buckler, and stand up for my help! Draw out also the spear and javelin and close up the way of those who pursue and persecute me. Say to me, I am your deliverance!

—PSALM 35:1–3, AMP

The King of kings and Lord of lords has redeemed us—we are His! Our heavenly Father gave us His written Word as an inheritance, a diary, a guidebook to what He has done, what He has promised, and what He will do!

Christ Jesus who died—who was raised to life again—is at the right hand of God the Father and is interceding for us. All we must do is believe, obey, and proclaim what the Spirit of the living God, the God of Abraham, Isaac, and Jacob, has written.

Take ownership of the Word of God. Declare God's position over every situation in your life. The phrase "to proclaim" comes from the Latin, which means to "shout forth." It is a strong word and is linked to another dynamic phrase or word in the New Testament, "to confess." Confession means to say with your mouth what God has already said in His Word.

REMEMBER THIS TRUTH...

When you trust in Christ, who is your blessed hope, you see the invisible, you will feel the intangible, and you can accomplish the impossible! Be more than a conqueror; learn to be an overcomer, for the God of Israel in on your side!

Proclaim your victory over the world, the flesh, and the devil because you are an overcomer by the blood of the Lamb and the word of your testimony. God's power is released in the supernatural when you speak His Word over your life, and that which is released in the supernatural affects the physical, where you live.

"Jesus is the High Priest of our confession. Whenever we say with our mouths what the Word of God says about us as believers in Jesus, we have released His authority and His blessings over our proclamations."[5]

God tells us to "fret not." Therefore, do not focus on the obstacles and problems of your life. Instead, magnify the God of promise, who has answers for every problem you encounter.

Focus on the Author of life and Giver of every perfect gift. Praise Him and proclaim His awesome Word. Remember, your problem did not take God by surprise. He is not worried about it, and He has already provided a way for you to overcome life's challenges.

You must do more than believe and have faith in the Word of the living God; you must also obey it. You must proclaim it over your life and the lives of your loved ones. You must have hope in the power of His promises.

Anyone can believe; demons believe. The Word of God says that the demons tremble at the mention of the Lord's name (James 2:19)! However, demons can't obey, and they don't proclaim the Word over their lives. But we can!

Don't lose sight of the promise! Don't ever make the mistake of associating your problem with God's lack of love for you. The greatest promise we have is God's unconditional love.

An overwhelmed young mother was seeing a secular counselor to help her cope with her daunting responsibilities. Attempting to employ stereotypical psychological questions during her session, the counselor asked, "Which of your three children do you love the most?"

The loving mother answered instantly, "I love all of my children the same!"

The counselor felt her answer came too quickly, so she began to probe. "You can't possibly love all the children the same," was the counselor's retort.

"Oh, but I do!" countered the mother.

The counselor sat forward in her chair and glared at the woman with a piercing stare. "Look, it is psychologically impossible for anyone to regard any three human beings exactly the same! If you won't be honest with me, I am ending this session now, and I will refuse to see you again!"

The young mother finally broke down under the counselor's badgering and began to cry. As she regained her composure, she looked at the counselor with sincerity and replied, "All right, I do not love all of my children the same."

The overbearing counselor leaned back in her chair and listened with a smug, self-satisfying smile at the mother's response. "When one of my three children is sick, I love that child more. When one of my three children is in pain or in need of my help, I love that child more. When one of my children is confused or lost, I love that child more. And when one of my three children is bad, I mean really disobedient, I mean really awful, I love that child even more."

The counselor sat in silence as the mother continued to share her true feelings. "Apart from those exceptions, I honestly love all my three children the same."

Our faith represents a God who loves His children all the same. His Word declares that He does not show "partiality" (Acts 10:34). He knows everything about His children. He knows when we are sick, in pain, confused, or lost, and when we are bad, really bad, *this is when He loves us even more*. During our time in the problem, no matter what the cause, God promises to love us as if there were no one else to love.

> God answers prayer, sometimes when hearts are weak,
> He gives the very gifts believers seek.
> But often faith must learn a deeper rest,
> And trust God's silence when He does not speak;
> For He whose name is Love will send the best.
> Stars may burn out nor mountain walls endure,
> But God is true; His promises are sure
> To those who speak.[6]
>
> —M. G. PLANTZ

ACCEPTING GOD'S PROMISES

I want to share with you a short yet profound teaching I have adapted from my dear friend Derek Prince on the appropriation of God's promises in the life of a believer.[7]

Faith is based on definite objective facts. Every promise in the entire Bible is a potential object of faith. For the believer there is nothing within the promises of God that is outside the scope of his faith:

> For all the promises of God in Him [Christ] are Yes, and in Him
> Amen, to the glory of God through us.
> —2 CORINTHIANS 1:20

> He who did not spare His own Son, but delivered Him up for us
> all, how shall He not with Him also freely give us all things?
> —ROMANS 8:32

All things means *all* things! It means all His blessings and all His promises are available freely to all who receive them through faith in Christ's atoning death and resurrection. There is no need, no trial, and no problem that are outside the scope of God's promises!

Every problem has a promise in God's Word that will bring provision to the believer once the promise is accepted through faith in Christ. When a problem arises:

1. Ask the Holy Spirit to direct you to the promises that apply to your problem (Ps. 5:3).
2. Obey the conditions that are attached to the promise (John 14:15).
3. Expect the provision in faith (Rom. 4:16).
4. Praise God while you wait on the provision (Ps. 71:14–17).

The secret in attaining the provision lies in knowing and applying the promises of God's Word. This is faith in action!

> His [God's] divine power has given to us all things that pertain to
> life and godliness, through the knowledge of Him [Christ] who
> called us by glory and virtue, by which have been given to us exceedingly great and precious promises.
> —2 PETER 1:3–4

Peter is in agreement with Paul; God has already provided us with all that we will ever need for the provision made available through Christ. We must claim God's promises for our lives.

> ## REMEMBER THIS TRUTH...
> *The provision is in the promise.*

Many Christians, however, are ready to claim the promises of God while ignoring the conditions that God has placed in His Word. These conditions must be met before the fulfillment of the provision is complete:

> Commit your way to the LORD, trust also in Him, and He shall bring it to pass.
> —PSALM 37:5

The first condition is to "commit your way," a single act. The second is to "trust also in Him," a continuing attitude. Therefore, we must:

1. Make a definitive act of commitment to Christ at the onslaught of the problem.
2. Maintain a continuing attitude of trust in Christ through the problem.

As these two conditions are met, we can possess the promise and wait on the manifestation of the provision. The appropriation of the following three successive steps of faith is the key to accepting the promises based on God's Word.

1. Find the promise associated with your problem in God's Word.
2. Meet the conditions associated with the promise.
3. Claim the fulfillment of the promise in faith.[8]

One of the most powerful proclamations you can make is the declaration of confidence in God's protection while you are in the problem. There is a promise over every problem you will encounter, and every one of these promises is found in God's eternal Word. If you are in the problem, I encourage you to declare the following proclamation.

PROCLAMATION OF GOD'S PROTECTION

No weapon that is formed against me shall prosper, and every tongue that arises against me in judgment I do condemn.

This is my heritage as the servant of the Lord, and my righteousness is from You, O Lord of Hosts.

If there are those who have been speaking or praying against me, or seeking to harm me, or who have rejected me, I forgive them. (Name them if you can.)

Having forgiven them, I bless them in the name of the Lord.

Now I declare, O Lord, that You and You alone are my God, and besides You there is no other, a just God and a Savior, the Father, the Son, and the Spirit, and I worship You!

I submit myself anew to You today in unreserved obedience.

Having submitted to You, Lord, I do as Your Word directs. I resist the devil—all his lies, his attacks, his deceptions, and every instrument or agent he would seek to use against me.

I will not submit to the evil one! I resist him, drive him from me, and exclude him from me in Jesus's name.

I reject the problem that has come against me in the name of Jesus and by the power of His blood! (Specifically state the problem you are in.)

I thank You, Lord, that through the sacrifice of Jesus on the cross, I will overcome the problem, and I will enter into the blessings of the provision.

I have inherited the blessings of Abraham, whom You blessed in all things—health, fruitfulness, prosperity, victory, and, ultimately, Your full favor.[9]

Chapter 4

DON'T GET TRAPPED
IN THE PROBLEM

THE CHILDREN OF ISRAEL WERE IN THE WILDERNESS FOR FORTY years when the actual journey could have taken them less than ninety days. Why? The answer to this question introduces another principle of *Life's Challenges—Your Opportunities*: how you react to the problem determines how long you stay in the problem.

Do you know people who have been trapped in the same problem for years? Often the son becomes trapped in the same problem of his father, and the daughter is trapped in the same problem of her mother. The Bible calls these problems *generational curses*.

When the same bad habits control you and those you love from generation to generation, you are mired in the pits of an inherited problem that can only be resolved by the supernatural deliverance of the Holy Spirit. (See Exodus 20:4–6.)

Don't become ensnared in your problem! It's time to break your down-spiral pattern. It is time to take the steps out of your bondage and prepare yourself to receive your promise.

EXCUSES OR RIGHT CHOICES

You can choose to take another lap around Mt. Sinai, extending your time in the problem, or you can determine that you are no longer going to tolerate a problem-ridden life. The children of Israel were faced with two choices: wander aimlessly in the wilderness for years, or go directly to their provision. We are faced with the same choices; in which direction are you going? Are you going to stay in your problem, or are you going to walk into your provision?

Remember, the Israelites had many reasons to rejoice. Pharaoh, the man who was worshiped as an earthly god, was drowned along with his mighty army, and the Jews were delivered from bondage.

> ## REMEMBER THIS TRUTH...
> *When we walk out of Egypt (bondage), through the Red Sea (water baptism), and enter the wilderness (problem), we will be faced with making right choices until we reach our provision (promised land).*

If anyone ever had the right to sing "He Set Me Free," it was the children of Israel. The Lord protected them with the fire by night and the cloud by day. Angel's food was prepared daily, fresh water was supplied from underground springs, yet nothing was sufficient for the murmuring crowd.

When confronted with another obstacle, they chose to *take another lap* around the wilderness by refusing to obey God's commands and by continuing to moan and complain.

I am certain that God in heaven looked over the balconies of heaven and shook His head in dismay. How many miracles would these slaves have to see before they could trust in Him? God cupped His hands to His mouth and shouted, "Take another lap!"

And around Mt. Sinai they went singing, "I'm bound for the Promised Land, but I'm trapped in the problem."

Is this you? Is your marriage trapped in unhappiness? Are you always mismanaging your finances? Are you constantly battling an addictive habit? God has already given you a pocket full of miracles, but you just can't seem to walk away from drugs or alcohol, you won't stop spending, and you refuse to be reconciled.

Aristotle said, "I count him braver who overcomes his desires than him who conquers his enemies; the hardest victory is the victory over self."

King Solomon said, "He that hath no rule over his own spirit is like a city that is broken down, and without walls" (Prov. 25:28, KJV).

You are not trapped in your problem because you are a bad person; you are trapped because you refuse to change and you continually fail to walk away from bad behavior. You would rather make excuses instead of right choices.

Making the right choices for the believer is not difficult. When you base your life on biblical principles, 99 percent of your choices are already made.

Glenn Van Ekeren, a noted speaker and featured author of *Chicken Soup for the Soul*, coins a term for the behavior adopted by many Christians while trapped in their problem: *Excusiology*.

"The exercise of making excuses is not new to our generation. We can trace this popular diversionary technique back to the Old Testament....[I]n the Book of Leviticus we find a sacred custom called the 'escaped goat' [scapegoat]."[1]

When the problems and trials of the people became overwhelming, a healthy male goat was brought to the temple, and in a formal ceremony, the high priest placed his hands on the head of the goat and read the list of troubles. This process was meant to transfer the agonies and anxieties of the people onto the goat. The goat was set free, taking the troubles with him out to pasture.[2]

REMEMBER THIS TRUTH...

What you walk away from will determine what God can bring you to. You must leave Egypt before you can reach your promised land.

Van Ekeren states that things have not changed much in four thousand years. Now people use a less formal process of placing blame for their problems on something or someone else; it's called *making excuses*. In fact, he has a name for the specialists in this field—*excusiologists*.

Having worked in adult and juvenile corrections, Van Ekeren states that "not one person was ever guilty of the acts, behavior, or crimes for which they had been accused." Everyone had an excuse. "I was in the wrong place at the wrong time." "I was framed." "I only wanted to rob the guy, but when he resisted I was forced to shoot him. It was his fault!"[3]

What does the Word of God say? "Truly, these times of ignorance God overlooked, but now commands all men everywhere to repent" (Acts 17:30).

Criminals are not the only practitioners of excusiology. Listen to some very real excuses used to redirect man's responsibilities. These are two classic excuses received for nonpayment of child support. "I can't afford to pay child support. I'm too far behind on my cable bill." And, "I will not allow my ex-wife to get rich on my money." (This man was paying $25 a week in child support.)

What does the Word of God say? "But if anyone does not provide for his own, and especially for those of his household, he has denied the faith and is worse than an unbeliever" (1 Tim. 5:8).

Some people have a problem holding down a job, yet they are all too ready to provide excuses for why they can't go to work. "My parrot spoke for the first time, so I waited for him to do it again so I could tape record it!" "My car got a flat tire and I couldn't come to work, so I took my kids to the park instead." "I thought Halloween was a national holiday!"

What does the Word of God say? "When the sun rises, they gather together and lie down in their dens. Man goes out to his work and to his labor until the evening" (Ps. 104:22–23).

EXCUSIOLOGY 101

People who stay trapped in their problems make excuses a ceremonial ritual, and when analyzing this habitual behavior one can discover a pathological pattern that keeps God's children from receiving their promise. They are deceived into believing that making excuses will somehow carry their problems away. Nothing could be further from the truth.

The first pattern that is adopted is *denial*. You refuse to admit any association, involvement, or wrongdoing in your problem. Children learn this technique early in their lives and often carry it with them into adulthood where they perfect the use of excuses. A little girl was being disciplined for misbehavior. In between her tears she admitted, "I didn't do it, and I promise I'll never do it again!" This may be acceptable behavior for a child, but not for a child of God! Your sins will surely find you out!

The second negative pattern is *refusing responsibility*. Finding someone else to blame is "scapegoatism" at its purest: "It's not my fault." "I have a problem because of my mother, father, children, boss, professor..."

The third pattern is what I call the *but syndrome*. "I did it, but..." We admit we are part of the problem, *but* we still blame the problem on anyone or anything.

Excusiology is a dead-end approach out of your problem. The quickest way out of the problem is to admit you have one, take responsibility, and stop blaming others.

Another choice while in the problem is to choose to spiritually perish while searching for a solution, or to take full possession of the promises of God and become better for it. The Israelites became apathetic to God's blessings and divine purpose for their lives. They lost sight of the goal and eventually lost faith in their spiritual deliverer as well. They became spiritually stagnant and lost their way to their Promised Land.

Have you been trapped in the problem so long that you have lost your faith in the God who gave you the promise? Have you become so stagnant in the problem that you have forgotten your promise? Are you so weary that you have become acclimated to your problem?

Do you continually feel sorry for yourself?

Don't indulge in self-pity—that is no place for a child of God! Self-pity conquers faith. Self-pity looks for man's approval and not God's direction. Self-pity is a death that has no resurrection, a pit that has no bottom. Self-pity is a decaying trap! Once you indulge in it, you will develop the wilderness complex.

Jonah protested his calling. Elijah was bitter because of his oppressors. Job sulked during his tribulation. All languished in self-pity. What they were really thinking was, "Lord, what have You done for me lately?" Or, "You have not given me what I want when I want it; therefore, You have failed me!" All of these men suffered from the wilderness complex.

Am I describing your life?

In his book *Escape From Freedom*, Eric Fromm said this of problems:

> Sometimes, the problems of life become so overwhelming that we despair of ever solving them. Should someone come along and say in a loud confident voice, "Follow me without question, do everything I tell you, and I will lead you out of this," many of us would find that a very tempting offer. When life becomes difficult, we want someone to say to us, "Don't worry your little head about it.

Let me do it for you, all I want in return is your gratitude and total obedience."4

When you believe that God has not heard your wilderness cry, you anxiously look for man to solve your problems and are willing to pay homage to him for doing so. You should instead listen harder for God's voice, for He is never far away. You should never fear the shadows of your problem. A shadow only means that God's light is shining somewhere nearby.

God forbid that we should seek our provision from someone or something other than God! He shares glory with no man. He wants us to make Him our sole provider. Our God is a jealous God. He said so Himself.

> You shall not make for yourself an idol.... You shall not bow down
> to them or worship them; for I, the LORD your God, am a jealous
> God, punishing the children for the sin of the fathers to the third
> and fourth generation of those who hate me.
> —EXODUS 20:4–5, NIV

God is our provider, not man! Take full possession of your promises. They belong to you and no one else. Thank Him for the problem, for it will bring you closer to Him. Look for ways to reach the provision, all the while bestowing gratitude to God.

REMEMBER THIS TRUTH...

You cannot solve a problem that you will not confront. When we confront the problem, we are destined to soon become free of it because the answer is not separate from the problem.

Your acts of thanksgiving are signs of spiritual life, trust, and well-being, and provide a swift way out of your wilderness. He rejoices in your praises (Ps. 27).

Another choice to make while you are in the wilderness is to *sit and stay*, or *stand and enter*. You can stand boldly on the Word of God and enter into His precious provision, or you can wait outside of your promises, sit in the wilderness, and never reach your provision. Your ability to embrace the promise of God without wavering is your *express ticket* out of the problem and into the provision (James 1:6).

Do you want to sit in the pit of despair and stay in the desolation of Egypt, or do you desire to walk into your reward while holding the hand of God? The choice is yours.

SEVEN ACTIONS TO SHORTEN YOUR STAY IN THE PROBLEM

1. Acknowledge the problem.

I know Christians who live with a white elephant in their living room. Everyone in the household, including the family dog, knows this massive intruder is in the house, but no one has the courage to confront it. Ignoring the problem will not cause it to disappear. Ignoring the problem will cause it to overtake you.

Do you practice the *Linus philosophy?* One day Linus and his friend Charlie Brown were chatting with one another. Linus turned to Charlie and said, "I don't like to face problems head on. I think the best way to solve problems is to avoid them. This is a distinct philosophy of mine. No problem is so big or so complicated that it can't be run away from."[5]

Ignoring the problem will not cause it to go away. The first step in solving any problem is to recognize that it exists. You won't find the solution until you discover the problem. When you go to the doctor with unusual symptoms, he admits you to the hospital and performs various tests to determine what is wrong with you. Once your physical problem is discovered, the doctor can prescribe the proper treatment to heal your illness. So it is with all problems.

Recognition of the problem is not surrender to it. Many Christians believe that *positive confession* requires that you not acknowledge the problem exists—nothing can be further from the truth! Positive confession is proclaiming God's promises in faith, believing that these promises apply to you, and knowing that His promises are sufficient for the victory over your problems.

How can He provide you with a healing miracle unless you acknowledge you are sick? Instead, speak to that illness in the name of Jesus

Christ, your Healer, and proclaim that, "My God promises to heal all of my diseases!"

How can He provide you with a financial miracle unless you acknowledge that you are in debt? Acknowledge your spending problem, your refusal to work, or your failure to obey the Lord in the tithe and offering. What to do? Obey God's Word immediately, rebuke the devourer, and proclaim in faith that, "My God shall supply all my needs according to His riches in glory!"

REMEMBER THIS TRUTH . . .

A problem acknowledged is a problem half solved! Acknowledge the problem, and He will show you the path to your provision.

You don't have to wait to improve your life. Begin by acknowledging the problem. Don't let it hold you hostage any longer. Deception is an evil companion; it makes you believe everything is all right while it is quietly seeking to destroy you.

Nothing is too big for God! You and He are a team. Each problem you have is a hidden opportunity so powerful that it dwarfs the very problem you are in. The greatest success stories were created by people who recognized a problem and turned it into an opportunity.[6]

Remember what Helen Keller said: "No pessimist ever discovered the secrets of the stars, or sailed to an uncharted land, or opened a new heaven to the human spirit."[7]

2. Take responsibility for your actions.

Winston Churchill said, "The key to greatness is responsibility." To free yourself from the yoke of your problem and to reach your divine destiny— your provision—you must take responsibility and accept the consequences of every thought, word, and deed in your lifetime.

Adam and Eve were expelled from the Garden of Eden not because they sinned but because they blamed their conduct on someone else. They refused to take personal responsibility for their actions.

When Adam and Eve ate of the forbidden fruit and attempted to hide their sin from God with their shabby fig-leaf attire, God called to them in the cool of the day, saying, "Where art thou?"

Now, let's listen to the drama in the Garden of Eden. Adam faced responsibility like a man; he blamed it on his wife. God gave Adam the opportunity to stand tall and take responsibility for his actions, but instead he whimpered, "This woman You gave me…!" (See Genesis 3:12.) "It's Your fault, God!"

God looked to Eve in her St. John's Fig Leaf original for her response. She was just as irresponsible as her husband. She said, "The serpent deceived me, and I ate" (Gen. 3:13). "The devil made me do it!"

Had they taken responsibility for their conduct and asked for forgiveness, they would not have been kicked out of the Garden of Eden.

Only when you take responsibility for who you are, what you have become, and the decisions you have made will you reach your divine destiny, your promised land flowing with milk and honey, your priceless provision.

You must accept responsibility for a problem before you can solve it. How many times have you heard someone say, "That's not my problem"?

REMEMBER THIS TRUTH…

When God asks you a question, He's not looking for information. Nothing you do has taken Him by surprise. He is probing your inner man to see if you will take responsibility for your deeds.

You will get trapped in the wilderness and live a life of absolute misery, attempting to avoid the very problem whose solution holds the key to your success. You can solve a problem only when you face the reality that it is yours to solve.

Stop going through life saying, "It's my mother's fault; she was never there for me." "It's my father's fault; he rejected me." "It's my professor's fault; he was too hard on me." "It was the policeman's fault; I was only doing 55 mph in a school zone, and he spoke harshly to me." You are trapped in the problem until you take responsibility for the problem.

The following story comes from *The Road Less Traveled* by Dr. Scott Peck and illustrates the refusal of individuals to accept responsibility for their problem.[8]

Dr. Peck tells the story of a career sergeant stationed in Okinawa who had a serious problem because of his excessive drinking. The sergeant denied that he was an alcoholic or that he even had a drinking problem and rationalized his problem by saying, "There's nothing else to do in the evenings except drink."

"Do you like to read?" Dr. Peck asked.

"Oh, yes, I like to read, sure."

"Then why don't you read in the evening instead of drinking?"

"It's too noisy to read in the barracks."

"Well, then, why don't you go to the library?"

"The library is too far away."

"Is the library farther away than the bar you go to?"

"Well, I'm not much of a reader. That's not where my interests lie."

"Do you like to fish?" Dr. Peck then inquired.

"Sure, I love to fish."

"Why not go fishing instead of drinking?"

"I can't go fishing. I have to work all day long."

"Can't you go fishing at night?"

"No, there isn't any night fishing in Okinawa."

"But there is," Dr. Peck said. "I know several organizations that fish at night here. Would you like me to put you in touch with them?"

"Well, I really don't like to fish that much."

"What I hear you saying," Dr. Peck clarified, "is that there are other things to do in Okinawa except drink, but the thing you like to do most in Okinawa is drink."

"Yeah, I guess so."

"But your drinking is getting you in trouble, so you're faced with a real problem, aren't you?"

"This God-forsaken island would drive anyone to drink."

Dr. Peck kept trying for a while, but the sergeant was not the least bit interested in taking responsibility for his drinking or even recognizing it as a personal problem, which he could solve either with or without help. Dr. Peck had no choice but to inform the commander that the sergeant was a hopeless case, and the sergeant was relieved of duty in mid-career. He was willing to lose his future rather than take responsibility for his problem.

It is not possible to live life without problems, but you don't have to be trapped in them, be it marital, financial, or emotional. Acknowledge the problem and become accountable for it!

3. Be willing to work.

God set the example and worked for six days in the creation of the universe. The first day God created light, and then He rested. The second day God created the firmament, and then rested. The third day God created the dry ground with the trees and grass, and rested. The fourth day God created the sun to rule the day and the moon to rule the night, and rested. The fifth day God created the fish in the seas and birds in the air, and then He rested. On the sixth day God created Adam and Eve, and no one has rested since.

REMEMBER THIS TRUTH...

The person who accepts responsibility for his or her problem is the person who will overcome it.

God rested on the seventh day, not because He was tired, but because He was establishing a prototype that is an essential part of physical and spiritual health.

Jesus Christ of Nazareth worked as a carpenter with His hands. His twelve disciples were working people who rose before dawn to drag smelly fishing nets through the waters of Galilee to earn a living. They worked hard! One was even a tax collector!

Saint Paul wrote, "If anyone will not work, neither shall he eat" (2 Thess. 3:10). Those words should be chiseled over the doors of the Welfare Department in Washington DC. Giving money to an able-bodied man or woman who can work but refuses to work is a violation of the law of God. The work ethic in America is dying. Our society's rejection of God's mandate to work is a symbol of our rejection of God and His plan for our lives.

Saint Paul writes to Timothy the words that would drive many modern-day "cotton candy" Christians out of the church: "But if anyone does not provide for his own, and especially for those of his household, he has denied the faith and is worse than an unbeliever" (1 Tim. 5:8). An able-bodied man who sits on the couch watching television every day while his wife works two jobs to provide for their family has "denied the faith" and is "worse than an infidel."

God created man to worship *and* to work. He who never works is unfit for worship, and eventually he who never worships is incapable of godly work.

How did America's welfare originate? For over one hundred years the U.S. Supreme Court ruled that it was illegal to take money from one citizen who would work and give it to a citizen who could work but would not work.

In an attempt to counteract the effects of the Great Depression, President Franklin D. Roosevelt created a peacetime domestic program called the "New Deal."

President Roosevelt established several new federal programs and agencies designed to reduce unemployment and restore prosperity. The fundamental legacy of the New Deal was increased government involvement in the lives of the American people.

Among the new federal strategies was the Works Progress Administration (WPA), which contained three major programs—a retirement fund, unemployment insurance, and welfare grants. These programs, coupled with a new subsidized housing program, began what some refer to as a welfare state.[9]

Roosevelt's New Deal was meant to temporarily open the public treasury to those in desperate need, but no one was ready for what evolved.

More than two hundred years ago, while the original thirteen colonies were still part of Great Britain, Professor Alexander Tyler wrote of the Athenian Republic, which had fallen two thousand years earlier:

> A democracy cannot exist as a permanent form of government. It can only exist until the voters discover that they can vote themselves money from the public treasury. From that moment on, the majority always votes for the candidates promising the most

benefits from the public treasury with the result that a democracy always collapses over loose fiscal policy, always followed by a dictatorship.[10]

Think of it...this statement was made more than two hundred years ago about a democracy that fell more than two thousand years ago! Is America destined to repeat history?

Our distortion of the federal welfare system has eroded the American dream. What is the result of this abuse?

Many of America's children don't have the confidence or belief that they can succeed on their own. The majority of welfare children grow up expecting the government to take care of them; they know no other way! The impact of increasing the lenience and generosity of welfare in undermining work and prolonging dependence has been confirmed by controlled scientific experiment.[11] Children who grow up in poverty because their parents refuse to work suffer from idleness, loss of personal integrity and self-esteem, and eventually loss of hope with no dependency on God! What do they see as the answer to their lack? Not work...not trust in God...but a vote for the politician who promises to supply the most.

We are ignoring God's work ethic, and until all Americans work who can work, our economy will fail. That is one of the reasons dark economic clouds are gathering over America.

Glenn Van Ekeren wrote a fascinating paper on work; allow me to share portions of it with you:[12]

In a national survey of 180,000 American workers, 80 percent indicated a dislike for their jobs. What a sad reflection on an activity that absorbs a major portion of our lives. Making matters even worse, few people who dislike their vocations will ever be a success at it.

Maybe it's time to consciously renovate our thoughts about work. We can choose to view work much like Thomas Edison: "I never did a day's work in my life. It was all fun." Edison believed the purpose of work was joy and fulfillment.

Or we can do as the foolish king who was condemned to hell forever because of his evil lifestyle. Each day he was required to push a large boulder up a mountain. At the end of each day, the rock rolled down again. Each day was a tortuous repeat of the day before.

Hordes of people view their daily responsibilities as replicating the uninspired fruitless experience of the foolish king.

It is estimated that more than 37,000 ways for making a living exist in the United States. We must stop looking at work as simply a means of making a living and realize it is an essential ingredient of making a quality life.

Martin Luther King Jr. said, "If a man is called to be a street sweeper, he should sweep streets as Michelangelo painted, or Beethoven composed music or Shakespeare wrote poetry. He should sweep streets so well that all the hosts of heaven and earth will pause to say, here lived a great street sweeper who did his job well."[13] We should work as if God is watching, because He is!

Will Rogers believed that, "In order to succeed, you must know what you are doing, like what you are doing, and believe in what you are doing." Roger's suggestions deserve a closer look.

1. Know what you are doing. Winners in life are willing to do things losers refuse to do. Winners prepare, study, train, apply themselves, and work to become the best at what they do. Choose one part of your job. Apply your talents. Become the expert and excel!

2. Like what you are doing. The secret to happiness, success, satisfaction, and fulfillment in our work is not doing what one likes, but liking what one does.

3. Believe in what you do. Successful people are not in a job for something to do…they are in their work to do something! Get beyond the job description, title, paycheck, or "to do" list. Be passionate and set your goal on the end result.[14]

God is never going to trust you with a better job unless you succeed at the one you have. Art Linkletter summarized what it takes to turn good into better, boredom into stimulating activity, and discontentment into commitment:

- Do a little more than what you're paid to do.
- Give a little more than what you have to.
- Try a little more than what you want to.
- Aim a little higher than you think possible.
- And give a lot of thanks to God for health, family, and friends.[15]

A president of a major corporation was asked, "Is it still possible for a young person to start at the bottom and get to the top, and if so, how?"

His answer? "Indeed, it is. The sad fact, however, is that so few young people recognize it." His outline for success? "Keep thinking ahead of your job! Do it better than it needs to be done. Next time, doing it well will be child's play. Let no one, or anything, stand between you and a difficult task. Let nothing deny you the rich opportunity to gain strength in adversity, confidence in mastery. Do it better than anyone else can do it. Do these things, and nothing can keep the job ahead from reaching out after you."[16]

Listen to the words of President Harry S. Truman: "I studied the lives of great men and famous women; and I found that the men and women who got to the top were those who did the jobs they had in hand, with everything they had of energy and enthusiasm and hard work."[17]

4. When you are wrong, admit it.

It takes profound moral and spiritual strength to utter the words, "I am wrong." A weak person will never admit he or she is mistaken. We all make mistakes; just don't make the mistake of proclaiming you have never made one.

How many marriages could have been saved by the willingness of one or both in covenant to confess, "I was wrong!" How many business deals go south, how many churches split, how many chief friends became bitter enemies because no one had the strength of character to humble themselves and say what weaklings can never say: "I was wrong!"

M. Scott Peck in his book *People of the Lie* describes those who would rather lengthen their stay in the problem than to admit they are wrong. They are:

Utterly dedicated to preserving their self-image of perfection, they are unceasingly engaged in the effort to maintain the appearance of moral purity. They worry about this a great deal. They are acutely sensitive to social norms and what others might think of them....they dress well, go to work on time, pay their taxes, and outwardly seem to live lives that are above reproach.

The words "image," "appearance," and "outwardly" are crucial to understanding the morality of the evil. While they seem to lack any motivation to *be* good, they intensely desire to appear good. Their "goodness" is all on a level of pretense. It is in effect, a lie. That is why they are people of the lie.

Actually the lie is designed not so much to deceive others as to deceive themselves. They cannot or will not tolerate the pain of self-reproach.[18]

These poor souls would rather die in the problem than to admit they are wrong. I challenge you—ask God to take the scales from your eyes and deliver you from this overwhelming bondage. He is waiting for you to take the first step, and He will do the rest!

REMEMBER THIS TRUTH...

Nothing in your life will work until you do!

Let me tell you the true story of a very rich man who made his fortune in the livestock business. This mighty man of wealth had a wife who was Hollywood beautiful. She was more than a head turner; she was a heart stopper. By appearances, he had all a man could want.

The rich man was Nabal, and his wife's name was Abigail. Nabal was known to be mean-spirited and unjustly cruel on his best days. Abigail was known to be gracious and loving even though married to this rich, arrogant, self-centered man whose very name literally meant "fool."

There was a young military commander who patrolled the area that included where Nabal's ranch was with all its thousands of heads of livestock. It was the presence of this young military commander and his men that kept thieves from raiding Nabal's bountiful ranch of its hundreds of sheep and cattle.

One day when they were running low on food, the young commander sent a messenger to Nabal and graciously asked if he could spare a few sheep for he and his men to eat. He was confident that Nabal would be deeply indebted to him for taking care of his property. This young commander would soon be king of Israel—his name was David.

What was Nabal's response to David's request? Nabal went into a tirade! He insulted David and his father with his angry reply: "Who is David, and who is his father, Jesse?" Nabal knew exactly who they were; he was being as rude and offensive as his obnoxious personality permitted.

When David heard of Nabal's outrageous denial, he commanded four hundred of his men to put on their swords and instructed them to take all the sheep they needed by force. David then made plans to kill Nabal.

Abigail, the beautiful wife of this empty-headed fool, heard of her husband's despicable words and David's intentions. This woman of valor and wisdom quickly gathered two hundred loaves of bread, two skins of wine, five slaughtered and dressed sheep, five sacks of roasted grain, one hundred clusters of raisins, and two hundred fig cakes and loaded them onto her donkeys.

She did not tell Nabal of her intentions. This woman of valor got her "wagon train" of provision into high gear in an effort to intercept David before he killed the fool to whom she was married.

She succeeded!

When Abigail saw David, she bowed to the ground and fell on her face before him. She was the absolute portrait of strength as she humbled herself on behalf of her husband in an attempt to save his arrogant life from an enraged David.

Abigail made one of history's greatest speeches on her face pleading for the life of Nabal, who did not have the strength of character to say, "I was wrong!"

This pure act of humility and contrition would determine her destiny, which was greater than anything she could have ever possibly imagined.

David accepted her request for pardon, and he and his men ate the delicious meal Abigail had prepared. David informed Abigail that had she not come, he would have killed her husband and every son he had by morning.

Thankful for David's mercy, Abigail mounted her donkey and rode home to her drunken, empty-headed husband who was hosting a great feast of his own.

Abigail knew that timing was everything.

She said nothing to Nabal that night, but at dawn she looked at his puffy face and red eyes and said to him, "David and his men were coming here last night to kill you and all your sons!"

What was Nabal's response? The "tough guy" had a heart attack and died ten days later. What happened to Abigail? David married her the same week.

Abigail was the woman who married the wrong man, but through her grace and strength, she stepped into the pages of history and became the beautiful queen of Israel. (See 1 Samuel 25.)

REMEMBER THIS TRUTH...

You know that you have passed from immaturity to maturity when you stop saying, "I don't have a problem," and say, "I am the problem."

When you're wrong, admit it; it will save your life from a tsunami of grief you'll never see coming, and it will shorten your stay in the problem.

5. Forgive.

The more things that change in our society, the more we must remember the things that never change, and that is God and His Word.

Jesus established a perfect model for prayer in Matthew 6. Within the Lord's Prayer are several supernatural principles; among them is the life-changing application of forgiveness.

The statement "Forgive us as we forgive those..." holds the golden key for many people who want to take a shortcut out of their problem.

Forgiveness is born in an act of confession followed by a purifying plunge into the fountain filled with blood drawn from Immanuel's veins.

When a friend, associate, or family member makes a mistake that offends you, don't rub it in—rub it out with the power of forgiveness.

What is forgiveness? Forgiveness is a full pardon from an offensive act that's been committed against you. It's a fresh start. It's another chance. It's the canceling of a debt. It's a new beginning.

There is no new beginning to your life without an ending to an offense, and there is no ending to your problem without a new beginning through forgiveness.

Forgiveness is the key that unlocks the door of resentment and the handcuffs of hatred. Forgiveness is a supernatural power that breaks the chains of bitterness, bringing joy that is unspeakable and full of glory!

Forgiveness is not softhearted foolishness. It's the first step to ending the spiritual and emotional problem you find yourself in right now.

Is this you?

You laugh, but your laughter is hollow. You smile, but behind the mask you're weeping. Are you going through the motions of life like a robot? Have you become mechanical, hiding your inner rage, your broken heart, and your deep resentment?

Are you frantically searching for relief in the magic formulas provided by your druggist, but you can't seem to quite find it? Are you ending every day trying to find an answer to your problem by taking one more pill, by drinking one more martini, one more glass of wine, or just one more bottle of beer? Are you in one failed relationship after another? You find no peace, no answer to your endless questions, only a deep-seated throbbing pain that will not go away.

REMEMBER THIS TRUTH...

Forgiveness is cleansing; it's not whitewashing!

The way out of the problem can be found in the simple mandate given to us by our Lord Jesus Christ: "Forgive us as we forgive those who trespass against us."

Forgiveness is not weakness; it takes great strength to forgive. Forgiveness is the first step toward happiness, toward hope, and toward healing. Forgiveness is a huge step out of the problem and into the provision of God.

Forgiveness is not for the benefit of the person who hurt you, who betrayed you, who lied about you, or who rejected you when you needed them most. Forgiveness is for *your* benefit.

Please hear me! God cannot forgive you if you will not forgive another. Jesus said, "For if ye forgive men their trespasses, your heavenly Father will also forgive you: But if ye forgive not men their trespasses, neither will your Father forgive your trespasses" (Matt. 6:14–15, KJV).

Forgiveness is not an option for the believer. Charles Swindoll said it perfectly: "Forgiveness is not an elective in the curriculum of servanthood. It is a required course, and the exams are always tough to pass."[19]

Even though the exam is tough, the Word of God gives us the necessary study notes to pass the test. The apostle Paul wrote, "And be kind to one another, tenderhearted, forgiving one another, just as God in Christ forgave you" (Eph. 4:32).

> Therefore, as the elect of God, holy and beloved, put on tender mercies, kindness, humility, meekness, longsuffering; bearing with one another, and forgiving one another, if anyone has a complaint against another; even as Christ forgave you, so you also must do.
>
> —COLOSSIANS 3:12–13

> And the prayer of faith will save the sick, and the Lord will raise him up. And if he has committed sins, he will be forgiven. Confess your trespasses to one another, and pray for one another, that you may be healed. The effective, fervent prayer of a righteous man avails much.
>
> —JAMES 5:15–16

The message is clear: if you won't forgive others, God can't forgive you. If God is perfect, and He forgave you, why can't you, with all your faults and failures, forgive others?

People say, "I can't forgive my husband…wife…mother…father, children…brother or sisters in Christ because…"

REMEMBER THIS TRUTH...

The will of God does not take you where the grace of God cannot keep you.

That's a lie from the father of lies! You can forgive; you just won't. Your unforgiving spirit is a weapon of control over people, and that, my friend, is the sin of witchcraft! Unforgiveness is a form of bondage that thrives on hate and resentment.

Sharing your bitterness with all who will listen takes your sin to another level. You become a two-legged viper, pouring your toxic poison into the lifeblood of friends and family, killing relationships, separating chief friends, and removing all possibility of reconciliation. Your toxic tongue will extend your stay in the problem indefinitely and will ultimately earn your ruin. God personally guarantees that you will live in torment until you forgive.

Jesus told the story of the unforgiving slave. The king called in his slave who owed him ten million dollars and ordered him to pay his debt immediately.

The slave said, "I don't have ten million dollars. That's ten times the total taxes of this nation. It is an impossible debt."

The king ordered him sold, along with his wife and children and all he possessed. The slave fell on his face, begged for mercy, and pledged to pay back everything he owed.

The king showed him mercy and forgave the slave of his debt and released him a free man.

After receiving this immeasurable amount of forgiveness from the king, the slave immediately went to the city gates and found a fellow slave who owed him twenty dollars and demanded immediate payment. When his friend could not pay, he had him thrown into debtor's prison.

The fellow slaves who witnessed this merciless act sent a message to the king. The king called the unforgiving slave before him and said, "You wicked slave, I forgave all your debt because you pled for mercy. Should you not also have had mercy on your fellow slave, even as I had mercy on you?"

Matthew continues to tell the story: "And the king, moved with anger, handed him over to the tormentors until he should repay all that was owed him." (See Matthew 18:23–34.)

Because it was impossible to pay the exorbitant debt to the king, the unforgiving slave was tormented on a regular basis for the rest of his life. He refused to forgive another and dearly paid the price. If you will not forgive, God will send the tormentors.

There is another sad part to this story; the slave who owed the twenty dollars never got out of jail either. Think about it! A minor act of forgiveness would have set both men free forever, but no forgiveness was extended, and both men spent the rest of their lives in torment.

Medical research proves that resentment and bitterness cause heart trouble, ulcers, high blood pressure, strokes, heart attacks, and even cancer. These are tormentors! Are you so angry...so resentful...so bitter...so high on hate that you are willing to kill yourself?

How many people have you sent to an emotional prison? How many have you held hostage because of a past offense that you refuse to forgive? You're concerned with your rights while God is concerned with reconciliation! Do you want to be right...or reconciled?

REMEMBER THIS TRUTH...

Your lack of forgiveness burns the bridge
that you must one day cross yourself.

A man tells a story that began while he was in college.

> I was part of a fraternity initiation committee that placed the new members in the middle of a long stretch of a country road. I was to drive my car with as great a speed as possible straight at them. The challenge was for them to stand firm until a signal was given to jump out of the way.
>
> It was a dark night. I had reached 100 miles an hour and saw their looks of terror in the headlights. The signal was given to jump out of the way and everyone jumped clear—except one boy.

I left college after that. I later married and had two children. The look on that boy's face as I passed over him at a hundred miles an hour stayed in my mind all the time. I became hopelessly inconsistent, moody, and finally became a problem drinker. My wife had to work to bring in the only income we had.

I was drinking at home one morning when someone rang the doorbell. I opened the door to find myself facing a woman who seemed strangely familiar, so I invited her into our home.

She sat down in our living room and introduced herself as the mother of the boy I had killed years before. She told me that she had hated me and spent agonizing nights rehearsing ways to get revenge.

I listened as she told me of the love and forgiveness that had come when she gave her heart to Christ. She said, "I have come to let you know that I forgive you, and I want you to forgive me."

I looked into her eyes that morning and I saw deep into her soul the permission to be the kind of man I might have been had I never killed her son. That forgiveness changed my whole life.[20]

Mark Twain said, "Forgiveness is the fragrance that the violet sheds on the heel that has crushed it."[21]

Forgiveness can transform lives, but the lack of it will wound and forever destroy. The church of Jesus Christ suffers from the lack of forgiveness. The church is crippled, not by Satan and his demon hordes...not by media attacks...not by the critical sarcasm of agnostics, but by Christians who hold other believers hostage over their past. Where is forgiveness in the house of God?

Hear me! The greatest proof the church could give a lost world that Jesus Christ is the answer for their lives is believers who will forgive one another and start loving one another as Christ mandated.

You don't even have to let the offender know that you have forgiven him or her. The mere act of pure forgiveness within releases you from prison. To erase the offense, to wipe the slate clean, to cancel a punishment, and to give up all claims of the one who hurt you is to be free from your bondage.

REMEMBER THIS TRUTH...

God is not concerned with what others do wrong;
He is only concerned with what you do right.
It is right to forgive.

The place called forgiveness is where you can find peace for your mind. Forgiveness is the manifestation of your promise! It's the place to find health and well-being. Forgiveness benefits your eternal soul. It's the beginning of the end of the problem and the first step into your promised land.

It's not what happens to you that matters; it's how you react to what happens to you that determines your success or failure while in the problem. It really does not matter what someone has done to you; what matters is how you react to that wrong.

6. Control your tongue.

There are seven gates or entrances into our senses. These *gates* allow different kinds of signals into the mind and, ultimately, our spirit.

Six of these gates are paired. The two eyes can behold the beauty of God's creation or the horror of man's evil; the two nostrils are able to smell the fragrance of a rose or the stench of corruption; the two ears have the ability to hear the good news of the gospel or listen to the assassination of another's character.

The final gate is the mouth. It stands alone and has the choice to speak blessings or curses through the power of the tongue.

The tongue causes us more problems than all the other six gates. There is no other area in our personality more directly related to our total well-being than the mouth and tongue. It is not possible to have a good life if you do not control your tongue.

James writes in his epistle, "If anyone considers himself religious and yet does not keep a tight rein on his tongue, he deceives himself and his religion is worthless" (James 1:26, NIV). James is saying that if we do not activate the promises in the Word of God and control our tongues from speaking evil, our religion is of no value.

When I was a child, my mother took us to the doctor who made the same opening statement every time he examined us: "Show me your tongue!" The doctor was able to determine if the body was sick by how the tongue looked. Likewise, God can determine the condition of your soul by what your tongue utters, for "out of the abundance of the heart the mouth speaks" (Matt. 12:34).

If you are able to control your tongue, you can control your whole life. In James 3:3–8 James gives us illustrations of little things controlling very powerful things. He writes that we put bits into the mouths of horses to make them obey us. With that small bit, we can control a very powerful animal.

James then compares the tongue to the rudder of a ship. A ship is a massive vessel that can carry tons of cargo through the raging surf of the sea, yet that powerful ship is controlled by a small rudder. If the rudder is used properly, it can guide the huge ship through turbulent storms and to its port of call. If the rudder is mismanaged, the ship can be driven into the rocks and destroyed.

Likewise, your tongue, a very small member of your body, controls the destiny of your life. If the rudder of the tongue is used properly, you will reach your divine destiny. If the rudder is used foolishly, your life will be shipwrecked, and your stay in the problem will be indefinite.

REMEMBER THIS TRUTH...

Your words determine your destiny!

The children of Israel were delivered from Egypt by the promise of God. They had endured the problem. They crossed the wilderness, and now it was time to stand and enter into the Promised Land.

Moses sent twelve men to spy out the provision God had promised to Abraham centuries before. One leader was chosen from each tribe to analyze the nature of the people, the size of their cities, and the kinds of resources available in this new land. The men were to return to Moses with a report of their findings.

The twelve spies spent forty days walking through the Promised Land. (See Numbers 13 and 14.) Listen to how most of them allowed their tongues to determine their destiny! Ten of the twelve spies told Moses, "Yes, it is a land flowing with milk and honey. Yes, the fruit is so heavy it took two of us to carry one bunch of grapes on a staff between us." But they concluded their report by releasing a curse on themselves and on the majority of the people they represented.

"But the people who live there are powerful, and the cities are fortified and very large. We even saw descendants of Anak there. The Amalekites live in the Negev; the Hittites, Jebusites and Amorites live in the hill country; and the Canaanites live near the sea and along the Jordan....We can't attack those people; they are stronger than we are" (Num. 13:28, 31, NIV).

After forty years of miracles, the ten spies doubted their provision and their Provider. They doubted God's promise. What was the consequence of their exclamation of doubt and fear? The fury of God turned on Israel because of their doubt and rejection of the promise. God pronounced a death decree on every Israelite twenty years of age and older. They were sentenced to die in the wilderness, remaining trapped in their problem forever. They were within walking distance of their provision, yet they failed to receive God's promise.

However, there were two spies who were spared from God's judgment. Joshua and Caleb saw what the others saw, but they believed in faith that God would help them defeat the giants who lived in the Promised Land. Joshua and Caleb did not speak in negative terms. They acknowledged the problem and stood on God's promise to take them into their provision. They endured the problem, acted on their faith, and walked into the Promised Land with those nineteen and younger. "Then Caleb quieted the people before Moses, and said, 'Let us go up at once and take possession, for we are well able to overcome it'" (Num. 13:30).

The next time you open your mouth...think! You are about to commit an act that can determine the quality of your present life and the success or failure of your future. Words can heal or they can wound; words can bless or they can curse; words can keep you trapped in the problem, or they can provide a shortcut to your provision.

Those who declare negative words and thoughts of trouble and defeat are treacherous. They come to the strong and consume them. They are like a bottomless pit. They are unquenchable. They are always parched, bitter, and resentful. They are contagious; they drain the lifeblood of those who listen to their toxic tongue.

REMEMBER THIS TRUTH...
Words are a mirror of your soul.

Yet those who proclaim God's promises with words and thoughts of hope and victory are inspiring. They strengthen the weak and motivate them. They are like an infinite resource of wisdom and understanding. They are contented, optimistic, and confident. They too are contagious; they elevate the faith of those who listen to their words of encouragement.

Make a habit of speaking good words, words of blessing and encouragement, words of healing and peace. Avoid using words of discouragement and defeat. If you keep saying that things are going to turn out bad, you have a very good chance of becoming a prophet, and your days in the wilderness will be long and full of despair.

7. Get off your pity pot.

As every cockroach knows, staying away from poison is the secret of success and a long life. Self-pity is poison. Self-pity allows our ego to get in the way of constructive criticism. Do you mount your pity pot, stick your thumb in your mouth, and whine for six months when a friend tries to point out a weakness that has you locked in your problem?

Self-pity is one of the worst enemies you can have. Don't try to make peace with it; conquer it! Self-pity is one of the the most disintegrating things you can do to yourself. Self-pity blinds the eyes of hope.

Self-pity is an overshadowing defect within a person. It is an obstacle to all spiritual progress. It will cut off all effective communication with others because of its excessive demands for attention, sympathy, and superficial praise. It is a form of self-imposed martyrdom.

Determine to get off your pity pot! Take heed of what Saint Paul said, and "stop comparing yourself to others." Set your mind on Christ, and self-pity will soon be a part of your past.

The most dangerous thing a person can receive is excessive praise from man. Why do some self-centered superstar athletes and high-paid movie stars break the law with impunity and whine when they are hauled into court? They do so because they have been corrupted by continual, gratuitous praise.

The Bible says, "Woe to you when all men speak well of you" (Luke 6:26). That's one verse in the Bible I've never had any trouble keeping!

Tom Selleck said, "Whenever I get full of myself, I remember the nice, elderly couple who approached me with a camera on a street in Honolulu one day. When I struck a pose for them, the man said, "No, no, we want you to take a picture of *us*!"[22]

Dr. Joyce Brothers writes, "An individual's self-concept is the core of his personality. It affects every aspect of human behavior: the ability to learn, the capacity to grow and change, the choice of friends, mates, and careers. It is no exaggeration to say that a strong, positive self-image is the best possible preparation for success in life."[23]

To which I say, "Amen!"

The opposite of self-pity is confidence. Confidence isn't something you hype yourself into. Confidence is what is left when all doubt is removed.

The word *confidence* comes from two Latin words: *con*, meaning "with," and *fideo*, meaning "faith." Confidence means living with faith! If you are going to be the best in your field, you have to believe in yourself when nobody else will. No one will follow a thumb-sucking whiner mounted on his or her pity pot!

REMEMBER THIS TRUTH...

Problems are inevitable, but self-pity is optional. Get off your pity pot!

Too many of God's children have *stinking thinking*.

Do you have a temperament that is unnaturally gloomy, melancholic, and filled with self-pity? Do you feel isolated, cheated in life, and always expecting the worst is going to happen to you? This is stinking thinking! You must stop this kind of thinking now!

Believe in the God who believes in you. The prophet Jeremiah wrote, "'For I know the plans I have for you,' declares the LORD, 'plans to prosper you and not to harm you, plans to give you hope and a future'" (Jer. 29:11, NIV).

Until you accept who you are and who you can become, you will never accept or attain God's destiny for your life.

Be careful not to be prideful, for the sin of pride will keep you in the wilderness. Ray Burwick, author of *Self-Esteem: You're Better Than You Think*, states, "Pride is an unrealistic appraisal of self. We think we are better than others. Low self-esteem is an unrealistic appraisal of self. We think we are not as good as others, and these two things, pride and low self-esteem, stifle God's best for us."[24]

How to Shorten Your Stay in the Problem

In review, the seven steps to shorten your stay in the problem are:

1. Acknowledge the problem.
2. Take responsibility.
3. Be willing to work.
4. When you are wrong, admit it.
5. Forgive.
6. Control your tongue.
7. Get off your pity pot.

The children of Israel had no intention of wandering in the wilderness for forty years, but they did so—one day at a time. They lengthened their stay in the problem by making one bad choice after another.

It's time for you to walk into your promise. Get excited about who you are in Christ and the plans He has for your future. You are a one-of-a-kind creation. He wants only the best for you. Make right choices, and don't be afraid to expect good things.

REMEMBER THIS TRUTH...

Life is too short to waste it staying trapped in the problem. Time waits for no man, and it certainly is not waiting for you.

Chapter 5

HOW TO SOLVE THE PROBLEM

E VERY CHAPTER IN THIS BOOK HAS PRESENTED VARIOUS problem-solving components. This chapter is lovingly dedicated to every person who has a lingering problem that is unresolved, who has a current problem that's driving you absolutely crazy, or who feels amazingly well for the moment but is wise enough to know that before the sun sets today they could be facing the greatest problem of their life.

God does not make His children immune to problems, but He promises, "I will be with him in trouble" (Ps. 91:15). It makes no difference how severe our trouble may be; nothing can separate us from our relationship with God.

Saint Paul wrote in Romans 8:37, "*In all these things* we are more than conquerors..." (emphasis added). The apostle Paul was not referring to imaginary things but to all kinds of problems that were very real, very dangerous, and life threatening.

Look at Paul's list of problems: "Who shall separate us from the love of Christ? Shall tribulation, or distress, or persecution, or famine, or nakedness, or peril, or sword?" (v. 35).

"Shall tribulation...?" Tribulation is never a wonderful or welcomed experience. Tribulation can be life threatening. Tribulation for Saint Paul was being stoned and left for dead in the street, beaten with a Roman whip with thirty-nine stripes, and bitten by a deadly viper on the isle of Malta.

Paul had great problems, but they were never greater than his Provider.

The bottom line is this: even life-threatening tribulations are not able to "separate us from the love of Christ." Your problems will never be greater than God's power! "For with God nothing will be impossible" (Luke 1:37).

"Shall distress…?" Can God's love hold fast, even when everyone and everything around us seems to be saying that His love is merely an illusion and there is no such thing as justice?

Paul and Silas were placed in prison for preaching the gospel. They had been beaten and their backs soaked in their own blood. Their reaction? They sang in their prison cell in the midnight hour. Distress cannot separate us from the Problem Solver, the God of Abraham, Isaac, and Jacob.

> For in the time of trouble He shall hide me in His pavilion; in the secret place of His tabernacle He shall hide me; He shall set me high upon a rock.
>
> —PSALM 27:5

THE NAME OF THE GAME IS *TEMPERANCE*

The secret of solving every problem is locked in the word *temperance*. Temperance is a bridle of gold that controls your wild-horse instincts, which, if left uncontrolled, will utterly destroy you. Temperance is the moderating of one's desires in obedience to the Word of God. Temperance is the foundation of health, strength, and peace. Temperance is moderation in the things that are good and total abstinence from the things that are bad.

REMEMBER THIS TRUTH…

Temperance is self-control, and the absence of self-control is the taproot of most of our problems!

Benjamin Franklin said, "Temperance puts wood on the fire, meal in the barrel, flour in the tub, money in the purse, contentment in the house, clothes on the children, vigor in the body, intelligence in the brain, and spirit in the whole constitution."[1]

Saint Paul wrote in 1 Corinthians 9:25 that we are to be "temperate in all things." In Galatians 5:22–23, he wrote, "But the fruit of the Spirit is love, joy, peace, longsuffering, kindness, goodness, faithfulness, gentleness, self-control. Against such there is no law."

In this age of advanced technology, we have learned to control everything but ourselves. We control the sun to heat our houses; we control mighty rivers to produce electricity for our cities; we control satellites in space to transmit communication signals to the nations of the world; we control deadly diseases with wonder drugs, but we have not learned how to control ourselves.

It is easier for man to control the universe than to control himself. Take the time to trace the source of most major problems men have on this earth and you will find the lack of temperance and the lack of self-control.

Every divorce was caused by one or both partners who had no self-control in one or more critical areas of their lives.

Every drunkard and drug addict stumbling down the streets of America's cities is a testimonial of man's absolute lack of self-control.

Every person buried by credit card debt sees his or her worst enemy when they look into the mirror. The war of self-control is a civil war of the soul. The inability to say, "No, I don't need that," or "No, I can't afford that," created that mountain of debt, resulting in the borrower becoming a prisoner to the lender.

Every war from the Book of Genesis until the most current one you will watch tonight on the national news was caused by the lack of self-control of a warlord or tinhorn dictator driven by lust and greed. War-crazed leaders have always been driven by the demonic urge for revenge and the lust of unlimited power!

Our technology has produced nuclear bombs so powerful we can atomize the earth. I'm not afraid of a nuclear bomb. But I am afraid of *any* bomb when man has his hands on it. If history teaches us anything, it teaches that man cannot control himself and in time will use that bomb to cremate the earth.

Self-control. Do you have it? Allow the power of the Holy Spirit to place within your mouth the golden bridle of temperance before you destroy yourself. The Bible teaches, "He who is slow to anger is better than the mighty, and he who rules his spirit than he who takes a city" (Prov. 16:32).

Your doubts betray your dreams. Your fears strangle your hopes and prevent you from climbing the stairway to the stars. Your habits, born of your free will, lead you to paradise or the gates of hell.

Developing self-control is one of the most treasured lessons of the Bible. Self-control is the ability to make yourself do the thing you have to do when it ought to be done. Self-control demands you do all with excellence, even when you don't want to do it.

Life is not doing what you want. Life is doing what you must. To do what you must and to do it well requires temperance and self-control. Do you have it? Without it you will live all your life perpetually in the problem.

Benjamin Franklin speaks of temperance as one of the virtues that breeds success. He gives thirteen virtues necessary for true success: temperance, silence, order, resolution, frugality, industry, sincerity, justice, moderation, cleanliness, tranquility, chastity and humility.

When faced with enduring and solving the problem, all of these virtues are needed at any given time or in one form or another, but temperance leads the pack!

There are times in everyone's life when success is born from adversity. You need to take a deep breath, shake yourself, and know that God cannot fail you. Every victory has stages of action before triumph prevails. Whatever choices you make or solutions you discover to solving your problem, you will need temperance to achieve your provision.

WHAT IS DISCIPLINE?

As a Christian, you are expected to demonstrate discipline in your appetites, your passions, your affections, your thought life, your attitude, your speech, your conduct, your habits, your desires, your companionships, and your amusements. Do you lack self-control in any of these areas? If the answer is yes, you are a time bomb that will explode, shattering your life and the lives of your precious family and friends.

Discipline is when you harness your raging emotions, your passions, your fears, and your frustrations to produce good fruit. Discipline is when you master the problem and refuse to allow the situation to master you.

Jesus Christ was the master of discipline. In the Upper Room He put a towel on His arm, knelt, and washed the dirty feet of His disciples. It was the portrait of absolute power under absolute discipline.

The ultimate example of discipline was demonstrated once again at the cross. As God Almighty, He had all power in heaven and in the earth. He could have called ten thousand angels to destroy the earth and reduce it to a spinning ball of dust in space.

Peter had cursed and denied Him. Judas sold Him for the price of a slave. Herod's men of war slapped Him, spit on Him, and mocked Him with a purple robe and a crown of thorns. Then they whipped Him until His back was a mass of bloody flesh hanging on to His rib cage, and with discipline He remained silent.

He carried His cross to Calvary, where Roman soldiers nailed the hands that had created man in the Garden of Eden. They nailed the sacred feet that had walked on water and at that very moment were crushing the head of Satan, bringing absolute victory to every believer forever.

What did Christ do with all that power? He who had all power in heaven and in the earth bowed His blood-soaked head and whispered, "Father, forgive them, for they know not what they do."

That's the kind of discipline that carries you through the problem. Do you have it? Without it you will destroy yourself and every dream you've ever had.

There's a great and eternal difference between discipline and punishment. Most people can't define either and confuse both.

Punishment is the consequence of wrongdoing.

Discipline is the determined will to do anything.

When you go to the university, you discover that everything you learned is, in fact, a discipline. When you get married, there is a discipline to marriage. When you join a New Testament church, you are presented a code of strict discipline based on spiritual authority. The church is not a democracy; it's a theocracy. You do not vote on the will of God. The will of God is written in the Word of God; you either obey or disobey. Obedience brings blessings, and disobedience brings consequences.

When you enter the military you begin with an experience called "boot camp." The purpose of boot camp is to take Mamma's fat little biscuit eater and transform him into a lean, mean, fighting machine.

When you arrive at this transformation camp, they shave your long, beautiful, curly hair off and give you baggy clothes in place of your designer jeans. They feed you food that you wouldn't feed to your dog—and give you fifteen minutes to eat it.

You are introduced to a drill instructor (DI) who marches you until your blistered feet bleed, and in less than twenty-four hours you are absolutely sure he is the Antichrist. You drop into your bunk dead tired, and your worst nightmare becomes reality—it's morning—the DI walks into your barracks at 4:00 a.m. screaming his head off as he hammers the inside of a garbage can with his swagger stick.

Mamma is not at the breakfast table to kiss you on the cheek, welcoming you to another new and exciting day or asking if you would like another large fluffy buttermilk biscuit with strawberry jelly.

This is discipline; it's not punishment!

Why is this happening?

It's happening because your DI is transforming his men from a group of self-serving, self-centered, prima donnas into a razor-sharp fighting unit tougher than a junkyard dog.

REMEMBER THIS TRUTH...
You are destined to become a giant-killer!

As a result of your endurance of this extreme discipline, you are not a big, fat target running around in a baggy green uniform looking for a new way to get killed in combat. Instead, you know how to endure severe problems, adapt to new environments, and overcome whatever situation develops in the combat zone.

So what's the point?

The point is—when we get saved, Jesus takes us by the hand and says, "Let's go to boot camp."

When He leads us into the problem, we pout, we whine, and we murmur to the members of our prayer group or church, saying something stupid like, "The devil is really after me!"

Wrong! This is not punishment; it's discipline! King Jesus has our self-centered and self-serving life in the rock-crushing machine. He is crushing our carnal nature. He is stripping us of our self-righteousness. We enter the problem dependent on no one but self; we graduate from the problem totally dependent on Him. Christ, our Commander, is going to march us through one adversity after another until He transforms us from religious wimps into anointed warriors.

As a giant-killer, you will have the anointing to tread on scorpions, cast out demons, command that sickness and disease be bound by the power of Christ, and live every day as more than a conqueror through Christ.

Nothing shall be impossible unto you as soon as you get off your pity pot, roll up your lower lip, put on the whole armor of God, and fight the good fight. You are a soldier in the army of the living God; act like it…think like it…talk like it…and fight like it.

You may be brilliant, but without discipline you're finished. You may be wealthy, but without discipline poverty is certain. You may be powerful, but without discipline you will live your latter years saturated in shame and disgrace. You may be the leader of people…the builder of a great business…an All-American athlete, but without discipline you are defeated before you begin in the race of life.

Ability will win one game; discipline will win the national championship or the Olympic gold medal. Talent may take you to the top; discipline will keep you at the top.

Recently the nations of the world were riveted to their television screens watching the Olympics in China. Americans were cheering for our talented and dedicated athletes. The entire nation was mesmerized by the unspeakable exploits of one Michael Phelps, who is now the most celebrated Olympian in the history of the world. There is one word that defines how Michael Phelps won a record number of gold medals…DISCIPLINE!

Michael's food intake was regulated to the last calorie. His hours of rest were measured, and his swimming skills were developed under the watchful eyes of dedicated coaches who pushed him hour after hour, week after week, year after year to be better than he thought he could be. Why? Because the price of championship is *discipline*.

Jesus demanded discipline in His followers. He said, "But why do you call Me 'Lord, Lord,' and do not do the things which I say?" (Luke 6:46). You are most likely a Christian if you are reading this book, but *are you a disciple?* You are a disciple of Christ *only* if *you do* what Christ asked you to do.

The rich young ruler came to Christ and asked to be one of His disciples. Jesus gave him one command: "Go, sell what you have and give to the poor, and you will have treasure in heaven; and come, follow Me" (Matt. 19:21). The rich young ruler turned and went away sorrowfully because even though he had great riches, he could not obey the command of Jesus. He believed Jesus was the Messiah; he simply could not obey Him.

Strap on your seat belt and hear this: Demons believe in Jesus. The Bible says that when they hear His name, they tremble in fear. Demons believe in Jesus; they just don't obey Jesus. Many people who call themselves Christians believe in Jesus; they just don't have the discipline to obey Him.

REMEMBER THIS TRUTH...

It's not what you can believe that distinguishes you as a Christian; it's what you can OBEY that separates you from the crowd.

The Bible says, "Obedience is better than sacrifice." (See 1 Samuel 15:22.) Discipline is godly obedience, not carnal willpower!

In my fifty years of ministry, I have often heard men driven by a macho mentality say, "I have a will of steel!" Pity! You are living in idolatry. You are, in fact, worshiping what *you* can do for you, not what *Christ* has done in you.

You hear the narcissistic arrogant spout, "I am the master of my fate and the captain of my soul." Wrong!

You can't take your next breath without God's help. You can't guarantee your next heartbeat. You certainly can't guarantee the destiny of your eternal soul without redemption through the cross of Christ. You are the captain of exactly nothing!

Carnal willpower can never conquer sin. The more time you give to conquering weakness through your willpower, the greater control that weakness will have in your life.

You don't believe that? How many times have you told yourself, "I'm going on a diet tomorrow, and I'm absolutely going to stop eating anything that's sweet." The more you think about not doing it, the more compulsively you desire to do exactly that.

You are like the secretary who told her friends at the office, "Tomorrow I'm going on a diet, because I'm big enough to get group insurance all by myself! I have the willpower to do it!" That night she thought of nothing but chocolate cake—she even dreamed of chocolate cake.

The next day she walked into the office with a beautiful chocolate cake dripping with icing. Her office mate asked, "I thought you were going on a diet today—one of those do-or-die diets where you're off sweets forever? Why did you buy that chocolate cake?"

"This morning as I was driving to work, I saw this beautiful chocolate cake in the window of the bakery. I told the Lord if He wanted me to have that cake to make a parking place available right in front of the bakery. And you know what? The tenth time I drove around the bakery, the parking place was there. Let's eat!"

Your sin cannot be conquered via willpower!

You cannot will yourself to go to heaven. Sin has been conquered by Jesus Christ at the cross. Willpower will never set you free from the attraction of sin. Only Christ can do that. "If the Son makes you free, you shall be free indeed" (John 8:36).

Discipline is proof you are in the family of God. If you reject the discipline of God, you are not His child. Here is scriptural evidence to support this fact: "If you endure chastening, God deals with you as with sons.... But if you are without chastening...then you are illegitimate and not sons" (Heb. 12:7–8).

Jesus demanded discipline and the crucifixion of the god of self in the lives of His disciples. Listen to His commands in the boot camp of Christian discipline:

- "Take up the cross, and follow Me" (Mark 10:21).
- "Take My yoke upon you and learn from Me" (Matt. 11:29).
- "Launch out into the deep and let down your nets for a catch" (Luke 5:4).
- "...you will find a colt tied....Loose him and bring him here" (Luke 19:30).

What's the message here? If you can't serve, you can't be a disciple. God has no superstars; we are all His servants for life. A servant in the Bible does what he's told, when he's told, exactly like he's told, as long as he's told. When you get to heaven, you will be received by God the Father with these words: "Well done, thou good and faithful SERVANT!" When I hear of pastors, singers, and musicians referred to as "superstars," I cringe. When I hear congregations sing the words of the gospel song, "O to be like Thee! / O to be like Thee / Blessed Redeemer, pure as Thou art," I wonder if we truly know the Jesus of the Bible.[2]

Jesus was born in shame and poverty in Bethlehem's manger. From His first sermon, He lived in a tornado of scandal from the established church.

He was hated by the sanctimonious, and plots to kill Him were devised by the Roman government. He fasted and prayed forty days and prayed all night many nights. He had power because of His prayer life, not because He was the Son of God.

Had there been a *Jerusalem Post,* He would have lived in a firestorm of constant criticism. The tabloids would write of His eating with prostitutes, telling His audience of Pharisees that they "are of your father the devil," and calling them "a generation of vipers." There would be pictures of Him being hauled into secular courts for breaking religious rules by healing people on the Sabbath.

He was crucified by the Roman government and hung between two thieves as an insurrectionist too dangerous to live. He was buried in a borrowed grave as His dearest friends denied Him, betrayed Him, doubted Him, and collected their thirty pieces of silver in the shadow of the cross.

Do YOU really want to be like Jesus? Are you disciplined enough to be His? Be assured, He will keep you in the problem until your self-centered, self-serving carnal will has been crucified and buried.

The apostle Paul was a disciplined Christian. He disciplined his body, saying, "I beat my body and make it my slave so that after I have preached to others, I myself will not be disqualified for the prize" (1 Cor. 9:27, NIV). He disciplined himself to loneliness, saying, "All forsook me" (2 Tim. 4:16). He disciplined himself to scorn, saying, "We are fools for Christ sake" (1 Cor. 4:10).

He disciplined himself to suffer, saying, "We are…persecuted, but not abandoned" (2 Cor. 4:8–9, NIV). He disciplined himself to die fearlessly, saying, "The time of my departure is at hand. I have fought the good fight, I have finished the race" (2 Tim. 4:6–7).

Where did we get the foolish idea that life was supposed to run smoothly all the time? We got it from Hollywood's "happily-ever-after endings," which are more delusional than truthful.

If you have the discipline to achieve your divine destiny, you will determine to overcome any obstacle set before you. If you want to succeed, you must erase any doubts you have. You must embrace the fact that God is on your side, and if God is on your side, you are destined for victory!

TAMING THE WILD HORSES

Victory over your problems is not possible without first harnessing your wild-horse emotions. How can we tame these instincts of human nature? The major religions of the world offer the following ways.

Self-assertion

First is the doctrine of *self-assertion*, which teaches man to give free rein to their natural instincts. Man's instincts are natural, therefore self-justifying. This doctrine also teaches that whatever is natural is beautiful, and whatever is beautiful must be right. If it feels so good, how can it be so wrong?

The only "sin" of this philosophy is to suppress a natural desire. This is called "the new morality" in the twenty-first century. The truth is...it isn't new, and it isn't moral—it's an old doctrine of paganism with a new name.

One of the apostles of this doctrine was German philosopher Friedrich Nietzsche, whose doctrine was:

> Be strong, assert your self; be a superman. Get rid of your pious priest and their weak lily livered gospel of mercy. Purge your soul of this devil called Christianity. Develop a master race of supermen.[3]

Adolf Hitler believed and obeyed the message of the apostate Nietzsche, and the Nazis of Germany birthed twelve years of hell on earth. The result was Dachau, Auschwitz, and Buchenwald as six million Jews were systematically slaughtered and fifty million others were drowned in a river of blood throughout Europe.

America is now embracing the message of Nietzsche: give free rein to your natural instincts; there is no right and there is no wrong.

Hitler labeled the Jews as less than human. When something is not human, it makes killing it seem not so evil. The American version of Nietzsche calls a baby in the womb of the mother a "fetus," a "blob of flesh." It's not human, so we can kill it without pain of conscience.

Moses shouts from Exodus 21:22–23, "If men fight, and hurt a woman with child, so that she gives birth prematurely...if any harm follows, then you shall give life for life." God calls that "fetus" a living soul, and anyone who kills it will stand on Judgment Day convicted of murder in the first degree.

Mother Teresa said, "A nation that kills its children in the womb has lost its soul."[4] Amen, Mother Teresa; I quite agree!

Hitler, following the doctrine of Nietzsche, executed the elderly. America now has assisted suicides for the elderly. Former Colorado Governor Richard Lamm said to the American elderly, "You have a duty to die and get out of the way!"[5] Hitler would have loved Gov. Lamm.

The state of Oregon supports assisted suicides for the elderly. The message? Your care and medical treatment are too costly...therefore you should die! Recently I watched a national news telecast in which a male senior citizen in Oregon who was seriously ill begged the medical community to help him save his life—not take his life.

Nietzsche said, "There is no God!" Nazi Germany bought it. America is now buying it.

It has been said, and bears repeating, "Those who do not remember the mistakes of history are doomed to repeat them." The Ninth Circuit Court of Appeals in California has ruled that the phrase "one nation under God" is unconstitutional. The Ten Commandments have been removed from state capitols, mocked, and banned from public schools lest, in the words of the Supreme Court, "any child reading them should be influenced by them." The result?

Our public school grounds now resemble battlefields littered with dead and dying children, shot by other children in their schools, who never read or heard the sacred words, "Thou shall not kill!"

REMEMBER THIS TRUTH...

When truth is rejected, all that's left to embrace is a lie. When light is rejected, all that's left is darkness. When the love of life is rejected, all that is left is the culture of death.

In Paducah, Kentucky, a fourteen-year-old boy methodically shot and murdered three students who bowed their heads in prayer in public school. He shot and wounded several others as he practiced the doctrine of Nietzsche, rejecting discipline and allowing the wild-horse instincts of humanity to run uncontrolled.

When we teach America's children for forty-plus years that there is no absolute right and no absolute wrong, we are destined to live with the consequences.

Letting the wild horses of human nature run without any form of control is moral and spiritual insanity. It has filled our penitentiaries and asylums for the criminally insane. It has produced a generation of child molesters and rapists. Teen pregnancies and suicides are running off the charts. The fabric of America is falling apart.

This is not beautiful. This is not progress. This is moral madness! "All nations that forget God are turned into hell."

How can this be turned around?

This doctrine of "There is no absolute wrong, and there is no absolute right" can be turned around with a revival of repentance, a revival of family values, and a revival of individual responsibility based upon the eternal truths of discipline and self-control as found in the Word of God. It can be turned around when the church of Jesus Christ decides to be what we are supposed to be—salt and light in a generation of darkness.

REMEMBER THIS TRUTH...

If Christians in America do not stand up and speak up, America's best days are behind us, and we will soon enter into a new era of apostasy that can only be adequately described as the new Dark Ages.

Jesus said, "If the salt loses its flavor...it is then good for nothing but to be thrown out and trampled underfoot by men" (Matt. 5:13). The reason the principles of righteousness are being trampled underfoot in America is because the church of Jesus Christ is more concerned about being a people pleaser than being a Father pleaser. Our light is being concealed and contained under the bushel of the church house when it needs to shine in the schoolhouse, the courthouse, and your house. It is time for believers to look at evil and say, "Enough is enough!"

Self-negation

The second method often adopted to control the wild horses of human nature is self-negation. This philosophy is the extreme opposite of self-assertion and states that our instincts are so fierce that we must find a way to destroy them. Buddhism and Hinduism are religions dedicated to the elimination of personal desire. The concept is this: If you have no desire, you will never be disappointed. When you kill all your desire, you arrive at Nirvana.

Self-negation is a problem. The Bible says, "Delight yourself also in the LORD, and He shall give you the desires of your heart" (Ps. 37:4).

Buddhism says, "Reduce your desires to zero, and you will be happy."

God says, "I am your Father in heaven, and I will give you your desires."

If you break the spirit of a horse, the horse is not worth having. If you break the human spirit, the person loses his passion and purpose for living.

WHAT IS THE SOLUTION?

The solution is not to let man run wild without any control; it's not to deny the desires that make you a person, but the solution is to harness your desires through discipline so you may reach your divine destiny. The biblical way for man to reach his highest purpose in life is the road of temperance, self-control, and discipline.

The same instincts that were in Napoleon were also in the apostle Paul. The difference? Paul's instincts were harnessed by the Holy Spirit. Napoleon's instincts were carnal wild horses that were never tamed or disciplined.

The answer is clear!

Harness the wild horse of human instinct with the golden bridle of temperance and discipline. Put these powerful forces to work. Ride them at full gallop yet under absolute control. Let trained and harnessed talents and God-given instincts carry you to staggering heights of divine accomplishment through every problem you face.

Look at the men Jesus chose to be His disciples. They were not waddling wallflowers or cowardly bystanders.

Consider Matthew the tax collector. Tax collectors worked for Rome collecting taxes from the Jews and were the most hated people in town. The tax collectors worked on commissions and bribes and taxed whatever they thought they could with the power of Rome to back them up.

Jesus looked at Matthew and said two words that changed his life forever: "Follow Me!"

The disciples were ambitious men. They not only wanted to get ahead in this world, but they also wanted to get ahead of each other. James and John said to Jesus, "Grant us that we may sit, one on Your right hand and the other on Your left, in Your glory" (Mark 10:37). Jesus didn't rebuke them for their ambition. Jesus did not fear men who were aggressive and ambitious. He simply harnessed their ambition with the golden bridle of temperance and put them to work in His kingdom, and changed the world.

Peter was a fighter! The Big Fisherman could take care of himself on the waterfront. He was impulsive. He had the habit of getting his mouth in motion before he got his brain in gear. Yet he was the only disciple who walked on water that night on the Sea of Galilee while the other eleven cautious cowards watched, expecting him to drown any second.

Peter, the impulsive and passionate apostle, was the anointed one who preached on the Day of Pentecost when three thousand stormed the gates of heaven as converts to Christ and His cross. Peter had courage under fire, and God used that raw, passionate, and fiery courage to shake the world.

Jesus ambushed Saint Paul on the road to Damascus. His name was Saul at the time, and he was a one-man terrorist organization against Christianity. He was putting Christians in jail, where they were beaten and often killed at his instruction.

REMEMBER THIS TRUTH...

God is looking for strong, aggressive, bold, and fearless warriors of the cross who are willing to fight the good fight, who will run the race of righteousness with temperance, who will resist the devil until he flees, who will endure hardness as a good soldier of Christ.

God saw this type A, turbocharged personality and said, "I choose him." God slapped Saul from his horse, blinded him, and commissioned him. The man whom many Christians considered the very worst man to lead the church was considered by God to be the very best man heaven could find. God changed his name from Saul to Paul, bridled this high-octane racehorse with the golden bridle of temperance, and shook the Roman Empire to the ground.

God is not looking for a frightened weakling, sucking his thumb in the corner while cowering and trembling at shadows with a Bible safely tucked under his arm. My father, who pastored for more than fifty years, said, "I would rather restrain a fanatic than try to resurrect a corpse."

When Nehemiah heard about the destruction of the gates of Jerusalem, he identified the problem, grieved, prayed and fasted before the Lord, and repented for Israel's sins (Neh. 1:3–4). God answered Nehemiah's prayer, turned the king's heart like streams in the desert toward him, and showed Nehemiah His divine favor (Neh. 2:1–10).

Nehemiah challenged the Jewish people to demonstrate their faith in God by their works. He led by example. Nehemiah received an assignment from the Lord, and, as is usually the case, problems followed.

Because of Nehemiah's disciplined leadership, the committed believers overcame laziness: "So we built the wall, and the entire wall was joined together up to half its height, for the people had a mind to work" (Neh. 4:6).

Through discipline, Nehemiah overcame criticism and mockery. "Whatever they build, if even a fox goes up on it, he will break down their stone wall" (v. 3). "But when Sanballat the Horonite, Tobiah the Ammorite official, and Geshem the Arab heard of it, they laughed at us and despised us, and said, 'What is this thing that you are doing?'" (Neh. 2:19).

What did Nehemiah do? "So I answered them, and said to them, 'The God of heaven Himself will prosper us; therefore we His servants will arise and build, but you have no heritage or right or memorial in Jerusalem" (v. 20).

Satan's number-one attack on your personal life is to discourage you through criticism of your life's work, your dreams, your appearance, and your past failures. It is essential to discipline yourself to listen to God's view of you, your accomplishments, and your future in order to pass this test.

Through self-control, Nehemiah overcame character assassination and conspiracy. "...you and the Jews plan to rebel; therefore according to these rumors, you are rebuilding the wall that you may be their king....Now these matters will be reported to the king" (Neh 6:6–7).

How did Nehemiah respond?

He prayed and remained true to his assignment. "So I sent messengers to them, saying, 'I am doing a great work, so that I cannot come down. Why should the work cease while I leave it and go down to you?'...Now therefore, O God, strengthen my hands" (vv. 3, 9).

Nehemiah persevered with his assignment even when his life was threatened. "Afterward I came to the house of Shemaiah the son of Delaiah, the son of Mehetabel, who was a secret informer; and he said, 'Let us meet together in the house of God, within the temple, and let us close the doors of the temple, for they are coming to kill you; indeed, at night they will come to kill you'" (v. 10).

Nehemiah showed discernment through his discipline. God revealed to him that the veiled threats were meant to deter him from his divine assignment. The wall was quickly completed; Nehemiah passed the tests set before him with the implementation of discipline and temperance, and as a result, the Lord was glorified:

> And it happened, when all our enemies heard of it, and all the nations around us saw these things, that they were very disheartened in their own eyes; for they perceived that this work was done by our God.
>
> —NEHEMIAH 6:16

Nehemiah remained faithful through the problem and accomplished his goal. He met his divine assignment. Life's successes are measured by the assignments we complete, not by what we begin. No one remembers the halftime score, only the final score. Whatever you do, don't quit before the miracle provision comes!

Moses never entered the Promised Land. Moses, the lawgiver of Israel, the poet, the prophet, and the liberator of the Jewish people had a problem...his uncontrolled temper.

It first manifested itself when he killed the Egyptian and was forced to flee Egypt for a forty-year course in self-control on the backside of the wilderness. Moses was in his problem!

His fiery temper manifested itself a second time when he came down from Mt. Sinai, where he had literally been in the presence of God until his face radiated His glory. When Moses saw the Hebrews making a golden calf, drunk, and committing sexual sin, he threw down the Ten

Commandments in rage. God told Moses that he would have to construct another set of Ten Commandments on his own.

The third time his anger exploded was when God told him to speak to the rock, and instead he smote the rock in anger. Had Moses spoken to the rock, the people would have seen it as the power of God, and God would have received the glory.

After all the years in the wilderness, after witnessing all the signs and wonders of the Lord, after speaking to God and hearing His voice, Moses could not rid himself of the bondage of anger. His anger cost him the privilege of walking into the Promised Land. Does this describe you? Do you hear from God, read of His incredible promises, and, after you enter into the problem, stay longer than you need because you refuse to let go of the imperfections that God wants out of your life?

There was once a good Quaker who owned a farm. He was trying to milk a stubborn cow early one morning when the cow suddenly lashed the Quaker's face with her tail. Maintaining his composure, he continued to milk the unwilling cow. This time she stomped the milk bucket, spilling his morning's work on the dusty barn floor. Doing his best not to lose his composure, which violated the tenets of his faith, he cleaned the bucket and attempted to continue his morning chore.

Finally, the belligerent cow kicked the Quaker and flung his body to the barnyard and into a pile of manure. Using every effort of self-restraint, the Quaker cleaned himself off, acquired another bucket, and quietly but firmly approached the milk cow with this veiled promise: "Cow, thou knowest that I am a Quaker and that I cannot lose my temper. But what thou knowest not is that I will sell you to a Baptist who will beat the devil out of you."

There are ways to pass the test.

Moses led the children of Israel through the wilderness as the unseen hand of God attempted to crush the spiritual and carnal imperfections within them that had developed in four hundred plus years of slavery. Yet, even Moses was kept from inheriting all God had for him because of his refusal to abandon the spiritual imperfections that kept him from his destiny.

Yet, an ever-faithful God took the saga of promise, problem, and provision and brought Joshua's generation, whose people were destined to be kings and priests unto God, into their Promised Land.

Moses was so frustrated with the people that he smote the rock, and they saw the miracle of the gushing water as a manifestation of Moses's power and not God's. God will share His glory with no one—not ever! God told Moses he would not be permitted to enter the Promised Land because he could not harness his temper. It was a severe penalty, just as yours will be if you do not allow the Holy Spirit to place the golden harness of temperance in your heart.

Consider King David. He too failed the discipline test.

King David conquered Goliath and terrorized the Philistines, but he could not control his lust for Bathsheba. As king, he invited her to his palace, and while her husband, Uriah, a loyal soldier of Israel, was in the field of battle, David impregnated Bathsheba.

David devised an elaborate conspiracy to hide his sin that led to the premeditated murder of Uriah. God's judgment was swift and certain. God told David he would not be allowed to build the temple because he had the blood of an innocent man on his hands. David's dream of building the temple was crushed because he was not able to control his sexual desires.

If Adam and Eve could talk to you, they would tell you that the price of the "forbidden fruit" is far more than you can pay.

If Samson could spend an hour with you by your fireside in the comfort of your home, he would passionately relate to you how his inability to control his all-consuming lust for Delilah destroyed his life. He confessed the secret of his power with God to Delilah, and his hair was cut off, as was his relationship with God. His eyes were gouged out, and he was forced to grind grain like an ox for the rest of his life as his enemies mocked him every day until the day of his death.

> Whoever has no rule over his own spirit is like a city broken down, without walls.
>
> —Proverbs 25:28

The Bible speaks of hardships to endure, crosses to be carried, and tribulations (problems) designed by God Himself to produce triumph as a result of the problem. When solving the problem, there is no quitting, no ducking the tough issues, no running from responsibility.

A winner never quits, and a quitter never wins. Jesus didn't quit on you—don't you quit on Him! You may memorize every problem-solving technique until you can recite them in your sleep, but without temperance and discipline in your life, you will never solve the problem.

REMEMBER THIS TRUTH...

Your success in life is ultimately measured by the problems you create or the problems you solve.

Chapter 6

THE QUICKEST WAY
THROUGH THE PROBLEM
IS STRAIGHT THROUGH

Dwight L. Moody said, "I'd rather be able to pray than be a great preacher; Jesus Christ never taught His disciples how to preach, but only how to pray."[1]

In the fifty years I have been in the ministry, I have been accused of doing things I did not do, saying things I did not say, and implying things I did not mean. I have been in many problems during my life, and I can say without question, I would still be in some of them had I not gone to the throne of God in prayer.

There is a physics principle that states that the shortest distance between two points is a straight line. This same principle exists in problem solving; the quickest way through the problem is to walk straight through it.

I gave some basic principles of prayer in chapter 2, but prayer is such an important element of the principle of *Life's Challenges—Your Opportunities* that I want to expound with personal testimonies. Why? Because personal testimonies bring the supernatural Word of God into the natural; they are faith builders. Testimonies make a faith deposit into our spiritual bank, and believe me, there will be days when you have to make a big withdrawal, and you will need a big balance to cover your needs.

My mother taught me to pray. She was and is a tremendous prayer warrior. That statement in itself is a miracle. When my mother was sixty-nine years old she was diagnosed with colon cancer. Her prognosis was grim. She was to undergo radiation treatment for eight weeks followed by colostomy surgery, which was to maintain a moderate semblance of life for one year, and after that was certain death.

My father, my three brothers, and I gathered around her bed and prayed the prayer of faith asking God to heal my mother. We all went straight to the Word of God and stood on Psalm 91. God promises in this psalm to be with us in our time of trouble, and He remained true to His Word.

The radiologist said my mother's delicate skin would be ravaged by the harsh treatment. For eight weeks Vada Hagee did not enter the radiation room without proclaiming Psalm 91, and at the end of treatment her skin was without sign or blemish.

The surgeon predicted four hours of surgery, ending with a colostomy bag. The surgery lasted less than two hours because the tumor was reduced from the size of an orange to the size of a small plum. The surgeon was able to snip out the intruder and reconnect the intestine without a colostomy.

My mother was back to work within a month and never had a sign of cancer again. Our God is with us during a time of trouble, and He will deliver us from that trouble!

Her miraculous life continues. At the age of ninety, my mother began forgetting everyday occurrences. She went to the doctor and was diagnosed with the first stages of Alzheimer's disease. She did not seem to be bothered by this diagnosis as much as her children were and went about her independent life taking what she called her daily "memory pill."

Four years passed, and she suddenly took a deep plunge into her inner world. We moved her to San Antonio and provided her with twenty-four-hour care.

As I saw the progression of other Alzheimer's patients around her, I was grieved to think of this remarkable woman's mind ravaged of its wisdom and love for the things of God. I prayed, "Lord, heal my mother or take her to Your bosom where she longs to be." I was confident that He would answer my prayer, which He did.

Her new doctor analyzed the progress of her dreaded disease. My wife, Diana, was present during the doctor's assessment. When the doctor gave her the news, she called me immediately and said, "The doctor has given me Mom's diagnosis. Come as quickly as you can!"

I must confess I assumed the worst. I arrived at my mother's room to find her conversing with her new doctor and Diana with a smile on her face. The doctor gave me her diagnosis: "Your mother does not have Alzheimer's." I was in shock, and Diana was in tears.

"Why the memory loss? What has happened to her mind? What is wrong with my mother?" I burst forth with one question after another.

"Your mother has delusional dementia often caused by living alone. I will adjust her medication, and you will see the veil lift from her mind. She may still forget a few things, but she does not have Alzheimer's." We rejoiced beyond measure. God had once again healed my mother!

The victory over one problem is often followed by another problem. Three weeks into her move to San Antonio, she developed an intestinal kink that put her in the hospital; her first stay since her healing from cancer some twenty-five years prior. I was traveling throughout the country keeping speaking engagements I had made a year prior, and Diana stayed at my mother's bedside. We would call each other several times a day waiting for the problem to resolve itself, but to no avail.

My mother made us promise years earlier that we would not keep her in this world one moment longer than God wanted her to stay. In attempting to keep this promise, her sons asked the doctor to avoid surgery. If the Lord was ready to take her home, we were ready to release her.

After nine days in the hospital, the surgeon came to Diana with a difficult choice. "If we don't operate within the next twelve hours, your mother-in-law will begin to experience a slow and painful death. But if we operate, her chances of dying while in recovery are great."

Diana prayed and asked God to provide an answer before trying to reach me, as I was in the middle of a presentation in California. As she ended her prayer, my dear friend Rabbi Scheinberg entered the hospital room to visit my mother. Diana shared her dilemma with him, and God used Rabbi Scheinberg to bring His answer.

"The Bible sets before us choices. God set before us life and death, and He asks us to choose life. Not to have surgery is certain death. No one chooses to have surgery to die; they choose surgery to live. If God decides, in His infinite wisdom, to take your mother-in-law home after surgery, it will be His doing and not yours. Choose for life."

Diana called me and gave me Rabbi Scheinberg's wise counsel. I shared it with my brothers, and we unanimously agreed. We would choose life. Diana called the surgeon immediately and, as only Diana can, gave him the whole testimony of her answered prayer. The surgeon was moved by her account and set the surgery for early the next morning.

Eight hours before surgery the surgeon called Diana. "I can't believe what I am about to tell you. The tests we have just administered to your mother-in-law in preparation for surgery show that the kink has resolved itself! She will be discharged within twenty-four hours." God answers prayer.

My mother went home, and three weeks later death paid another visit. Without warning or prior history, my mother suffered a massive double pulmonary embolism. We admitted her to the hospital once again, and the specialists came in to say that they were not familiar with treating such a massive embolism because, "Frankly, Pastor Hagee, no one ever survives them!"

After another nine days in the hospital, they sent her home under the care of hospice.

Hospice put her on a twenty-four-hour watch because they felt death to be "imminent." Her sons surrounded her bed and had a prayer of release. As she lay in a deep sleep, we began to sing the old songs of the church, songs that she was familiar with, like "No One Ever Cared for Me Like Jesus," "It is Well With My Soul," and "Holy, Holy, Holy."

Suddenly we could see signs of life coming back to her body. The most notable signs were her feet. My mother had been the church organist during the years she and my father pastored. Now, as she listened to her sons sing, her feet began to move as if they were pumping the organ pedals to the music. She then began to raise her hands in praise to the God of her salvation. After several hours, she opened her eyes, sat up in bed, and began to eat and drink.

Within ten days, hospice met with us and declared that my mother had "graduated" from hospice like very few people do; she lived! She comes to church every Sunday and sings the songs of the church while clapping her hands in praise. My mother has forgotten many things, even forgetting my name at times, but not once has she forgotten who she is in Christ. She remembers the songs of the church. She remembers her healings and her blessings. She remembers how to pray. She remembers the Lord's Prayer, which she recites every day. Her comment on the Lord's Prayer: "If it was important to Jesus, then it is important to me."

My mother continues to pray for her family and for those who work and live around her. Her caregivers bring their problems to her, and she lays her wrinkled hands on them, asking God to intervene. God always answers.

On occasion, my mother asks me, "Why has the Lord left me on this world for so long?" And I answer her with a promise, the promise that she adopted as her own and proclaimed every day for months. This promise comes at the end of Psalm 91.

> He shall call upon Me, and I will answer him; I will be with him in trouble; I will deliver him and honor him. With long life I will satisfy him, and show him My salvation.
> —Psalm 91:15–16

Our God is a promise keeper, and He promises to take us straight through the problem if we stay connected to Him in prayer. Prayer to God is communication with God, which means that as we talk to God, He also speaks to us. What He has to say about our character or attitude may not be exactly what we want to hear or what we want to do, but it is always true and always unfailing.

THE POTTER'S WHEEL

I have been to Israel twenty-five times, and each time I enter this land flowing with milk and honey I learn something that forever changes my life.

In one of our visits, Diana and I visited Hebron and watched a potter take a worthless lump of clay and make it into a beautiful one-of-a-kind vase, much like Jeremiah describes in the Bible. In fifty years of ministry, I have never seen so many spiritual principles applied so quickly and powerfully.

REMEMBER THIS TRUTH...

God does everything through prayer.

I was intrigued by what I saw, and thought, "Lord, I am that lump of clay, and You are the Master Potter." Little did I know that God was about to teach me a lesson that would help me get through the many problems that would later come my way.

As the potter slowly pumped the pedals beneath his feet, the wheel began to spin. The potter took a mound of what seemed to be worthless mud and slapped it on his wheel. The gifted hands of the potter then began to feel for imperfections in the shapeless mass of clay. As he found them, he would smash the mud with his hand, crushing the flaws until they blended perfectly with the rest of the clay.

Have you ever felt the hand of Jesus crushing the imperfections in your life? I have! It's not pleasant, but if you want to become the product of His will and not your will, you must yield to His hand of correction with absolute submission and be willing to become broken by Him. Yes, it will hurt. No, it is not pleasant. But it is necessary to attain your goal and His divine destiny.

REMEMBER THIS TRUTH...

God can only use broken vessels.

It is the torn ground ripped asunder by the plow that produces the harvest. It is the pressed grape that makes the new wine. It is the crushed rose petal that makes the most delicate perfume. It was the broken alabaster box whose precious spikenard spilled over the head of Jesus and created a memorial so great that God would not allow mankind to ever forget.

King David penned the words none who seek to walk into the inner chambers of God can ever forget: "The sacrifices of God are a broken spirit, a broken and a contrite heart—These, O God, You will not despise" (Ps. 51:17).

How can He put the Word of God *into* our hearts if our hearts aren't broken first?

God must break us from our arrogance and independence, which deceives us to believe that we can live life successfully without Him or that we don't need Him to achieve our provision.

The personal act of surrendering your life to the supremacy of Jesus Christ is a must in reaching your destiny, your promised land flowing with milk and honey.

Have you broken away from your independence of God?

If not, the rest of your activity is religious pretense. You will be very busy continuing to spin on the wheel of life, but all your motion will not get you to your destiny. The dividing line between the wilderness and your promised land is this: Will you give up *YOUR* way for *HIS* way? Will you surrender to Jesus Christ, placing no conditions on how you arrive to your promised land?

The desire, passion, and power of your walk with Christ come from purposely signing away your own rights and becoming a bondservant to Jesus Christ. Until you do that, you will live looking back to Egypt and will be seduced by the gods of this world, as were the Hebrews who made the golden calf. Every mistake they made, you will make!

When the potter in Hebron had finished crushing the lumps of imperfect clay and the vase was beautifully formed, just as he had planned from the beginning, he placed the vase in the roaring fire of the kiln.

"How long do you leave the vase in the fire?" I asked.

He looked at me, smiled through his thick beard, and extended his clay-covered hands toward me, saying, "I leave it in the fire until it has the ability to sing."

"Sing?" I queried.

"Yes...sing. When I take it out of the fire, I flick the rim of the vase with my fingernail, and if it sings, it's ready. If it doesn't sing, I put it right back in the fire. The purest sound is produced by the hottest fire."

My spirit leaped within me! What was God showing me?

REMEMBER THIS TRUTH...

If God has you in the problem, and He pulls you out of His refining fire, the last thing you want to do is roll out your lower lip and complain! Do yourself a favor, and do not whine or murmur. Sing! Sing for joy!

Sing even if you don't feel like singing. Slap yourself if you have to; just don't complain. Sing in faith, as Paul and Silas sang in the jail at Philippi. Sing as loud as you can. Soon your problem will supernaturally vanish, and your promised land will suddenly appear on your horizon.

THE SUPERNATURAL TRILOGY—
THANKSGIVING, PRAISE, AND WORSHIP

Thanksgiving

Thanksgiving and praise *to* God are partners with the worship *of* God. Thanksgiving acknowledges God's goodness. Praise acknowledges His greatness. And worship acknowledges God's holiness.

Being thankful is a command:

> And let the peace of God rule in your hearts, to which also you were called in one body; and be thankful. Let the word of Christ dwell in you richly in all wisdom, teaching and admonishing one another in psalms and hymns and spiritual songs, singing with grace in your hearts to the Lord. And whatever you do in word or deed, do all in the name of the Lord Jesus, giving thanks to God the Father through Him.
>
> —COLOSSIANS 3:15–17

When you are in the problem, ask this of yourself: "Can what I am thinking, what I am saying, or what I am doing be thought, said, or done in the name of Jesus and with thanks to the Father?" If what you are doing can't meet these conditions, then don't do it!

Paul gives us another "to do" list during our time in the wilderness. And believe me, I know through personal experience that by doing what is mandated in this verse you will go straight through to your provision.

> Rejoice always, pray without ceasing, in everything give thanks; for this is the will of God in Christ Jesus for you.
>
> —1 THESSALONIANS 5:16–18

The first mandate is to *always be joyful*. Many years ago, a little boy was given a priceless possession—his beloved grandfather's gold pocket watch, and he treasured it. One day while working in his father's barn, he lost the watch amidst the straw and debris. He became frantic.

He desperately searched for the prized watch but could not find it. Almost in tears, he suddenly realized what to do. He stopped scurrying around and became very still. In the silence, he heard the watch ticking. He found what he was searching for.

God has given each of us the priceless gift of joy in Jesus. How easy it is to lose this invaluable gift while scurrying around within the rubble of our own recourses seeking an answer to our problem. The answer is always found within the promises if we would just stop worrying, become very still, and take the time to listen to His voice, for *there* is the fullness of joy.

The second mandate is to *pray without ceasing*.

My mother taught me an invaluable lesson: Little prayer, little power. Some prayer, some power. Much prayer, much power.

I have had many questions asked of me regarding prayer throughout my years of ministry. My hope is that the answers I have given my parishioners will in some way help you.

Some ask the question, "When should I pray?"

Owen Carr gives the answer: "Prayer should be the key of the day and the lock of the night."[2]

I have been asked, "Why do I have to pray all day?" O. Hallesby answers this question: "As impossible as it is for us to take a breath in the morning large enough to last us until noon, so impossible is it to pray in the morning in such a way as to last us until noon. Let your prayers ascend to Him constantly, audibly or silently, as circumstances through-out the day permit."[3]

Others ask, "Why should I pray?" One good reason to pray is because when the knees are not often bent, the feet soon slide. Charles Haddon Spurgeon says, "One night alone in prayer might make us new men, changed from poverty of soul to spiritual wealth, from trembling to triumphing."[4]

REMEMBER THIS TRUTH...

*You learn to pray by praying; you learn
to pray well by praying more.*

Oswald Chambers gives another reason for prayer: "It is not so true that 'prayer changes things,' as that prayer changes me and I change things. God has so constituted things that prayer on the basis of Redemption alters the way in which man looks at things. Prayer is not a question of altering things externally, but of working wonders in man's disposition. We have to pray with our eyes on God, not on the difficulties."[5]

Another question is: "How do I pray while I am in the problem?" The answer is to pray in faith believing and allow the Lord into your problem, giving Him the right of entry to your needs and permitting Him to implement His supremacy in dealing with them and you.

We are to give thanks in all things. Thanksgiving has taken me through many a problem. The most difficult and yet most productive time for thanksgiving is when we are smack dab in the middle of the problem.

We don't feel like offering thanksgiving while we are in the wilderness. It never crosses our minds. It is against our nature to thank God for the problem. This is where I hear my parishioners shout, "Thankful for what?"

I am amused by the vegetable juice commercial where you see a person, listless and without energy, eating everything but what they should, and suddenly it hits him: "I shoulda had a V-8!"

Imagine this visual example in the spiritual realm. We are dragging along, pulling what seems to be an insurmountable problem, doing everything we should not do. We become fearful; we murmur; we worry. We complain and indulge in self-pity, creating lots of motion in the problem but making no progress out of the problem. Then all of a sudden it hits us! "We should be thanking God!"

It has been said, "Better to lose count while naming your blessings than to lose your blessings by counting your troubles."[6] Learn to give thanks to God for everyday blessings. Each day is a gift, and within each gift is a blessing; you must learn to untie the ribbon with thanksgiving.

Famed poet Robert Louis Stevenson wrote of blessings, "The best things are nearest: breath in your nostrils, light in your eyes, flowers at your feet, duties at your hand, the path of God just before you. Then do not grasp at the stars, but do life's plain, common work as it comes, certain that daily duties and daily bread are the sweetest things of life."[7] Give God thanks for all things—even problems.

Many of my major problems and disappointments in life have turned out to be some of my greatest blessings. It is my responsibility to look through the eyes of God at the opportunities these problems afford me. This task can be only accomplished within the atmosphere of thanksgiving.

> ## REMEMBER THIS TRUTH...
>
> *God allows problems to come into your life*
> *not to drown you but to cleanse you. A problem*
> *is often God's blessing in disguise. Saint Basil said,*
> *"Many a man curses the rain that falls upon his head,*
> *and knows not that it brings abundance*
> *to drive away hunger."*[8]

When Golda Meir, former prime minister of Israel, was asked what blessings she was thankful for, she replied, "Not being beautiful was the true blessing. Not being beautiful forced me to develop my inner resources. The pretty girl has a handicap to overcome."[9] We can give thanks for all things!

Praise

The second part of the supernatural trilogy is praise. Praise acknowledges the greatness of God.

> Great is the LORD, and greatly to be praised in the city of our God, in His holy mountain.
> —PSALM 48:1

> Enter into His gates with thanksgiving, and into His courts with praise. Be thankful to Him, and bless His name. For the LORD is good; His mercy is everlasting, and His truth endures to all generations.
> —PSALM 100:4–5

There are countless reasons why we should offer up thanks and praise to God. Allow me to list three ageless reasons why we praise Him:

> For the LORD is good; His mercy is everlasting, and His truth endures to all generations.
> —PSALM 100:5

I quote my friend and mentor Derek Prince often because his teachings are simple yet profound. He paints a beautiful portrait of entering into the presence of God through praise.

Isaiah describes the city of God in chapter 60:18:

Violence shall no longer be heard in your land, neither wasting nor destruction within your borders; but you shall call your walls Salvation, and your gates Praise.

The wall surrounding the presence of God is Salvation. But all the gates have just one name: Praise. If you want to get in through the walls, the gate you have to go through is praise. No praise, no access. Praise is the only way into the immediate presence of God.[10]

One of my favorite scriptures about praise is Psalm 22:3: "But You are holy, enthroned in the praises of Israel." The word *enthroned* in Hebrew means "to inhabit." Therefore God manifests Himself within your praises. Imagine that! While you are in your problem, and you utter praises unto God, He promises to come into your presence, and His presence instantly dwarfs your problem.

Both David and Paul reveal how thanksgiving and praise bring God's people out of their problem and take them triumphantly into their provision.

Save us, O LORD our God, and gather us from among the Gentiles,
to give thanks to Your holy name, to triumph in Your praise.
—PSALM 106:47

Now thanks be to God who always leads us in triumph in Christ.
—2 CORINTHIANS 2:14

Diana and I make it a habit of offering thanksgiving and praise to God while we are in the problem. It is often the only way to remain spiritually grounded. I challenge you. If you are in the midst of a problem as you are reading this book, stop; take a pen and paper, and begin to list the things you are thankful for. If you cannot think of a thing, then begin by thanking God for the breath in your lungs, your eyesight, your hearing, and soon more and more blessings will come flowing from your mouth, and suddenly, the peace of God will surround you.

Thank Him for His promises, and thank Him ahead of time for the provision. Begin to praise Him for who He is—for His majesty, His greatness, and His marvelous works. I promise you based on personal experience that you will begin to walk straight out of your problem and into your God-given destiny.

REMEMBER THIS TRUTH…

*Make a conscious decision with your will—
and not your emotions—to praise God for
His greatness and majesty while you're in
the problem, and soon you will see the light
of the promised land on the horizon.*

You may ask, "When should I praise God?" We should praise Him every day, forever and ever, and at all times (Heb. 13:15–16). "How shall I praise Him?" We are to praise God with our whole hearts (Ps. 111:1); with understanding (Ps. 47:7); with lifted hands, mouth, and joyful lips (Ps. 63:4–5); as an evening sacrifice (Ps. 141:2); with dance (Ps. 149:3); with the timbrel and dance (Ps. 150:4).

"Who is to praise God?" Everyone who has breath should praise the Lord (Ps. 150). In fact, there is only one class of people who cannot praise the Lord—the dead (Ps. 115:17).

Worship

The final part of the supernatural trilogy is worship. Thanksgiving acknowledges God's goodness, praise acknowledges who God is, and worship acknowledges God's holiness. While thanksgiving and praise are vocal utterances in the form of speaking, singing, or even shouting or dancing, worship is a condition of the heart involving your whole being.

There are actual positions of worship. I love to witness the nights of "extravagant praise" at our church. It is a time when we come together for one purpose and one purpose only—to give thanks and praise unto God and then gradually enter into worship before Him.

As the pastor of the church, I can actually witness the three phases of the trilogy in the actions of the people. Thanksgiving usually involves joyful clapping and singing. Praise progresses into the lifting up of hands in pure homage to the King of kings and Lord of lords. Then a remarkable thing happens.

The congregation begins to bow their heads, some kneel, and yet others lay prostrate before the Lord as an atmosphere of worship permeates the air. It is a beautiful sight. At times I begin to weep when I see God's people in worship, because I know it pleases God, and they in turn will be blessed. John Bunyan describes worship this way:

> He that is down need fear no fall,
> He that is low, no pride;
> He that is humble, ever shall
> Have God to be his guide.[11]

Worship is a way your spirit becomes integrated with God's Spirit. Worship is the only place to find peace with the problem.

Thanksgiving, praise, and worship are the supernatural trilogy that, when perfected, takes us straight through the problem to our provision.

There are many examples in Scripture of people just like you and me to whom God gave a promise, led them into a problem, and there they wrestled with their carnality trying to reach their provision. Can you see yourself in these people?

CONSIDER ABRAHAM

God gave Abraham a promise that impacted the destiny of every nation on the face of the earth up to this very moment. The impact of Genesis 12 is the reason why the despots of this world are working night and day to "wipe Israel off the face of the earth."

Israel is the only nation that, by its very presence, proves there is a God of promise. Israel is the only nation created by God and protected by God, for "He that keepeth Israel shall neither slumber nor sleep" (Ps. 121:4, KJV).

God promised Abraham, "I will make you a great nation; I will bless you and make your name great; and you shall be a blessing. I will bless those who bless you, and I will curse him who curses you; and in you all the families of the earth shall be blessed" (Gen. 12:2–3).

Examine the seven magnificent promises God made to Abraham.

1. I will make you a great nation.
2. I will bless you (personal blessing).
3. I will make your name great.
4. I will bless you so much you will have the power to be a blessing to the nations.
5. I will bless those (Gentiles) who bless you.
6. I will curse those who curse you.
7. I will bless the whole earth through you.

I could write a book about God's seven promises to Abraham, but allow me to give two illustrations that affect every person on the face of the earth. Many of you have heard my teachings on Israel and the Jewish people, but they bear repeating.

The seed of Abraham became known as the Jewish people. Their name is derived from the tribe of Judah. The Jewish people have blessed the earth beyond measure.

Consider the debt of gratitude Christians owe the Jewish people. The Jewish people have given to us:

1. The Word of God
2. The patriarchs: Abraham, Isaac, and Jacob
3. The Old Testament prophets: Isaiah, Jeremiah, Ezekiel, Daniel, Hosea, Joel, Amos, Obadiah, Jonah, Micah, Nahum, Habakkuk, Zephaniah, Haggai, Zechariah, and Malachi. Not a Baptist in the bunch!
4. The Jewish people have given to us the First Family of Christianity: Mary, Joseph, and Jesus.

Jesus embraced His Jewish roots. He was trained as a rabbi. He taught the Torah. He kept the seven feasts of Israel. His last request to the church was recorded this way: "Inasmuch as ye have done it unto one of the least of these my brethren, ye have done it unto me" (Matt. 25:40, KJV). The "least of these" refers to the Jewish people.

The Jewish people have given to us the disciples and the apostles. For this reason Jesus said, "Salvation is of the Jews" (John 4:22). What does that mean? It means that if you take away the Jewish contribution to Christianity, there would be no Christianity.

The Jewish people have been blessed, and indeed, have blessed all the earth. They represent less than 3 percent (1/1000th) of the earth's population, yet Israel, the one-hundredth-smallest country in the world, can lay claim to the following:

- Israel has the highest ratio of university degrees, compared to the world population.[12]
- Israel's $100-billion economy is greater than the combined economies of all of its immediate neighbors.[13]
- Israel ranks third in the industrialized world—after the United States and Holland—in the percentage of their workforce with university degrees. Twenty-four percent of Israel's workforce holds university degrees, with 12 percent holding advanced degrees.[14]
- Israel is the only democracy in the Middle East.
- Relative to its population, Israel is the largest immigrant-absorbing nation on earth. Immigrants come in search of democracy, religious freedom, and economic opportunity.[15]
- According to industry officials, Israel designed the airline industry's most impenetrable flight security.[16] U.S. officials now look to Israel for advice on how to handle airborne security threats.
- In 1991, during the Gulf War, the Israel Philharmonic Orchestra played a concert wearing gas masks as Scud missiles fired by Saddam Hussein fell on Tel Aviv.[17]
- In medicine—Israeli scientists developed the first fully computerized, non-radiation, diagnostic equipment for breast cancer.[18]

- An Israeli company developed a computerized system for ensuring proper administration of medications, thus removing human error from medical treatment.[19]
- Israel's Given Imaging developed the first ingestible video camera, so small it fits inside a pill. Used to view the small intestine from the inside, the camera helps doctors diagnose cancer and digestive disorders without exploratory surgery.[20]
- In technology—Israel has the highest concentration of high-tech companies in the world (apart from the Silicon Valley).[21]
- In response to serious water shortages, Israeli engineers and agriculturalists developed a revolutionary drip irrigation system to minimize the amount of water used to grow crops.[22]
- Israel has the highest percentage in the world of home computers per capita.[23]
- Leading the world in the number of scientists and technicians in the workforce is Israel, with 145 per 10,000, as opposed to 85 in the United States, over 70 in Japan, and less than 60 in Germany. Israel has over 25 percent of its workforce employed in technical professions, thus placing first in this category as well.[24]
- The cell phone was developed in Israel by Motorola, which has its largest development center in Israel.[25]
- Most of the Windows NT operating system was developed by Microsoft-Israel.[26]
- The Pentium MMX Chip technology was designed in Israel at Intel.[27]
- Voice mail technology was developed in Israel.[28]
- Four young Israelis developed AOL Instant Messenger.[29]
- An Israeli company was the first to develop and install a large-scale solar-powered and fully functional electricity generating plant, in southern California's Mojave Desert.[30]

All of the above and much, much more was accomplished as Israel and her people were engaged in regular wars with an implacable enemy that seeks its destruction, and an economy continuously under strain by having to spend more per capita on its own protection than any other country on earth. All this was accomplished by a people and a country just sixty years old, reborn from the ashes of the Holocaust, and having begun its life with a promise from the Word of God.

God created Israel with a covenant promise. Israel has endured more than its share of problems, yet God has faithfully and continually led the nation and the Jewish people to their provision: "And all the peoples of the earth shall be blessed through you."

Listen to this story found in American history that has been forgotten by most of us. It portrays the Jewish contribution to the birth of our own nation.

When George Washington and the Continental Army were camped at Valley Forge, the situation was dire. Our soldiers were without food, without proper clothing for the harsh winter, and without sufficient weapons and ammunition to defeat a well-equipped British army that had camped for the winter.

A Jewish banker, Haym Salomon of Pennsylvania, went to the Jewish community in Europe and America and raised millions of dollars on behalf of George Washington and the ragged and hungry Continental Army.

Haym Salomon gave the much-needed money to General Washington without a legal document requiring repayment. It was a gift that would give a young, struggling nation the opportunity to survive.

With that money, provisions were purchased, and the Continental Army defeated the British, giving birth to "life, liberty, and the pursuit of happiness."[31]

George Washington, wanting to make sure America remembered the Jewish blessing on our nation, instructed the engravers of the one-dollar bill to make a lasting tribute to the Jewish people.

Take a dollar bill out of your wallet and look over the head of the American eagle, and you will see the six-pointed star of Israel. The starburst around it is symbolic of the Shekinah glory that dwelled over the tabernacle while the Jewish people were in the wilderness.

Abraham was given a promise that was so staggering it has literally shaped the destiny of men and nations. God keeps His promises to those who stay obedient while being tested in the problem.

Before Abraham received his covenant promise, God told Abraham to:

1. Get out of your country.
2. Get away from your family.
3. Get away from your father.
4. Go to a land that I will show you (Gen. 12:1).

"So Abraham departed..." (Gen. 12:4). Abraham obeyed! He left father, family, and country and stepped out in faith toward his promise. Later, Abraham was asked of God to sacrifice his only son of covenant, Isaac, the son of promise, and Abraham obeyed immediately. The next morning, without question, Abraham gathered the implements for the unthinkable sacrifice and headed for Mount Moriah in the foothills of Jerusalem where, thousands of years later, Jesus Christ, the Lamb of God, was offered up for your sins and mine. He was the lamb Isaac spoke about as he and his father climbed Mt. Moriah in total obedience to God.

What does that have to do with you?

Much in every way!

One of the secrets of success to solving your problem is found in Isaiah 1:19–20: "'If you are willing and obedient, you shall eat the good of the land; but if you refuse and rebel, you shall be devoured by the sword'; for the mouth of the LORD has spoken."

Are you "willing and obedient"? Are you willing to live your life God's way? Are you willing to live in absolute obedience to God's will and His Word?

Abraham was determined that absolutely nothing would stop him from doing exactly what God wanted. Not family, not father, not home, not even the life of his precious son of promise...NOTHING!

Abraham passed the test. He obeyed God and walked into his provision. Until you become absolutely "willing and obedient" while in the wilderness, you will never get through the problem and into your promised land.

The purpose of the problem is to crush everything in you that resists God's lordship over your life. Our God is Lord of all, or He's not Lord at all. While in the problem He will bring you to a place where you absolutely have to decide for or against total obedience to Him. God's children are prone to quarrel with Him about the problem that seems too difficult, uncertain, or impossible. Our right response to the problem is not to argue with God, but to trust totally, to obey absolutely, and to follow Him faithfully. If God commands something of your life, it is because He is confident you can accomplish it.

REMEMBER THIS TRUTH...

If God gives you a million-dollar promise, He will give you the ability to endure a million-dollar problem.

Paul declares in Philippians 3:10, "I want to know Christ..." (NIV). "To know God is to experience His love through Christ, and to return that love in obedience."[32] If you are now in the problem, surrender your will to Jesus Christ immediately, absolutely, and irrevocably so you can get through the problem and into your provision!

CONSIDER KING DAVID

David the shepherd boy had the favor of God and rose from the dusty pasture to the palace of Israel. David was a psalmist, a prophet, a priest, a statesman, and a warrior king.

David gathered the scattered tribes of Israel and made them a nation under his leadership. It was David, the man after God's own heart, who climbed up a water shaft with his warriors to deliver the city of Jerusalem from the Jebusites three thousand years ago.

The promise of kingship came when David was anointed by the prophet Samuel. David's problems began soon after, as a jealous and demonized King Saul demanded his death. Saul and his execution squad hunted David just as a pack of wolves hunt a wounded deer.

David was stalked for years! Although he was the anointed king of Israel, he lived in caves, separated from his family and his friends. He was denied the basic comforts of home and hearth. It was a bitter and barren time while the King of kings transformed a keeper of lambs into a lion of God.

I have often asked myself this question: If David was so good with a sword, why didn't he kill King Saul and end his problems in one swift move? If someone is trying to kill you, don't you have the right to protect and defend yourself?

Then I saw the answer one day in the Scriptures. David fought eighteen wars in his military career. He fought thirteen for Israel and five for himself. He was not afraid of the fight. David didn't kill King Saul lest he offend the God that had anointed Saul king of Israel. David was willing and obedient to the Word of God, which states, "Do not touch My anointed ones, and do My prophets no harm" (1 Chron. 16:22).

David walked into the throne room of Israel, his provision, years after the oil from Samuel's horn had soaked his shepherd's tunic. David later fell into sexual sin with Bathsheba and even committed premeditated murder against her husband in a futile attempt to hide his immoral conduct. God forgave David because he acknowledged his sin and confessed it.

We all dream of absolute forgiveness of our transgressions. To attain this pardon, we must do our part, and He promises to do His. I wonder if we believe that God's part is harder than ours. Nothing could be further from the truth!

The most difficult part is acknowledging and confessing our sin, and then we release the Lord to forgive and forget. It may be difficult for us to forget, but not for God—for nothing is impossible to Him!

The story is told in Spain of a father and his teenage son who had a strained relationship. As a result, the son ran away from home in anger. His father, however, began a journey in search of his rebellious son.

Finally, while in Madrid, in a last desperate effort to find his beloved son, the father put an ad in the newspaper. The ad read: "Dear Juan, meet me in front of the newspaper office at noon. All is forgiven. I love you. Your father."

The next day at noon in front of the newspaper office, more than eight hundred "Juans" showed up. They were all seeking forgiveness and love from their fathers. Our Father is a God of complete forgiveness for those who seek it.

The proof of God's love and total forgiveness for the man who endured the problem for twelve years is stated in Ezekiel 37:24: "David My servant shall be king over them, and they shall all have one shepherd; they shall also walk in My judgments and observe My statutes, and do them."

True to His promise, David is going to rule as a viceroy over Israel under the messiahship of King Jesus during the millennium.

CONSIDER JESUS

Jesus of Nazareth was the seed of the woman, promised in Genesis chapter 3, who would crush the head of the serpent. He was proclaimed by the prophets of Israel to be the Lamb of God and the Savior of the world.

He was born in a cattle stall, surrounded by donkeys, sheep, and goats. His cradle was a stone crib where livestock ate their forage. His mother was not carried to her labor and delivery by royal coach but on the back of a mangy donkey.

There were no nurses encouraging this first-time mother through the pain and travail of birthing her child. There was no attending specialist to administer an epidural at the first sign of suffering.

As a Jew, the Son of God was born into an atmosphere of racial hatred. He was born into the political oppression of the Roman government, whose brutality stained the soil of the nations in rivers of innocent blood.

The legitimacy of Christ's birth was in question from His first breath. When He began His ministry, the recognized spiritual leaders called him a heretic. He was called a drunkard, a demonized miracle worker who functioned under the power of Beelzebub.

Mary saw Him as an infant in Bethlehem's manger. John the Baptist saw Him as a candidate for water baptism. The disciples saw Him as their Jewish Rabbi. The Roman government considered Him an insurrectionist too dangerous to live and executed Him with their masterpiece of brutality known as crucifixion at the place called Calvary.

His provision came on the cross, when He shouted, "It is finished!" What was finished?

Sin was finished, for, "If the Son therefore shall make you free, ye shall be free indeed" (John 8:36, KJV). Our last and worst enemy, death, was totally defeated. On the Resurrection Morning, when death's prison bars are broken, when the trump of God shall sound, the dead in Christ shall rise and we shall "see Him as He is."

When we see Him standing in the clouds of heaven receiving the church triumphant, we shall see Him as He is. We shall see Him as our precious Lord and Savior. We will see Him as the Fairest of ten thousand, as the Bright and Morning Star; as the Alpha and Omega, the First and the Last.

We shall see Him as the Lion of the tribe of Judah. As the Great I AM, the Great Physician, and the Great Shepherd of the church. He is Immanuel, God with us. He is the Friend that sticketh closer than a brother. He is the fountain filled with blood drawn from Immanuel's veins. He is the Life, the Light, the Love, the Lion, the Lamb, and Lord of glory!

He is the One who can guide you through the battleground that has become your problem. He is the Guiding Light that will lead you through the darkness to your promised land.

Remember the words of that grand old song of the church:

> Turn your eyes upon Jesus,
> Look full in His wonderful face,
> And the things of earth will grow strangely dim
> In the light of His glory and grace.[33]

PERSEVERANCE

The desires of your heart are often confronted with problems. In order to get straight through the obstacles these problems present, we must embrace an unquenchable spirit, hard work, energy beyond what we think is possible, and an unwavering commitment and faith in God.

When you are faced with your roadblock, don't view it as a stop sign. See it as an opportunity for patience and perseverance to have their perfect work. You may be thinking, "When do I know that I have sufficiently persevered?" You will inherit your promise when you have gone the distance needed to enter your provision. "That you do not become sluggish, but imitate those who through faith and patience inherit the promise" (Heb. 6:12).

The following individuals understood the need to "go the distance."

- Dr. Seuss's first book was rejected by twenty-seven publishers; his books went on to sell six million copies.[34]
- Vince Lombardi didn't become a head coach in the NFL until he was forty-six.[35]
- During the first year of business, the Coca-Cola Company averaged sales of nine drinks per day.[36]

- Henry Ford's first car company went bankrupt, and his second car company failed.[37]
- Michelangelo endured four years lying on his back on a scaffold to paint the Sistine Chapel.[38]
- Michael Jordan was cut from his high school basketball team.[39]
- In 1905, the University of Bern rejected a PhD dissertation, saying that it was irrelevant and fanciful. Albert Einstein was disappointed but not defeated. He persevered.[40]
- For eight years he wrote a myriad of routine reports for the navy. He later wrote an array of stories and articles that never got published. Several years later he wrote a book that touches the world. Alex Haley and *Roots* made history.
- Cyrus H. K. Curtis lost over $800,000 on the *Saturday Evening Post* before it realized a dollar profit.[41]
- Frank Woolworth borrowed $300 to open his first store, and then saw three of his first five chain stores fail.[42]
- David W. Hartman went blind at age eight. His dream to become a medical doctor was thwarted by Temple University Medical School, when he was told that no one without eyesight had ever completed medical school. He courageously faced the challenge of "reading" medical books by having twenty-five complete textbooks recorded for him. At the age of twenty-seven, David became the first blind student to complete medical school.[43]
- A junior naval officer dreamed of becoming an admiral but was discharged from the service because he had cancer. He endured four bouts with the disease, and at one time was informed he only had two weeks to live. He beat the cancer, but navy regulations forbade him from being reinstated. Then he learned it would take an "act of Congress" to get him back in the navy, so he went after it. President Truman responded to his dogged determination and reinstated him.

This man, Irwin W. Rosenberg, became rear admiral of the U.S. Seventh Fleet.[44]

A high school basketball coach was attempting to motivate his players to persevere through a difficult season. He stood before his discouraged team during halftime and shouted, "Did Michael Jordan ever quit?"

The team responded, "No!"

"What about the Wright brothers? Did they ever give up?"

"No!" resounded the team.

"Did Tiger Woods ever quit?"

Again the team yelled, "No!"

He asked a final question of the excited team. "Did Elmer McAllister ever quit?" There was a long silence.

Finally, one player was bold enough to ask the enthusiastic coach, "Who is Elmer McAllister? We never heard of him."

The coach snapped back, "Of course you never heard of him…he quit!"

Harriet Beecher Stowe said, "Never give up, for that is just the place and time that the tide will turn."[45] The provision of God is right before you. The darkest hour is just before the dawn. The best is yet to be. Joy comes in the morning.

Life is not one mountaintop experience after another. You will encounter flat plateaus and, at other times, deep and dark valleys. As children of God, we pray for mountaintops, tolerate plateaus, and avoid the valleys. But when valleys are inevitable, don't get discouraged. Don't be dismayed. Don't be deceived. Press on. Press on. Press on. For within your valley you will find the signposts that lead you out into the sweet sunshine and your promised land.

REMEMBER THIS TRUTH…

The quickest way out of the problem is straight through it!

Chapter 7

SIGNPOSTS TO THE PROMISED LAND

A S WE LEARNED IN THE LAST CHAPTER, HOW WE CONDUCT OURSELVES in the problem determines how long you stay in the problem. The children of Israel were in their problem for forty years. Jesus was in the problem for forty days. What made the difference?

Jesus walked straight through the wilderness by following the signposts found in Scripture. The children of Israel made a career of their wilderness experience by refusing to obey the Lord's direction. Even after they walked out of the land of their captivity, their hearts remained full of idolatrous habits and negative attitudes, formed by four hundred years of slavery. They were out of Egypt, but Egypt was still in them.

Don't stay in your problem longer than you need to. Saint Paul said it best: "Forgetting those things which are behind...I press toward the goal for the prize of the upward call of God in Christ Jesus" (Phil. 3:13–14). Your problems cannot be solved by reliving the failures of the past. Looking back at the past only serves to limit your vision for the future.

Even though the past is never entirely gone, your atonement and redemption from yesterday's mistakes and failures can be the bricks and mortar of today. You are making a faith deposit into your spiritual faith bank every time He takes you through a problem. This accumulation of faith will help you through today's problems and give you hope for tomorrow.

You need to dream of things that never were and press toward the goal God has ordained for your life. You must leave Egypt before you can reach your promised land. Remember, God took the children of Israel *out* so He could bring them *in*. You must leave the past behind before you can arrive into your provision. The only reason you should look back is to remember the good God has done for you.

Let me ask you a question: Have you truly left Egypt? Are you looking back at a past relationship, a lost promotion, a bitter experience? Is your mind so fixed on a person or a situation that it keeps you from going forward with your life? What was once hard to bear is often sweet to remember. "Do not say, 'Why were the former days better than these?' For you do not inquire wisely concerning this" (Eccles. 7:10).

Quit looking back at "what might have been" and refusing to enter into God's gracious provision of "what can be," because God will leave you "in" your problem until you follow the signposts found in His Word that lead you "out" of the problem.

THE IMPORTANCE OF SIGNPOSTS

Many historians consider the D-day invasion the greatest military achievement of the twentieth century. The invasion of Normandy on June 6, 1944, launched the Allied assault—consisting of twenty U.S. divisions, fourteen British divisions, three Canadian divisions, a French division, and a Polish division—on Nazi-occupied Northern Europe.[1]

"On the first day of the invasion…about 120,000 Allied troops landed at five beach locations along the coast of the French province of Normandy after crossing the English Channel from bases in southern England. The Allies faced a force of about 50,000 Germans and suffered nearly 5,000 casualties on the first day alone but succeeded in securing the beaches from which they launched their offensive.

"…Once a beachhead was established, the plan was to pour in the supplies needed to sustain an offensive and then break out into the French countryside. Executing the plan was not simple. Crossing the treacherous English Channel with its unexpected storms, enormous tides, and tricky currents would be just the first step in the amphibious assault."[2] This was indeed a problem.

Once the Allies got off the beach and began to penetrate into the French countryside, mass confusion erupted. What the Allies did not foresee was that Adolf Hitler understood the importance of signposts to either guide his troops to or direct his enemies away from a specific geographical position. He knew that a soldier out of position was a soldier without purpose.

So Hitler's battle plan called for turning all the road signs around so the Allied soldiers would follow the opposite direction they had been commanded to go. Allied troops, believing the signposts were accurate, were, in fact, vigorously marching in the wrong direction in an attempt to achieve their combat mission.

Satan is a master at turning the signposts of life around as you struggle with your problem. The enemy wants to prevent you from reaching your promised land and God's glorious provision for you.

Let me give you an illustration from the life of Christ. His mission in life was the cross. Satan tried to turn the signposts around when Jesus was in the wilderness through a series of temptations.

Each time Satan tempted Him, Jesus responded, "It is written." Then Satan twisted the Scriptures, trying to keep the Son of God from fulfilling His mission at the cross.

If Satan twisted Scripture with Jesus Christ, he will most assuredly twist Scripture with you. The false doctrine taught in many churches today is nothing less than the prince of darkness turning the signposts around as the pastor leads his entire congregation away from God's purpose and prevents them from entering into His provision for their lives.

If you will follow God's signposts, you will shorten the time it takes to reach your provision. The signposts are clearly marked on the road map you've been given, and that road map is the Word of God.

YOUR ROAD MAP: THE WORD OF GOD

In His Word, God tells us what we need to know and what we need to do. Christians must believe and recognize that the Word of God is absolutely true and that commands from God are a reality. Those committed to secular humanism, on the other hand, do not believe God's Word has any more significance than the *New York Times*. When they pray, they say, "Listen up, Lord, for I am speaking," not, "Speak, Lord, for thy servant heareth."

For the believer, there is no question; for the secular humanist, there is no real answer. Secular humanism does not believe that God gives us signposts to direct us on the path of life. Secular humanism believes it speaks *for* God...not *to* God. Since communication with God is—in their pseudo intellectual opinion—blurry at least, the will of God therefore cannot be known to man.

This is a most comforting position to the followers of secular human-ism and all others whose lifestyle mocks the truth of God's Word. Secular humanists hate the Bible because it clearly defines right and wrong. When you can state specifically what is right and wrong, you discover something called *sin*. If there is sin, there must be a Judgment Day for the repentant by an almighty God that leads to either heaven or hell. This is unthink-able to secular humanism.

As Christians, however, we believe the God of the Bible speaks to us clearly and directly. His will and purpose for our lives can be known and joyously pursued through the Word of God.

Christians believe that Jesus of Nazareth is God incarnate. He came to Earth to save us from our sins. He died, rose from the dead, and now rules and reigns at the right hand of God the Father, and He will soon appear in the clouds of heaven in an event known as the rapture of the church.

The Rapture will happen in the twinkling of an eye. In an instant, every righteous person will leave the earth and ascend into the clouds to meet the Son of God. Those practicing the faith in secular humanism will be left behind to work out their utopian salvation with the assistance of their messiah, the Antichrist.

REMEMBER THIS TRUTH…

When you begin to follow God's signposts out of your problem, you must firmly grasp the initial concept—God expects you to heed the directions in the road map you've been given: obey His Word.

The Bible presents God the Father as one who commands and requires human beings to practice obedience. Deuteronomy 28 confirms this simple and never-changing law of God, which confirms that our obedience brings blessing and our disobedience brings curses. I urge you to read this chapter slowly to discover the blessings God promises—and the certainty of judg-ment that comes if you disobey the law of God.

This concept that God requires and commands human beings to obey originates in the Book of Genesis. After making a covenant with Adam and Eve, God commanded the man, saying, "Of every tree of the garden you may freely eat; but of the tree of the knowledge of good and evil you shall not eat, for in the day that you eat of it you shall surely die" (Gen. 2:16–17).

In Genesis chapter 17, "The Lord appeared to Abram and said to him, 'I am Almighty God; walk before Me and be blameless. And I will make My covenant between Me and you…to be God to you and your descendants after you.… You shall keep My covenant" (Gen. 17:1–2, 7, 9).

The intensity of the message that the created are expected by the Creator to do exactly what He says, when He says, like He says is recorded in 1 John 2:4: "He who says, 'I know Him,' and does not keep His commandments, is a liar, and the truth is not in him."

"If you are willing and obedient," the Bible says, "you shall eat the good of the land" (Isa. 1:19). Notice the two words, *willing* and *obedient*. You can be willing to receive God's blessing and never receive it because you are not obedient to God. The carnal mind cannot comprehend this, but let me be very clear: you will never win a spiritual battle with human logic.

Believe it or not, there are those who are obedient, but they are not willing to receive God's blessing. They feel that they do not deserve it! Well, in some ways they are right. The favor of God was created for the children of God who are obedient to His Word. It is for those made righteous by the blood of His Son, Jesus Christ, not by what they have done. Once you discover who you are in Christ—His joint heir—you will be more than willing to receive every blessing the cross affords you.

Signpost #1—Faith

The first signpost out of the wilderness is *faith*—not faith that God can do it, but faith that God will do it—for you, and do it right now.

Faith opens the windows of heaven and closes the gates of hell. By faith, Abraham offered up Isaac on Mount Moriah. By faith, Abraham received the covenant that still stands today. By faith, Joseph, while dwelling in Egypt, saw the future. He saw freedom while he was living in slavery. He saw financial abundance while the Jewish people were living in poverty. He saw a future where the Jewish people would live in a land flowing with milk and honey and all their enemies would be defeated.

By faith, Moses refused to be called the son of Pharaoh's daughter, rejecting the crown of Egypt for "the crown that fadeth not away."

By faith, the massive walls of Jericho fell down. The enemies of Israel were destroyed by a victorious shout given in faith by the Jewish people.

By faith, the fathers of the church subdued kingdoms, worked miracles, and closed the mouths of lions in the priceless name of Jesus and His blood.

By faith in Jesus, His death, and His resurrection, you and I received salvation and eternal life.

Everything God offers to man in the Bible comes on the wings of faith. There are a thousand ways to please God, but none of them can happen without faith.

Faith is the daring of the soul to see further than the natural eyes can see. The Bible says, "As it is written, the just shall live by faith" (Rom. 1:17).

If you don't believe it, you will never achieve it. The Bible says, "For with God, nothing shall be impossible." If God sends you fishing for Moby Dick with a cane pole, take the tartar sauce—it's going to be a great day for fishing. I'd rather be willing to try something great for God and fail than to do something small and succeed. Even the errors of the past are the successes of tomorrow, for a mistake is the evidence that at least you tried to do something.

Problems and failure are obstacles to keep you from your divine destiny. Listen to what some of the most successful people in history have said about problems and failure:[3]

- Statesman Bobby Kennedy said, "Only those who dare to fail greatly can ever achieve greatly."
- Thomas J. Watson, the founder of IBM, said, "Would you like me to give you the formula for success? It's quite simple, really. Double the rate of failure. You're thinking of failure as the enemy of success. But it isn't at all. You can be discouraged by failure—or you can learn from it. So go ahead; make mistakes. Make all you can. Because remember, that's where you'll find success." (This is one of my favorite attitudes about failure and success.)
- Famed physician and developer of the polio vaccine, Dr. Jonas Salk, said, "As I look upon the experience of an experimentalist, everything you do is, in a sense, succeeding. It's telling you what not do as well as to do. Not infrequently, I would go into the laboratory, and people

would say that something didn't work. And I'd say, 'Great, we have made a great discovery! If you thought it was going to work and it didn't work, that tells you as much as if it did.' So my attitude is not one of pitfalls; my attitude is one of challenges and, 'What is nature telling me?'"

What is God telling you? He says you can do all things through Christ who strengthens you. That is money in the bank!

Faith reverses the natural order. In the natural, we see and then we believe. Hence, we say, "Seeing is believing." By faith, we first believe it, and then we see it in the natural. That's why the Bible says, "We walk by faith and not by sight."

Mark 9:23 says, "Jesus said to him, 'If you can believe, all things are possible to him who believes.'" The sequence is this: you believe first and receive later. The carnal man wants to receive it first and then believes he has it after it's in his hand.

Hebrews 11:1 says, "Now faith is the substance of things hoped for, the evidence of things not seen."

Faith is not feeling. You can walk into a hospital room and see someone you dearly love suffering on a bed of affliction and cry emotionally for an hour. Your tears may give you emotional relief, but they will do nothing for your loved one. Nothing! Yet one minute of faith released in prayer to a loving God can stop sickness and disease in its tracks.

Hebrews 11 states that faith has "substance." Faith is real. It is measurable. What does it mean for our faith to have substance? It means that our faith is not "rabbit's foot faith." Rabbit's foot faith certainly didn't do the rabbit any good, and it won't do you any good either. Substance in this case means that we have an assurance that God will do for us today what He has done for His people previously.

What God has done in the past, He can do in the present. God's past performance gives us absolute assurance for our future. God said in His Word, "I am the LORD, I do not change" (Mal. 3:6). Scripture also says that Jesus Christ is "the same yesterday, today, and forever."

Whenever you are trying to walk through your problem to the promised land, the first signpost is to recognize that your faith is a substance proven and validated by what God has done in the past.

We know that God answers prayer with supernatural and miraculous manifestations. God answered the prayer of Elijah, who called fire from heaven at Mount Carmel. God heard the prayer of Joshua and held the sun in its place, and time literally stood still.

The God of Abraham, Isaac, and Jacob muzzled the mouths of lions for Daniel because of his prayers. The New Testament church experienced a supernatural explosion because of their prayers. The Bible says, "And when they had prayed, the place where they were assembled together was shaken" (Acts 4:31).

No matter how intimidating your problem happens to be, God is ready to hear and answer your prayer *right now*. He is ready to release your miracle—but first you must expect a miracle! Corrie ten Boom said, "Faith sees the invisible, believes the unbelievable, and receives the impossible."[4]

REMEMBER THIS TRUTH...

Our faith is not mysticism. Our faith is not positive thinking or religious psychobabble. Our faith is rock solid, based on the historical evidence that God in heaven will faithfully perform what He has promised.

Are you in a major health crisis? I know from Scripture and from personal experience that God supernaturally heals. Jesus healed the deaf, the blind, and the mute. Jesus healed blood diseases when He healed the woman with the issue of blood. Jesus healed diseases of muscles and nerves when He healed the paralytic by the pool of Bethesda. He healed the man with the withered hand. He touched the untouchable, and lepers were instantly given skin as clean and pure as that of a newborn baby.

If Jesus Christ, the Great Physician, did those things in the past, He will do them for you in the now! The integrity of the Word of God guarantees it.

Are you looking for a mighty breakthrough in your business to survive in these times of financial crisis? I am praying for you as you read this book. I am believing that barriers to your financial success will be broken, that you will not fear your competitors or your future. That you will know in the depth of your soul that God is already in your future working out the problems that are tormenting you and your family *today*.

God will give you the confidence to begin a bigger and better project than you and your company have ever considered in the past. Don't fear a monster project! When God gave Noah the concept of building the ark, no one on Earth had done it before. It was indeed a monster project that Noah brought in on time, on budget, and without a government loan or OSHA supervision!

Don't limit yourself with petty excuses. There are two kinds of people in the world—those who make good and those who make excuses. Throughout my ministry I have listened to people say things like, "I can't succeed in this problem because I'm not an expert." Let me remind you that the *Titanic* was built by experts and the ark was built by an amateur with faith in God. Which one of those boats would you like to charter for your next cruise?

The *object* of your faith is critical to your walking through the problem and receiving your provision. The Bible says, "Have faith in God."

Some people have faith in faith. They take the attributes of God and make them objects of worship and abuse them. For instance, in my fifty-plus years of ministry, I have had people come to me and quote the Bible verse "God is love." Then they go on to rationalize that the adulterous relationship they're involved in is a "love relationship" and is therefore acceptable to God because God is love. They are dead wrong!

They are taking an attribute of God, in this case, love, and using it to justify their immoral actions. Therefore, they are worshiping their distorted view of an attribute of God instead of God Himself. This is, in fact, theological idolatry. You have chosen a different God to worship. The object of our faith must be God and God alone.

Those who have faith in faith believe more in the crucifix hanging around their necks than the Christ hanging on the cross. A crucifix around your neck without Christ in your heart is nothing more than faith in faith; it is not faith in God.

Faith in God consists of more than wearing jewelry. It's more than crossing your fingers and saying, "I hope, I hope, I hope." Faith in God is *substance* based on the Word of God and the *evidence* of God's past performance. Not only is the object of your faith important, but so is its source.

The Bible says, "Faith cometh by hearing, and hearing by the word of God" (Rom. 10:17, KJV). The Greek word *cometh* is a progressive verb, which implies a faith that is continually increasing and growing.

When you become a new Christian, God gives you a measure of faith. This measure of faith increases to more faith until, over a period of years, as you have walked through your problems and experienced God's provision, your faith grows and matures even more.

Proverbs 3:8 says, "It shall be health to thy navel, and marrow to thy bones" (KJV). The navel is the source of nutrition for the baby in his mother's womb. Proverbs is saying here that the Word of God is the source of life to the spiritual man. Read it and live! Marrow is the place where red blood cells are reconstituted, and life, the Bible says, is in the blood. The marrow refreshes and restores life in the body, and so does God's infallible Word.

Therefore, the message of Proverbs 3:8 is that God's Word is the source of life and the source of physical and spiritual restoration. If you really want to do something healthy today, read the Word of God. It will refresh and restore your heart, soul, mind, and body. There's not a health spa in America that can make that happen.

In 1929, J. C. Penney became critically ill and was admitted to a sanitarium for treatment. One night he reached the depths of despair and began to write farewell letters to his loved ones. In the letters to his wife and mother he expressed doubt that he would see the sunrise.

J. C. Penney did, however, survive the night, and the next morning he experienced a life-changing event. He wrote: "When I awoke the next morning, I was surprised to find that I was still alive. Going downstairs I heard singing in a little chapel where devotional exercises were held each morning. I can still remember the hymn they were singing: 'God Will Take Care of You.'

"Going into the chapel, I listened with a weary heart to the singing, the reading of the scriptures, and the prayer. Suddenly, something happened...I felt as if I had instantly been lifted out of the darkness of a dungeon into warm brilliant sunshine. I felt as if I'd been transported from hell to paradise. I felt the power of God as I had never felt it before. I realized that God with His love was there to help me."[5]

J. C. Penney felt the presence of God and accepted it in faith. Faith in God changes things. Faith in God makes us new; it takes the poverty of the soul into spiritual wealth and leads us to His provision for our lives.

God answers prayer, and His Word is absolutely true. He has healed in the past; therefore, you have a biblical basis for believing that God will heal you and the members of your family of any disease or affliction known to man.

When you are in the problem and Satan whispers, "You can't get well," you have the positive affirmation written by the prophet Jeremiah that shouts back, "For I will restore health to you and heal you of your wounds" (Jer. 30:17).

One of the most remarkable miracles that has taken place in our church, and we have had many, was the healing of Lizzy Gross. In fact, when we pray with others, we encourage them to listen to her testimony as a faith builder for their own miracle. Lizzy is the daughter of John Gross, minister of music at Cornerstone, and his wife, Lestra. The following is the amazing testimony of "Lizzy's supernatural miracle."

> Lizzy began to complain of having double vision in mid-December of 1990. It really didn't seem to bother her very much, and we weren't sure that it wasn't just the imagination of a ten-year-old girl. Nevertheless, we asked about her double vision on a daily basis, and she would confirm that it was still there. We took her to an ophthalmologist, and he concluded that indeed there was an imbalance in her eyes. The doctor explained that even though we couldn't see it, one eye had shifted a bit to the outside, which was causing the double vision, and explained that this condition, often referred to as a "lazy eye," was quite common in children Lizzy's age.
>
> The doctor suspected that she would grow out of it, but if she didn't, he told us that a simple surgery would easily correct her problem. He also said that there was a remote possibility that her condition could be caused by a neurological infection. He told us to go home and to watch her closely, indicating that we should probably notice an improvement within a few weeks.
>
> The contrary happened. Her eye began turning outward more, although Lizzy never complained, and her double vision was getting more intense.
>
> We took her back to the ophthalmologist, and he maintained his diagnosis that she had typical "lazy eye" and that it would correct itself within a matter of weeks.

Not satisfied with that diagnosis, we wanted to get a second opinion. Lestra made an appointment with another ophthalmologist who came highly recommended. When he examined Lizzy, it didn't take him very long to determine that this was potentially a very serious condition. He would not give us a definitive diagnosis without further tests, but he indicated that she either had myasthenia gravis, multiple sclerosis, or a brain tumor.

Our lives were turned upside down, and we became very upset with what might be happening to our precious baby. The doctor recommended we see a pediatric neurologist immediately, and in a matter of hours Lizzy was in his office. The neurologist examined her thoroughly and put her through a series of tests for coordination and motor skills.

By this time, her eye condition had worsened. She couldn't hold her eyelids open without propping them with her little fingers. The specialist administered a Tensilon Test, which would determine whether she had myasthenia gravis or ocular myasthenia.

The doctor diagnosed ocular myasthenia and said that children often grow out of this condition. He didn't indicate that Lizzy's infirmity would worsen.

We didn't want our daughter to suffer with this illness or any other, so we began to call upon the Lord and searched the Scriptures concerning healing.

Meanwhile, the neurologist ordered an MRI of Lizzy's brain stem to be taken on February 6 as a precaution.

We will never forget that ominous day when we received this report: "I've got bad news for you. The MRI shows a tumor. It looks bad, it's in a terrible location of the brain, and you need to admit your daughter to the hospital immediately."

Pastor Hagee and Diana were waiting by my office door as I hung up. I told them what the doctor had said, and we stood, held hands, and prayed the prayer of healing over Lizzy. I met Lestra at our house before taking Lizzy out of school. In her typical strong spirit, she said, "We are going to commit this to the Lord! I will not fear no matter how bad it looks." That was the first time of many dark moments when my wife's faith encouraged me.

We picked up Lizzy at school and told her she needed to go to the hospital because there was something in her head that was making her eye crooked, and the doctors wanted to fix it. We added a very important fact before we admitted her to the hospital: *we told Lizzy that we were trusting God to heal her.*

When we arrived at the hospital, the neurologist showed me the MRI. The film showed what looked like a white rock in the dead center of her brain. The neurologist said the tumor was about the size of a walnut or maybe a small orange.

"Is it malignant?" I asked.

The doctor replied, "It doesn't matter if a tumor is malignant. It's there, and it's eating up the brain. However, in almost all cases they are malignant, which simply means that it has the ability to metastasize. The consensus of the experts who looked at the MRI is that the tumor is, indeed, malignant."

I declared, "Well, it looks like a job for God!"

Lestra and I spent the rest of the afternoon watching our beautiful daughter as she playfully sat on her hospital bed. We tried to grasp the fact that we were the parents of a terminally ill child but could not. There were times when we couldn't restrain our emotions, and we took turns going into the hallway, bursting into tears, and regaining our composure to return to the hospital room to play with Lizzy and talk with visitors who came by.

It was then that we experienced the first of what would be an incredible support from the body of Christ. Through the entire course of events, including medical visits, hospital stays, and everything in between, there was always someone from our prayer group praying and believing with us for Lizzy's healing.

Pastor Hagee began to preach a series on healing and asked our church to corporately fast every Monday for Lizzy's healing and the healing of other members in the church family who were struggling with any form of disease. The spiritual battle was on for the life of my daughter!

The doctors ordered a special CAT scan, which has the ability to show what an MRI doesn't. However, the CAT scan did not show as much as the MRI. The doctor officially informed us that chemotherapy and radiation were not options in terminal cases such as Lizzy's and that there was nothing they could do to save her life.

We were left with no hope. He told us that our daughter would die within nine months to a year. Her symptoms would worsen every day and would be so alarming that it would drive us to the point of insanity. He described excruciating headaches and loss of mobility, until finally she would not be able to breathe. Her condition would eventually result in death.

The doctor recommended one more MRI and a spinal tap on the off chance of a multiple sclerosis diagnosis. They would send the tests to the Mayo Clinic for results. He told us to go home and enjoy our daughter while we still could.

Before we left the hospital, we met with another doctor who was chief of staff for the doctors on Lizzy's case and well respected. Ultimately he became our daughter's personal physician. He reaffirmed that there was nothing that could be done. A biopsy to determine what kind of chemotherapy to use was not possible because of the location of the tumor. Radiation was also not possible because it would destroy vital brain tissue surrounding the tumor. There was nothing medical science could do—we were engaged in a raging battle for the life of our daughter.

In a situation like this, you have to believe that it is God's will to heal. We knew God had healed before—there was no question about that. We had heard testimonies after testimonies about God's healing power. But we needed to know *if He was going to heal Lizzy*! You aren't satisfied with, "Well, if it's His will…" when you are dealing with the possible death of your ten-year-old daughter. There was no room for *IF*!

We began to delve into the Scriptures with passion and purpose. Isaiah 53:5 says: "He was wounded for our transgressions, He was bruised for our iniquities; the chastisement for our peace was upon Him, and by His stripes we are healed." The Word says: "He Himself took our infirmities and bore our sicknesses" (Matt. 8:17). The Word promises: "Who forgives all your iniquities, who heals all your diseases, who redeems your life from destruction" (Ps. 103:3–4). His Word proclaims: "I am the LORD who heals you" (Exod. 15:26).

We believed the many promises in God's Word. We knew that Christ went to the cross so that we could have the promise of healing. We knew that Christ promises to be no respecter of persons, and we knew that He promises to be the same yesterday, today, and forever.

Lestra prayed to the Lord: "I know what Your will is, and that is to heal my daughter. You said in Mark 11:22 to 'have faith in God.' You said, 'I say to you, if you have faith as a mustard seed, you will say to this mountain, "Move from here to there," and it will move; and nothing will be impossible for you' (Matt. 17:20). You said that whatever we ask in prayer believing, we will receive it, and it will be ours."

We chose to stand on the promise that it was God's will to heal Lizzy. We had to believe that no matter what the doctors said to us about her, God's Word was true. So we began a crusade to build our faith. We completely saturated our lives with the Word of God. We didn't watch television, listen to the radio, or read newspapers and magazines. Every spare minute, except for our daily activities and the necessary part of running a household with three children, was spent in the Word of God.

We wrote scriptures on construction paper and taped them to the walls of our house. Pastor Hagee created an audiotape by reciting all the healing scriptures in the Word of God, and I played background music for it. We listened to that tape day and night. We had the audible sound of the scriptures playing in our house twenty-four hours a day—especially at night in Lizzy's room while she slept. We were convinced that there was power in the spoken Word, and that there is supernatural power in simply hearing God's Word.

Our church continued to fast and pray. Many people came at 7:20 each Monday morning to kneel at the altar and proclaim the healing Word of God as they prayed for Lizzy's healing along with us. We isolated ourselves from people who came in fear instead of faith that God would heal our daughter. We were bound and determined to listen only to what God's Word said, and not to consider what man said.

At the end of February, Lizzy was getting worse. Her droopy eyelids were more pronounced. Her left eye had drifted so much it was difficult to see its beautiful blue color, and she began to lose feeling on the left side of her face. Even her doctor was alarmed at the loss of feeling in her face.

A few days after that doctor's visit, Pastor Hagee asked me how Lizzy was doing. "Not great," I said. "It seems like she may be getting a bit worse."

I remember his response: "Johnny, I'm going to start speaking to that tumor. I'm going to command that cancer, in the name of Jesus Christ, to come under the authority of the Word of God and to dry up and die! I'm going to curse it at the roots, and I'm going to demand that it leave Lizzy's body!"

We all joined with Pastor Hagee on this spiritual warfare tactic. We began to speak right to that place where the tumor lived with the power of the Word of God. It was such an intense spiritual warfare.

I remember times when Lizzy would come into our room exhibiting horrible symptoms. We would comfort her, and when she left our room, Lestra and I would kneel at our bedside and command the symptoms to leave. They had no place in our daughter's life.

In the middle of March, we began to notice that Lizzy's eye looked much straighter. We were careful about being overly optimistic—even to the point of not mentioning it to one another. Finally, I whispered to my wife, "Do you notice her eye being straighter?"

And she said, "Yes, I do!"

We went to see Pastor Hagee again, and he confirmed what we saw. Her eye was getting better. He said, "Johnny, take Lizzy back to the doctor; we have a miracle here!"

In the course of the next two weeks, each symptom of the tumor gradually disappeared. By the time of her doctor's appointment, her eye was completely straight, her double vision was almost gone, her hooded eyelids were open, and she was as bright-eyed as ever.

The doctor examined here and said, "God, she looks good."

I asked, "How is it possible for a person to have a tumor like Lizzy's on the brain stem to get better?"

"It's not possible," the doctor responded. "She should be getting worse. Let's take another MRI."

On April 26, 1991, Lizzy had her last MRI! Her symptoms were completely gone. She was restored by the power of God. During the MRI, a friend of ours was in the technician's room as the MRI was being administered, and he overheard the radiologist say, "There's supposed to be a tumor in this little girl's brain. Where is it? It's gone!"

Our friend shared what he heard with us. It was what we were expecting. We had already been rejoicing for weeks. We went into the back room with the radiologist and viewed all the images. She explained to us that the enhancement showed the tumor was gone. She further explained that there was associated swelling around the area where the tumor had been, and she felt it was water on the brain, indicating that there had been some invasive matter within her brain.

We have learned a lot about a doctor's point of view—especially those who read scans. The facts they have about tumors indicate that they don't go away on their own!

All I can say is it's been eighteen years since Lizzy was healed! I believe God's Word is true, and His promises endure to all generations. She is now married and has two beautiful children. As she grew older, we explained all that happened to her, and together we praise the Lord for the power and integrity of the Word of God. God keeps His promises!

Indeed the Bible says, "Beloved, I wish above all things that you prosper and be in good health." God's ultimate goal is the healing of the soul, not just the healing of the body. There came a time in our journey when we not only focused on Lizzy's healing and what God could do for us—we focused on loving God for who He is.

Often it's not until you do that you see the results you are looking for! The greatest commandment is to "love the Lord thy God with all your heart, soul, mind, and body." We are to "seek first the kingdom of God, and all these things will be added unto you."

You can't expect the promises of God to be yours until you completely submit every area of your life to the Lord Jesus Christ and unconditionally make Him the Lord of your life.

The seven kinds of faith

When you are in the problem and the prince of darkness whispers, "You don't have enough faith," remember the words of Saint Paul: "God has given to every man a measure of faith." (See Romans 12:3.) That includes you.

REMEMBER THIS TRUTH…

When you are in the wilderness, and you don't feel you can take another step, a little voice will whisper in your ear, "Don't you feel weak today?" The Word of the living God thunders back with your answer: "The Lord is the strength of my life; of whom shall I be afraid?" (Ps. 27:1).

We don't simply survive in the wilderness; we mature into overcomers! "In Him we live and move and have our being" (Acts 17:28). We are made strong through Jesus Christ and the power of God's Word. "But in all these things we overwhelmingly conquer through Him who loved us" (Rom. 8:37, NAS).

In order to better identify this very important signpost, God describes several forms of faith in His Word.

The seven kinds of faith

1. *Natural faith.* When traveling, you have natural faith that the pilot knows the difference between Chicago and Cuba. You have natural faith that your doctor knows the difference between a tonsillectomy and a hysterectomy or your left leg from your right. When you go into court, you have natural faith in your lawyer that he knows the law fully and completely. You have natural faith in your banker that the money you put in his bank will be there the next time you make a withdrawal. Try living without natural faith in your fellow man, and in short order you will find yourself in a padded room, pounding your head against the wall.

Isaac had natural faith when he trusted in his father, Abraham, who said that God would provide the sacrifice, while Abraham had supernatural faith in God the Father to provide the lamb.

2. *Little faith.* Matthew records Jesus saying to His disciples, "O ye of little faith" (Matt. 6:30, KJV). Little faith can only accomplish little things.

Little faith always worries about "things." God is attentive to little things, for He attends the funeral of every sparrow that falls in flight. If the sparrow in the field knows God will be there for him, why don't you? Aren't you more important to God than sparrows? Worry conquers faith.

3. **Mustard seed faith.** Matthew 17:20 states, "So Jesus said to them, '…if you have faith as a mustard seed, you will say to this mountain, "Move from here to there," and it will move; and nothing will be impossible for you."'

The strength of a mustard seed is so strong that it transforms the taste of whatever it is mixed with. A mustard seed is intense, pure, and potent! When mustard seed faith is focused on God's ability, it has the power to cast mountains into the sea.

4. **The measure of faith.** The Bible says that God gives a measure of faith to every believer in Christ (Rom. 12:3). You have a measure of faith right now. It's up to you to read the Word of God to increase your faith. It's up to you to choose to believe that the Word of God is true. It's up to you to pray and fast for God's direction out of your problem. God will give you the necessary amount of faith it takes to walk out of your problem. Your measure of faith will never increase unless you exercise it.

5. **Great faith.** What is the difference between a measure of faith and great faith? Great faith is the ability to pray in one place and believe that God can answer your prayer on the other side of the world. That requires faith that has grown up and matured.

The Bible gives the example of Jesus praying for the centurion's servant. Jesus declared that the centurion possessed "great faith."

The centurion said to Jesus, "Lord, I am not worthy that You should come under my roof. But only speak a word, and my servant will be healed" (Matt. 8:8). Jesus answered, "Assuredly, I say to you, I have not found such great faith, not even in Israel!" (v. 10).

The power and superiority of this kind of faith is found in the centurion's expression, "Speak the word only." Your faith is great faith when it believes that God can do something from a great distance away. It takes the Word of God at face value.

6. **Faithless faith.** The Bible records: "He said to Thomas, 'Reach your finger here, and look at My hands; and reach your hand here, and put it into My side. Do not be unbelieving, but believing'" (John 20:27). People who have faithless faith say, "Seeing is believing." They are ruled by the flesh.

They are ruled by their five senses: things they can taste, touch, smell, see, or hear. They will never experience the power of God because they have faithless faith that must see before they believe.

7. *Visible faith.* The Bible says, "And when He saw their faith…" The fact is God can see your faith. He can hear your faith in what you say and how you pray. He can see it in what you do.

Think of Peter walking on water:

> And in the fourth watch of the night He came to them, walking on the sea. When the disciples saw Him walking on the sea, they were terrified, and said, "It is a ghost!" And they cried out in fear. But immediately Jesus spoke to them, saying, "Take courage, it is I; do not be afraid."
>
> Peter said to Him, "Lord, if it is You, command me to come to You on the water." And He said, "Come!" And Peter got out of the boat, and walked on the water and came toward Jesus. But seeing the wind, he became frightened, and beginning to sink, he cried out, "Lord, save me!"
>
> Immediately Jesus stretched out His hand and took hold of him, and said to him, "You of little faith, why did you doubt?"
>
> —MATTHEW 14:25–31, NAS

Peter exhibited two kinds of faith. First, he showed visible faith by believing what Jesus said and getting out of the boat and onto the water.

While Peter had his eyes on Christ, he was able to walk on the water. Once he took his eyes off the Master and what He had promised and looked on the problem (the storm), Peter immediately sank. Jesus identified this kind of faith as "little faith."

Are your eyes on Jesus and what He promises in His Word, or are you looking at the problem and becoming fearful, sinking in your unbelief?

Visible faith is the willingness to walk out into the unknown, stand boldly on the Word of God, and believe that God will do what He promised to do.

If you're going through the problem, cling to the promise, because your provision will never become reality unless you are willing to stand boldly and with confidence on the Word of God.

Visible faith in God is the kind of faith that gets results; it is bold. This kind of faith will give you a fighting spirit that will not give up or give in to the problem. When your faith in God's Word is aggressive, you will never settle for second best. When your faith is bold, you will not settle for the torment of living in the problem.

Visible faith is determined. The three Hebrew children stood before Nebuchadnezzar and said, "Our God whom we serve is able to deliver us." After they declared their bold promise, they defied the order of the king.

Consider this dramatic scene. They are standing before King Nebuchadnezzar, who had erected a ninety-foot statue and demanded that they bow down to it. They stood on the first commandment of the Word of God, which says, "You shall have no other gods before me."

These three observant Jewish men defied the most tyrannical man on the face of the earth who had the most formidable army in the most power-ful government on the earth by believing: "Our God is able to deliver us."

That's determined faith! That's bold and aggressive faith! What visible faith!

Visible faith produces a proclamation. The Bible says, "That whosoever shall say unto this mountain, Be thou removed, and be thou cast into the sea; and shall not doubt in his heart, but shall believe that those things which he saith shall come to pass; he shall have whatsoever he saith" (Mark 11:23, kjv).

A proclamation is what you say. A proclamation releases the power of God to attack your problem. The Bible says, "And they overcame him [Satan] by the blood of the Lamb and by the word of their testimony [proc-lamation]" (Rev. 12:11).

Let me give you a Bible proclamation that will take you out of your trouble and into your provision.

> *Through the blood of Jesus, I am redeemed out of the hand of the devil.*
>
> *Through the blood of Jesus, all my sins are forgiven.*
>
> *Through the blood of Jesus, I am continually being cleansed from all sin.*
>
> *Through the blood of Jesus, I am justified, made righteous, just as if I'd never sinned.*

Through the blood of Jesus, I am sanctified, made holy, set apart to God.

Through the blood of Jesus, I have boldness to enter into the presence of God. The blood of Jesus cries out continually to God in heaven on my behalf.

If you will speak this proclamation, it will give you supernatural power to go straight through your problem to your personal land flowing with milk and honey. I encourage you to make this declaration right now, and believe what it says, and I am confident that you will become renewed and spiritually energized!

SIGNPOST #2—DILIGENCE

The Christian life is intended to be a life of *diligence*. Diligence is characterized by steady, earnest, and energetic effort. Diligence is like an intense laser beam focused on a specific goal.

Diligence is Saint Paul saying, "This one thing I do." Paul didn't dabble in a dozen different areas and preach the gospel on the side. With laser-beam intensity, he focused on the "prize of the high calling of God in Christ Jesus" (Phil. 3:14, KJV). He counted the riches of this earth as a dung heap that he might please the Lord who called him to be a servant in the kingdom of God.

In this politically correct generation, many Christians are afraid to carry their faith into the business world, the schoolroom, the university, or even into their social lives. They have lost their sense of diligence.

Far too many twenty-first-century Christians put their faith on like a Sunday suit of clothes. They go to church, robotically sing "Amazing Grace," and nod their heads approvingly as the Word of God is preached. Yet in their mind they're already playing the golf game planned for that afternoon. This is not diligence.

The Christian life is a process of growth. You don't confess your sins, receive Christ, and walk out of the church a mighty spiritual tree laden with ripened fruit bearing the nine gifts of the Holy Spirit. These elements of maturity are developed while in the problem through the process of spiritual struggle.

The growth process of a mighty oak begins with a tiny acorn falling into the soil and dying to itself in order to birth the magnificent tree. The tiny sapling thrusts it head through the rocks and soil to fight for the light of day. It then struggles through the snow, the heat, and the drought and raging storms to sustain its growth.

After decades of success, it spreads its massive branches to form a cool and comforting shade. It grows its roots deep into the ground to keep it in the times of the storm. Someone passes by and stops beneath its arching branches and says, "This is a mighty oak." But do we bother to ask, "What price did this oak have to pay to reach its divine destiny?"

The price it had to pay is the one you will have to pay while in the problem. There is a dying process. There is a birthing process. There is a willingness to fight for the light of day for God's guidance. There will come adversities of snow and heat and drought. There will be times of success and times of failure. Finally, after years of struggle, you will become what God intended for you to become: a mighty spiritual oak.

> It is not the critic who counts, not the man who points out how the strong man stumbled, or where the doer of deeds could have done them better. The credit belongs to the man who is actually in the arena, whose face is marred by dust, and sweat and blood, who strives valiantly, who errs and comes short again and again, who knows the great enthusiasms, the great devotions, who spends himself in a worthy cause, who, at the best, knows in the end the triumph of high achievement, and who, at the worst, if he fails at least fails while daring greatly, so that his place shall never be with those timid souls who know neither victory nor defeat.[6]

How diligent are you in your service to Christ? How diligent are you in your covenant with your spouse? How diligent are you in the provision and protection of your family? Diligence is not an option; it is a command of God. Diligence is a vital signpost out of your problem.

> Keep thy heart with all diligence; for out of it are the issues of life.
> —Proverbs 4:23, kjv

SIGNPOST #3—EXCELLENCE

Everyone possesses the potential for greatness. You are the divine creation of a majestic God, who is committed to excellence. There is within you His divine spark of excellence, waiting to explode into its blazing and brilliant potential.

The story is told of an American Indian who found an eagle's egg and put it in the nest of a prairie chicken. The eaglet hatched with the brood of prairie chickens and grew up with them.

All his life the eagle, thinking he was a prairie chicken, did what other prairie chickens did. He scratched in the dirt for seeds and worms. He clucked and cackled. When he dared to fly, it was only for a few feet, because that's what the other chickens were doing and that's all he believed he could do.

Years passed, and one day he saw a magnificent bird far above him in the cloudless sky, flying with majestic grace on the powerful wind currents. It soared with scarcely a beat of its powerful wings. The prairie eagle said to the other chickens, "What a beautiful and majestic bird. What kind of bird is that?"

"That's an eagle, the chief of birds," the prairie chickens clucked. "But don't dare think you can fly like an eagle; you can never be like them. You are just a prairie chicken."

So the deceived, earthbound eagle never gave it another thought. And the eagle died, thinking he was a prairie chicken. What he thought about himself completely controlled his potential, his provision, and his divine destiny.

What a waste! God designed him to soar into the heavens. He was engineered by the divine architect for high adventure. Yet he wasted his life pecking for worms and scratching in the dirt, cackling and clucking his days away because he believed he could do no better.

You will do the same if you do not see yourself as God sees you. You are God's divine creation, and locked within you is the spirit of excellence.

You are designed for high flight. The Bible says, "But those who wait on the LORD shall renew their strength; they shall mount up with wings like eagles, they shall run and not be weary, they shall walk and not faint" (Isa. 40:31). It's God's will for you to achieve excellence, even while you are in the middle of the problem. Psalm 16:3 states, "As for the saints who are on the earth, they are the excellent ones, in whom is all my delight."

God's divine assignment for you is a land flowing with milk and honey. You have a special purpose on this earth that only you can accomplish. You must choose to accomplish it with excellence for the glory of God and the realization of your dream.

Excellence in your life is a basic form of Christian witnessing. Every job you do is the portrait of the person who does it. Saint Paul said in Colossians 3:17, "And whatever you do in word or deed, do all in the name of the Lord Jesus." What's the message? Do it with excellence, or don't do it.

Don't wish for your job to be easier. If it was easier, everyone would be doing it, and you would be unemployed. Ask God to crucify your prairie chicken temperament—your sloppy, slovenly attitude that allows you to accept a mediocre effort. Let the divine spark of excellence explode within you; do your job with excellence. The secret of joy in your work is contained in one word: *excellence*. To do something with excellence produces the priceless sense of accomplishment.

Excellence is not a project, act, or job description; excellence is a way of life. It includes going beyond the normal call of duty, stretching our perceived limits, and holding ourselves responsible for being our best.

Excellence is simply doing your very best, in everything, in every way, in every situation. Consider these four attributes of excellence:

1. Consider your commitment.

"The quality of a person's life," said Vince Lombardi, "is in direct proportion to their commitment to excellence, regardless of their chosen field of endeavor." Isaac D'Israel put it this way: "It is a wretched taste to be gratified with mediocrity when the excellent lies before us."

2. Pay the price.

Excellence in any endeavor is not automatic. As Dr. Stephen Covey says, "Real excellence does not come cheaply. A certain price must be paid in terms of practice, patience, and persistence—natural ability notwithstanding." Review those three Ps again—each is necessary for paying the price.

3. Exceed expectations.

Challenge yourself to exceed self-imposed and other limitations. Go a step beyond the customary or ordinary. Give just a little more than normal. Bishop Gore said, "God does not want us to do extraordinary things; He wants us to do ordinary things extraordinarily well." When people perform the common things in life in an uncommon way, the world will sit up and take notice.

4. Never settle for good enough.

Winston Churchill exemplified this quality. He said, "I am easily satisfied with the very best."

Former Secretary of State Henry Kissinger asked an aide to prepare a report. The aide worked day and night to analyze the information and complete his report. Shortly after receiving the finished product, Mr. Kissinger returned it to his aide with a note: "Redo it." The aide diligently went about his task, turned it in, and again was told to redo it. After the third time the aide asked to see Kissinger. "I have completed this report three times," he said, "and this is the best job I can do." Kissinger replied, "In that case, I'll read it now."

Excellence comes from striving, maintaining the highest standards, paying attention to little details, and being willing to go the extra mile.[7]

SIGNPOST #4—KNOWLEDGE

> But also for this very reason, giving all diligence, add to your faith
> virtue, to virtue knowledge.
>
> —2 PETER 1:5

The word for *knowledge* in 2 Peter is the Greek word *gnosis*, meaning "to know God and his salvation."[8] "Grace and peace be multiplied to you in the knowledge of God and of Jesus our Lord" (v. 2).

In verse 2, the word *knowledge* was the Greek word *epignosis*, meaning, "super knowledge."[9] Saint Paul, writing to the Colossian believers, prayed that they might have the *epignosis*, meaning the super knowledge of God (Col. 1:9). The Gnostic heresy, which covered the earth in that day, claimed to impart super knowledge through the secret rituals.

However, for both Peter and Paul, *knowledge* meant growth and development in the Christian life, and super knowledge was their goal as the Holy

Spirit confirmed the Word of God to the individual believer. Let me give you a personal example of Holy Spirit–directed knowledge.

My grandfather, John Christopher Hagee, married Laverta McElvany, the daughter of the headmaster of the Methodist Bible College in Oklahoma at the turn of the twentieth century. God gave to their union ten sons and one daughter. My father was the second son, and the lone survivors as of this date are Uncle Tad, an attorney in California retired from Atlantic Richfield, and Aunt Sue, the baby of the family and only girl.

The fifth son was named Joel Lavon. His brothers nicknamed him "Tinker" because he was always tinkering with anything that was not nailed down. One day the brothers were hunting, and Uncle Tinker climbed up a tree to look down a dry creek bed. The limb he was perched on snapped, and Tinker plunged into the creek bed beneath him. He landed feet first, and a stick penetrated deeply into the bottom of his bare foot.

Immediately Tinker's brothers carried him home, and within hours, he was running a high fever. His foot began to swell, and ugly, dark streaks started creeping up his leg.

Grandfather called for the doctor, who examined Tinker and announced to the family, "Tinker has blood poisoning, and if it doesn't improve soon, we must cut off his leg to save his life."

My grandfather was a man with an awesome prayer life. He asked the doctor to give him until morning to seek the face of God for the answer. As grandfather prayed through the night, God gave him a word of knowledge concerning Tinker. It was "super knowledge."

The word of knowledge, which is a knowing in your spirit that conquers all doubt, revealed to my grandfather that there was a ball of moss in Tinker's foot that was on the end of that stick—and that was the source of the infection.

My grandfather woke my grandmother and asked her to get her knitting needle and bring it to him. He sterilized the knitting needle and gently pushed it through the open wound of Tinker's foot until he felt the moss. Grandfather twisted the needle and carefully pulled the plug of moss out of Tinker's foot. Instantly, the corruption of poison flowed through the gaping hole and out of Tinker's foot.

Tinker's leg began to diminish in size, and his fever broke before morning. By daylight, he was doing much better. When the doctor returned the next morning, he examined Tinker and declared that he was on his way to recovery from the blood poisoning.

The point of this story is that God can give you "super knowledge" that will give you the ability to solve mind-boggling problems in your life.

I have personally witnessed the working of this super knowledge in the lives of Spirit-filled believers for decades. God has the power to tell you what is going to happen before it happens and the power to tell you what has happened when it is a mystery to the human mind.

This is not exclusively a New Testament phenomenon. In 2 Kings 6 the Bible records that the king of Syria called his men together and asked them, "Which one of you is on the side of the king of Israel?"

Why did he ask his military command staff this question? He was looking for a spy because every time he set a trap for the army of Israel, the prophet Elisha told the king of Israel where the trap would be set so they could stay away from that exact location. Elisha did this repeatedly through the word of knowledge or super knowledge.

The military commander of Syria answered the king: "None, my lord, O king; but Elisha, the prophet who is in Israel, tells the king of Israel the words that you speak in your bedroom" (2 Kings 6:12).

The man of God was telling God's people, the Jewish people, what was going to happen, when it would happen, and where it would happen—as the words were being spoken by their enemies miles away. That, my friends, is super knowledge.

God can give you the word of knowledge if you will seek His face in the day of your problem. The word of knowledge is a supernatural revelation of information pertaining to a person or an event, given for a specific purpose, usually having to do with an immediate need.[10] The God whom we serve is the God who reveals secret things to His children. This is promised in Deuteronomy 29:29: "The secret things belong to the LORD our God, but the things revealed belong to us and to our children forever" (NIV).

Your denomination may not believe in the word of knowledge, but I assure you on the authority of God's Word and the teaching of Saint Paul, it's very real and very available if you're willing to seek the face of God to know the unknowable and to do the impossible. It is God's laser beam that will guide you straight through the problem.

Signpost #5—Patience

If God left His precious, perfect, and only begotten Son in the problem for forty days, why do you believe that God has failed you if in the next forty minutes He doesn't solve the problem you've embraced for the past forty years? Like the children of Israel, we ignore God when we are problem free but demand that He take us out of our troubles just minutes after we come into them.

Let me share a true story with you. One day I was late for a major appointment, and I got caught at the longest traffic light in San Antonio. It is a long light even when you are not in a hurry—and an eternal flame when you are.

I was the second car in line. The car in front of me was driven by a little old lady who was staring at the light in front of her like a bird dog pointing to a covey of quail.

The light changed from red to green, and she didn't move. I could not believe it. I was already five minutes late, and now I was furious! The light went from green to red, and my urge to scream was throttled in my throat. I can assure you all the reserves in my "patience bank account" were exhausted in a matter of seconds.

The light went from red to green a second time, and she did not move. It was as if she was frozen in position, staring at the light. That ripped it! I started honking my horn with my left hand and slapping the dashboard with my right hand. I rolled down my window and screamed, "Drive, lady, drive!"

It did absolutely no good. I might as well have been talking to the man in the moon. The light went back to red, but no more red than my face. I needed this delay like a giraffe needs strep throat.

At that awkward moment, when I was honking my horn and pounding the dashboard and screaming to the top of my lungs, a car pulled up next to me. I looked out my window and to my dismay saw that the car was full of Cornerstone church members. They rolled down their windows, and the church member behind the wheel said with a sanctimonious sense of sarcasm, "Why, hello, Pastor Hagee." The teenagers in the back were laughing like it was *Saturday Night Live*.

I was totally busted! Guilty as charged! I was caught red-handed at a moment when I had completely lost all patience. Finally, by the grace of God, the light changed again, and I went through the intersection on to my appointment...late.

Most people have the wrong concept of the word *patience*. Patience is, in fact, the ability to endure when trials come while you're in the problem. Patience is, in other words, endurance.

Saint Paul wrote that we are to "endure hardness as a good soldier of Jesus Christ" (2 Tim. 2:3). According to the apostle, God expects you to demonstrate endurance.

Endurance is divine. The Bible says in Matthew 24:13, "He who endures to the end shall be saved." In James 5:11, we see the result of endurance: "Behold, we count them happy which endure" (KJV).

What is endurance? The Greek word for *endure* is *hupomono*, meaning, "to have fortitude and to persevere."

Let me tell you a true story given to me by my dear friend Dr. W. A. Criswell, for many years the pastor of the First Baptist Church in Dallas and the president of the Southern Baptist Convention. Dr. Criswell preached the dedication sermon for Cornerstone Church. Dr. Criswell and I shared a mutual love for Israel, and I loved him dearly for he was one of the great preachers of the twentieth century.

Dr. Criswell told the story of a friend who had two big bird dogs in his backyard. One afternoon a little bulldog came snorting down the alley and saw those big bird dogs. The little bulldog snorted and climbed under the fence, and the fight was on!

There were yelps, barks, growls, bites, and scratch marks as the little bulldog went home severely whipped. The next day he laid out in the sun, allowing his battle wounds to heal.

But the next afternoon, at the same time, he came snorting down the alley, scratching and pawing the gravel as he snorted in defiance. He crawled under the fence and charged those two big bird dogs, and once again, the furious fight was on, and was once again the little bull dog was whipped.

Day after day, he would lie out in the morning sun letting his wounds heal and in the afternoon come down the alley, scratching and pawing the ground, determined to win the fight.

About the fifth day, the two big bird dogs saw him coming down the alley, and both ran down into the basement of their owner's home, whimpering, to hide from the triumphant little bulldog who simply would not give up. His patience endured the problem.

He was not the biggest, he was not the best, but he was the winner. He was the winner because he just refused to quit. Endurance is the road less traveled, but it is the road to all accomplishment. Endurance is a choice you make every day of your life.

> Knowing this, that the trying of your faith worketh patience. But let patience have her perfect work, that ye may be perfect and entire, wanting nothing.
> —James 1:3–4, kjv

We must learn to endure the winds of adversity for they lead us to the highest pinnacle of success.

Endurance will carry you through the problem you are in to the provision you must have! It's always too soon to quit! Remember the famous quote of Sir Winston Churchill: "Never, never, in nothing great or small, large or petty, never give in."[11] He followed his own admonition, never giving up during the dark days of World War II when it seemed Hitler was unstoppable and victory was impossible.

During the battle for London, when the Nazis were bombing London relentlessly, Churchill walked the bomb-riddled streets of his beloved city with a cigar between his teeth and his stubby fingers lifted high with the V for victory sign.

A strong case can be made that Sir Winston Churchill saved Western civilization by slowing the Nazi blitzkrieg and exposing Communism as the iron curtain was falling across Europe. With his amazing brilliance and his bulldog endurance, he dragged Europe to the realization that appeasing the Nazi monsters was not the answer. The answer was victory through endurance and patience.

What made this unusual man a hero for the ages? Three words: perseverance, endurance, and patience.

SIGNPOST #6—INTEGRITY

Integrity has become a rare and precious commodity in America. *Integrity* is defined in Webster's Dictionary as "adherence to a code of moral or other values."

I love the words of the following poem written by Josiah G. Holland.

> God give us men. The time demands
> Strong minds, great hearts, true faith and willing hands;
> Men whom the lust of office does not kill;
> Men whom the spoils of office cannot buy;
> Men who possess opinions and a will;
> Men who have honor, men who will not lie;
> Men who can stand before a demagogue
> And dam his treacherous flatteries without winking;
> Tall men, sun-crowned men, who live above the fog
> In public duty and in private thinking.[12]

The Bible demands integrity for all successful leaders. Proverbs 11:3 says, "The integrity of the upright shall guide them: but the perverseness of transgressors shall destroy them" (KJV).

You pass or fail in life based on your personal integrity! Without integrity you will never reach the promised land.

The story is told of John Smith, who had worked for many years as foreman for a very successful building contractor. One day the building contractor called him into his office and said, "John, we are going to build one last house together, and I want it to be the finest house we've ever built. You will be the foreman on this very special project, and I want you to order the very best materials and the finest fixtures available. I want you to spare no expense in making this a truly magnificent home! I'm going to Europe with my wife for a one-year vacation, and I want the home finished when I return."

John accepted the assignment, and his boss left for Europe. Then came the integrity test! He thought, "If I'm really in charge and the boss is away, I can cut corners on the materials and the fixtures and put the extra money in my pocket. Who will know the difference? Once the house is painted, it will look just great!"

John set about his scheme. He ordered second-grade lumber, but his reports indicated that it was top grade. He ordered inexpensive concrete for the foundation and put in cheap wiring and secondhand lighting and fixtures, yet his report read as if they were top quality.

The house was finished, and his boss returned from Europe anxious to see the magnificent home. John took his boss from the front door through every room and ended the grand tour on the massive back patio.

His boss smiled at John, shook his hand, and said, "John, you've done a magnificent job. You've been such a good and faithful foreman all these years. You have been a man of integrity. John, here are the keys to this magnificent home...it's yours! It's an expression of my gratitude and appreciation for your loyal service. Live in it with my compliments!" John lost his integrity when he needed it most.

The Bible makes it clear that integrity will also bring blessing to your children.

Proverbs 20:7 states, "The just man walketh in his integrity: *his children are blessed after him*" (KJV, emphasis added).

Are your children being blessed by your integrity?

Several years ago, I was invited to a local country club by one of San Antonio's leading businessmen. I had no idea what he wanted or the nature of the lunch.

I was on time for the lunch; the businessman was late! I found our table and sat down to wait. Within minutes the businessman arrived with a Cheshire cat smile covering the entirety of his face.

He tossed a slick magazine on the table in front of me that showed every new private jet that was being made in America at the time.

"What is this?" I asked.

"I want you to pick out the jet you would like to have, and I'll buy it for you."

I wasn't born late last night; I smelled the integrity test coming. "What's the catch?" I asked, totally bewildered.

"I will buy you the jet of your choice if you will steer all the business in your church toward me in the future!" He could hardly contain his joy.

Without hesitation I responded, "That would be dishonest and lacking in integrity on my part. In the decades I have been a pastor, I have been approached by numerous businessmen who have asked me for the name of our church members for their business interest. The answer is always the same: NO!"

The all-consuming smile left his face as I left the table and the country club and, instead, ate a double-meat, jalapeno cheeseburger alone but with my integrity intact.

What's the point?

Every Sunday it is my absolute pleasure to look out over a congregation of thousands. There are five very special people in that great audience who mean the world to me…my children. They are all blessed of God and serving the Lord. They are living proof of Proverbs 20:7: "The just man walketh in his integrity: his children are blessed after him" (KJV).

I close this signpost marked "integrity" with this story. A client went to his attorney and said, "I am going into a business deal with a man I do not trust. I want you to craft an airtight contract that he can't break and that will protect me from any sort of mischief he may have on his mind."

The attorney replied, "Listen, my friend. There are no group of words in the English language that will take the place of integrity between two men that will fully protect either of you if you plan to deceive each other."

Without integrity you will never walk out of your problem and into God's provision for your life.

Chapter 8

YOUR VISION DETERMINES YOUR PROVISION

YOUR VISION FOR YOUR LIFE DETERMINES GOD'S PROVISION *IN* YOUR life! Your attitude molds who you are and what you expect out of life. When you trust another person, you won't be suspicious of that person's motives. If you are generous, you won't suspect that others are cheating you. If you are honest, you won't anticipate deceit from others. If you show mercy, you don't expect others to be judgmental.

One of the best outcomes of your problem is the positive altering of your attitude about your life and how you perceive the world around you—including your problems. If you believe the promises of God are for you, then you won't be intimidated by your problem when it comes. In fact, without intimidation and fear, you are halfway to your provision.

If you choose to have a negative attitude, thinking only in narrow-minded terms, then you don't have a chance to come through your problem—you are defeated before you get out of the starting gate. You have, in a sense, destined yourself to stay trapped in your private wilderness for a very long time.

An immature or negative attitude attempts to manipulate God; a mature and positive attitude seeks to align with God's divine will for your life.

God, who is your Father, has all power in heaven and in earth. He loves you deeply, and He has made a promise to each of His children: "I will give you the desires of your heart!" God intends to keep that promise, and your future is just as bright as the promises of God. That alone should give you a positive attitude about your life now and future life in Christ.

If you can't define the desire of your heart, then you can't define your destiny. If you're going nowhere, any road will take you there, but what road takes you to your divine destiny? Don't let problems or failures dictate your future. Instead, let your Father in heaven design your life.

REMEMBER THIS TRUTH...

A good attitude is more important than good aptitude.

What did King Solomon say of adversity and problems? Proverbs 24:10 states, "If you falter in times of trouble, how small is your strength!" (NIV). Other translations describe your strength as "small" or "limited." This wise saying is certainly true if we rely on our own strength to see us through the problems of life. But what happens when we depend on the strength and wisdom of our Creator? What then?

Abraham, the father of all who believe, and Isaac, his only son of covenant, climbed Mount Moriah for a sacrifice of obedience to God. The purpose of this *mission impossible* was for Abraham to prove to God his willingness to obey God completely in every dimension of his life. The Bible promises, "If you are willing and obedient, you will eat the best from the land" (Isa. 1:19, NIV). Abraham, in pure faith, was painstakingly walking toward his provision.

As father and son climbed the mountain, Isaac asked Abraham, "Where is the lamb for the burnt offering?" (Gen. 22:7, NIV).

Abraham responded with a pronouncement of faith that all Bible believers know and speak often: *"Jehovah Jireh."*

The meaning and theology behind this declaration is "God sees." It presents the concept that God can see your need, and He will meet your need. The Bible confirms this promise with the verse: "You do not have because you do not ask" (James 4:2).

Those who have turned the world upside down for God have been men and women with a positive vision in their hearts and a Bible in their hands. They have asked for, and believed in, God's promises to be made manifest in their lives. They have acknowledged that their strength is not sufficient, but with God nothing is impossible.

Say it out loud: *His vision leads to your provision.* Imagine that thought for a moment. God's omniscient (all-seeing), omnipresent (all-present), and omnipotent (all-powerful) plan for your life will determine the magnitude of your provision. That is huge!

When you approach problem solving in your own strength, you will stumble over the pebbles of life. You will never get the opportunity to scale the mountains because you will keep your eye on the smallest obstacles and not on the supernatural goal of your provision. When you approach the problem through your own strength, you fail to recognize adversity as the springboard to great achievement.

A small town chamber of commerce invited a guest speaker to address its annual dinner. The community's economy was weak, people were discouraged, and the chamber of commerce wanted the motivational speaker to give the community a boost.

During her presentation, the speaker took a large piece of white paper and put a black dot in the center of the paper using a marking pen. Then she held the paper up before the group and asked them to describe what they saw. One person quickly replied, "I see a black dot."

"OK, what else do you see?"

Others joined in agreement: "A black dot."

"Don't you see anything but the black dot?" the speaker asked.

A resounding "No" came from the audience.

"The most important thing has been overlooked," replied the speaker. "No one noticed the sheet of paper! Listen carefully," she pleaded. "In our business, family, personal, and social lives, we are often distracted by small, dot-like failures and disappointments. There is a tendency to forget the wonderful things around us. Those blessings, successes, and joys are far more important than the little black dots that monopolize our attention and energies."[1]

God our Father, who possesses all strength, all vision, and all power is not moved or surprised by your problem. In fact, He is excited about it, because He knows the successful outcome. He sees the whole picture, not just the black dot. He knows the promotion is on its way. He knows that your healing will soon be manifested. He knows that your child will be free from the bondage of drugs. He knows that your marriage will be restored and made new!

One man said that the difference between an obstacle and opportunity is, "Our attitude toward it. Every opportunity has a difficulty, and every difficulty has an opportunity."[2]

REMEMBER THIS TRUTH...

A small positive change in your outlook is needed to convert a large challenging problem into an opportunity.

People of faith search for the unique purposes within their problems, for it is by coming face-to-face with the problem that they can realize their opportunities and potential.

A small businessman owned a modest clothing store in the middle of a city block in Middle America. A national superchain came into his city and informed him in no uncertain terms, "Sell out to us, or we'll drive you out of business."

"I will not sell out!" said the small clothing store owner.

The superchain, true to its word, built a massive building around the small businessman's clothing store, which covered from one end of the block to the other. On opening day, the superchain stretched a huge banner in front of their store that read: "GRAND OPENING!"

The small businessman responded by putting up a sign stretching from one side of his store to the other, located right in the middle of the block. His sign read: "MAIN ENTRANCE!"

How you see the problem *is* the problem. This man's vision determined his provision. Examine the difference in the following "woe-is-me" businessman who rehearsed to his friend why business was so bad from month to month.

> January is bad because people spent all their cash for the holidays.
> February is bad because all the best customers have gone south for the winter.
> March is bad for business because it is unseasonably cold.
> April is never a good month because of income tax season.
> May is worse than March because it is too rainy and the customers are depressed and won't go shopping.

June has too little rain and the people are discouraged for the drought.

July is entirely too hot and everyone is exhausted.

August is a very weak month because everyone is on vacation.

September is worse than August because they spent all their money while they were away.

October is so slow because my customers are waiting for the fall clearance.

November is depressing because the people are discouraged over the election results.

December seems to be slow because everyone is saving their money for the holidays.

One man's vision produced successful results, and the other man's attitude produced excuses for failure.

PROVISION IN ACTION

How does the concept of promise, problem, and provision work out in your daily life? Have you learned to see your challenges as opportunities to experience the provision of God? The following illustrations are *vision* and *provision* in action.

A marriage transformation

God gives you a promise, a word, a knowing in your spirit that He is going to save your alcoholic husband. Your response? You shout, "Glory, hallelujah, God will soon answer my prayers!"

Then hours later you get a call from Baptist Hospital notifying you that your husband has been in a serious car wreck and is in the hospital in a full body cast.

What is this? This is a problem!

Remember—when you are in the problem, there is a right way and a wrong way to respond. The right way sends you straight through the problem, and the wrong way gets you another lap around Mount Sinai with an extended stay in your wilderness.

How will you respond to the news that your alcoholic husband is in a full body cast? This is not how you thought your provision would come.

You envisioned him coming home to you, falling on his knees, and asking your forgiveness for his years of drinking and abuse, then pledging to rededicate his life next Sunday at the Shallow Water Church where both of you seldom attend.

This is the wrong way to respond: "Well, if this is how God answers prayer, maybe I'll just go down to the liquor store and buy both of us a quart of Wild Turkey and sing, 'I'll Fly Away.'" This kind of attitude will guarantee both of you an extended stay in the problem.

The right way to respond to the problem is: "Thank You, Lord, for Your faithful promise. Old lush lips, the king of the lounge lizards, is flat on his back in Baptist Hospital in a full body cast. Your Word says, 'He makes me to lie down in green pastures.' 'This is the day the Lord hath made.' I just feel like something good is about to happen. Glory to God, my provision is on the way!"

God looks over the balconies of heaven and hears the words of this faithful wife and commands His angels, "Did you hear what My child said down there in the midst of the problem? She didn't whine, murmur, or complain about My plan. Go down to her, angels, and give her wells she didn't dig, houses she didn't build, and vineyards that she didn't plant. Give her the husband she has been praying for. Make her marriage like heaven on earth! Bless her with My favor, which is more precious than silver and gold."

Saints of God, hold on to the promise of God while you are in the problem with an attitude of praise and thanksgiving, and be prepared to receive your blessed provision. Again I say, hold on! If you are willing and obedient, you will eat the fat of the land! God will command His blessing to overtake you like a tidal wave overtakes a child's sand castle. Get happy! Rejoice and be glad! Good things are about to happen…to YOU!

Financial makeover

Recently I received a letter from a church member that began with the words, "Thirty-nine hours ago I was fired!" Needless to say, I believed I was in for a discouraging story, but I was wrong. This testimony illustrates how your attitude in the midst of your trouble can transform your problems into blessings.

Dear Pastor Hagee,

Thirty-nine hours ago I was fired as an area sales manager of a large home contracting company. Three men from corporate headquarters walked by my office, and one of the men paused by my door and said, "Bryan, can you come with me?" I immediately sensed something was wrong.

I walked in the conference room where the marketing director sat at the table alongside the corporate accountant and one of my associates. I immediately thought of all the rounds of layoffs the company had experienced over the last ten months.

I remembered the disappointment that our leaders had voiced about the lack of success of a recent $500,000 promotional purchase. I assumed they were going to release the associate that persuaded the management team to make the deal.

I sat down and waited awkwardly. I searched the table for a friendly face as the branch manager gave me a nod and a half-reassuring smile, but then quickly diverted his gaze to the blank wall behind me.

My face and neck were burning hot. I could hear my heart beating in my ears with what sounded like the constant whooshing roar of water going through a lead pipe. I felt like I was in front of an execution squad waiting to be shot.

My mind was racing: "Am I getting fired? Please, Lord, no! I just spoke to the vice president of sales whom I directly report to, and she didn't lead me to believe anything was wrong." I waited for what seemed an eternity.

Eleven months ago I sent an e-mail to our entire division suggesting that we start a prayer group every Monday morning because the bottom had dropped out of the new home sales market in our city.

We created every type of promotion we could possibly conceive, but the only thing we hadn't tried was prayer. We began with over twenty people, and then dwindled to a steady five attendees per week who stood in faith that the Lord would intervene.

My mind went back to the meeting at hand. We continued to wait in our self-imposed silence. Suddenly the awkward quiet was broken. One of the men asked, "Is everything good?" The branch manager continued to stare at the baseboards and responded with a barely audible noise that sounded more like "humph" than a proper answer.

I remember thinking, "It is not easy to terminate an employee, even when it is justifiable." I felt for my friend. I wanted to tell him, "I'm sorry. I know this is not coming from you."

At that moment, the corporate representative assertively entered the room, and with what seemed to be a megaphone he announced, "Gentlemen, I believe we all know each other. Senior management in the company has decided to make changes to the management team. You are included in those changes. Please empty your desks by the end of the day. That's all we have to say."

He left the room as abruptly as he entered as the branch manager began to explain our termination packages. The two of us who were fired listened quietly and were then escorted back to our offices. The corporate accountant walked with me in silence as I began packing my personal belongings.

I finally asked, "Is this performance related, or are we going through more layoffs?" He responded with, "Naw, we are changing management down here to see if we can't turn this thing around." I continued to pack. "What did he mean by 'changing management?' 'Turn things around?' Our sales have increased dramatically over the last three months! We are the top-selling division in the country!" My mind was working in overdrive at this point.

I exited through the shortest hallway in the building to ensure the fewest sightings. I did not want a *glance of pity* to set me off. I held my breath, walked to my truck, and sat for a moment, then exhaled.

I began to pray, "Thank You, Lord, for whatever is going on. I know that You will get me through this. Amen." I told myself, "When one door shuts, another one opens." I have armed myself over the years with countless biblical promises to encourage myself and others in moments like this. "God doesn't want me here anymore, so He removed me. He is going to replace good with better. He has promised to take care of me and my family because we have been obedient." I spoke to myself with the reassuring promises of God and assessed the last several months for what seemed to be a very, very long journey home.

I thought of how I had lost joy and passion for my job months prior to this day. One of my associates and I had been competing for the vice president's position, and our division chief was putting us through competitive tests. The contention had been difficult for all of us.

I was near burnout from very long days when I learned that I and other sales managers were invited to a corporate retreat to discuss sales strategies.

There was a problem; it was the same weekend of our daughter's participation in our church's Christmas pageant. I was *advised* that I should not miss the retreat; either I attended the meeting, or I would no longer be with the company.

My wife and daughter were very disappointed that I would not be attending the pageant but understood that I had no choice. I was working longer hours for less pay, and it was taking a toll on our marriage and my time with my family. If it were not for our shared faith, we would have been in deep trouble.

I arrived at the retreat and was disappointed when we only met for one hour and got little accomplished.

I did, however, have lots of time to pray and reflect.

The other meetings involved the division presidents, and as I observed them, I noticed that this was a group of men who sacrificed a lot of time away from their families. I thought, "The higher I climb, the less time I will have for Tracy and the kids."

I decided that weekend that I did not want the vice president's position. We wrapped up the retreat early, and I was able to return in time to watch Taylor perform in the Christmas pageant, which was the highlight of my weekend.

The position of vice president was given to my contender, and I remained sales manager and continued to work long hours. I was still in overdrive without making progress.

Several weeks passed, and Tracy excitedly shared something wonderful that had happened to her. She had been working two jobs, juggling kids' schedules, and still being a supportive wife to me. She was as burned out as I was. I was unaware that she had been praying to the Lord for joy to return to her life. He gave Tracy the desire of her heart shortly after she began praying, and she was so eager to share her provision with me; her joy was back!

I had noticed a change in her attitude for the good, but, to be honest; I was too self-absorbed to ask why. Her example resonated with me, and I too prayed, "Lord, please bring joy back to my life and passion for my work."

As I waited for His answer, I began to establish a weekly training program for our sales team. I reviewed countless hours of videos of our sales people in action. I remembered that my college football coaches at Rice University spent hours upon hours reviewing game films in order to establish strengths and weaknesses. Our practices were then designed around refining the strengths and correcting the weaknesses.

I gave this information and strategy to the new vice president, and we began training. Within ninety days, our average sales per month increased from 135 to 160. I began to write a training manual for new home sales, and, before I knew it, my passion and joy for my job was back!

The morning I was fired my wife had awakened me from a dream so that I would have enough time to take our daughter to school. In my dream, I was riding in a school bus on the way back home from a late football game. Sitting in the front of the bus was a man who tried to hand me a long, wide scroll to read. This man seemed to be a coach of some sort. He appeared confident, cheerful, encouraging, and seemed to be very much in command.

I was tired and angry and refused to accept the scroll. He asked me again to read it, and this time he placed the paper in my hands. He told me again, "Read it. It is Psalms 40–45." Then I awoke from my dream feeling helpless.

After dropping my daughter off at school, I prayed, "Lord, help me." Immediately, I remembered the dream. Psalms 40–45! I was no longer angry. I prayed, "Lord, what are You going to show me now?" I returned home, excitedly picked up my Bible, and read Psalms 40–45.

I waited patiently for the LORD; and He inclined to me, and heard my cry. He also brought me up out of a horrible pit, Out of the miry clay, and set my feet upon a rock, and established my steps. He has put a new song in my mouth—praise to our God; many will see it and fear, and will trust in the LORD.

Blessed is that man who makes the LORD his trust, and does not respect the proud, nor such as turn aside to lies. Many, O LORD my God, are Your wonderful works which You have done; and Your thoughts toward us cannot be recounted to You in order; if I would declare and speak of them, they are more than can be numbered.

Sacrifice and offering You did not desire; my ears You have opened. Burnt offering and sin offering You did not require. Then I said, "Behold, I come; in the scroll of the book it is written of me. I delight to do Your will, O my God, And Your law is within my heart."

—PSALM 40:1–8

Pastor, you have taught "Promise, Problem, and Provision" to our congregation before, and I have always listened, but this time I put what I learned into action. I asked for *joy* to return to my work, and I received it. I received *the promise* that He would give me joy through the storm. Guess what came next? That's right; *the problem* was getting fired unexpectedly.

After being faced with the problem, Tracy and I prayed immediately and thanked God for what was to come. We knew that God had something good planned for us, and in faith we praised Him for *His provision* ahead of time.

Soon after my discharge, I learned that not only would I be paid for my remaining vacation, but I was also given two months salary as part of a severance package.

Psalm 40:1–8 encouraged me then, and it continues to help me overcome the resentment that still arises from time to time. *Cry out;*

wait; receive deliverance; praise the Lord; and be greatly blessed! What great promises from the Lord in a time of need!

In addition to my severance package, Tracy and I were allowed to *cash out* of a profit-sharing plan, which provided enough money to pay off all of our debt except our mortgage and home equity loan. We are praying and believing to become debt free. I am confident that our second lien on our home will be the next debt to fall away from our lives!

The provision continues! The day after I was fired, I received a phone call from a builder who contacted me as soon as he learned that I was available and offered me a job. My salary increased by 9.2 percent, and my workload decreased by 67 percent. Praise the Lord!

Thank you, Pastor, for your teaching on "Promise, Problem, and Provision."

Tracy and Bryan chose not to get trapped in their problem. They chose to sing while in the fire. They chose to follow the signposts out of their wilderness, praise God for His bountiful blessings, and have faith in our God who never fails.

YOUR ATTITUDE DETERMINES YOUR OUTCOME

Have you chosen a negative attitude to your circumstances? Has it accomplished anything other than bringing you discouragement? What good did it do to be bad tempered today? Did your complaining drive your problem away? Did you achieve more than you normally do because of your pessimistic attitude? If your bad approach toward your problem did not smooth the path to your divine destiny, then why adopt it? Your attitude determines the outcome of most everything in your life.

Harvard psychologist William James said, "The greatest discovery of my generation is that a human being can alter his life by altering his attitudes of mind."[3]

For as he thinks in his heart, so is he.

—PROVERBS 23:7

Attitude affects quality of life. A positive attitude won't make you do anything, but it will help you do everything better than a negative attitude will. I've worked with winners and encountered losers. I've experienced the epitome of optimism as well as negativism. There have been people who lived life to the fullest and people who just existed. My conclusion is that what people possess inside will affect what is happening outside.

Author James Allen put it this way: "[A person] cannot travel *within* and stand still *without*."[4] Like it or not, we become on the outside what we are inside. "Attitude is the reflection of a person," commented Earl Nightingale, "and our world mirrors our attitude."[5]

Attitude is a choice. Much of his life, Robert Louis Stevenson laid in bed with tuberculosis. After hearing him hacking loudly one day, his wife said to him: "I suppose you still believe it is a wonderful day." Stevenson looked at a window filled with sunlight and responded, "I do! I will never let a row of medicine bottles block my horizon."[6]

We cannot control circumstances. Life's events happen. It is our responsibility to choose our responses and our attitude. "Situations may color your view of life, but you have been given the power to choose what the color will be."[7]

We must learn to choose carefully because we are free up to the point of choice; then the choice controls the chooser.

ATTITUDES ALTER ABILITIES

Professor Erwin H. Schell, one of America's most respected authorities on leadership, says, "Obviously, there is something more than facilities and competence that makes for accomplishment. I have come to believe that this linkage factor, this catalyst, if you will, can be defined in a single word—*attitude*. When our attitude is right, our abilities reach a maximum effectiveness and good results inevitably follow."[8]

> A little boy was overheard talking to himself as he strutted through the backyard, baseball cap in place, toting ball and bat. He was heard to say, "I'm the greatest hitter in the world!" Then he tossed his ball into the air, swung at it and missed. "Strike one!" Undaunted he picked up the ball threw it into the air and said to himself, "I'm the greatest baseball hitter ever," and he swung at the ball

again. And again he missed. "Strike two!" He paused a moment to examine his bat and ball carefully. Then a third time he threw the ball into the air. "I'm the greatest hitter who ever lived," he said. He swung the bat hard again, missed a third time. He cried out, "Wow! Strike three! I'm the greatest PITCHER in the world!"[9]

A POSITIVE ATTITUDE ANTICIPATES ADVERSITY

Optimistic people do not have their heads in the clouds believing nothing will go wrong because they have a positive attitude. Actually, the opposite is true.

Positive people know challenging events, adversity, and tough situations are inevitable. J. Sidlow Baxter, in his book *Awake, My Heart*, beautifully addresses this concept. "What is the difference between an obstacle and adversity? Our attitude toward it. Every opportunity has a difficulty and every difficulty has an opportunity. If the best things are not immediately possible, then immediately make the best of the things that are possible."[10]

POSITIVE PEOPLE KEEP SUCCESS AND FAILURE IN PERSPECTIVE

Positive people tend to remove the word *failure* from their vocabulary. Words such as *experience, results, challenge, temporary setback,* and *unsuccessful attempt* are preferred.

But you say this is just a matter of semantics. No, it is a process of conditioning our minds to use failure as a stepping-stone to success.

I am convinced that with the right attitude, all the setbacks in the world will not make you a failure. On the flip side, with the wrong mental attitude, all the help in the world will not make you a success.[11]

You are who and what you are today because of the attitude you choose. Will the future be a repeat of the past? The choice is yours.

What did David sing to the Lord while in one of his many problems? "For in the time of trouble He shall hide me in His pavilion; in the secret place of His tabernacle He shall hide me; He shall set me high upon a rock" (Ps. 27:5).

What did David sing to the Lord while in the wilderness? "You are my hiding place; You shall preserve me from trouble; You shall surround me with songs of deliverance" (Ps. 32:7).

And what did the Lord God of Israel promise David? "I will instruct and teach you in the way you should go; I will guide you with My eye" (v. 8).

Saints of the Most High God, are you going through a fiery trial right now? Listen to the comforting words of 1 Peter 4:12–13:

> Beloved, do not think it strange concerning the fiery trial which is
> to try you, as though some strange thing happened to you; but re-
> joice to the extent that you partake of Christ's sufferings, that when
> His glory is revealed, you may also be glad with exceeding joy.

PRESS ON! The darkest hour is just before the dawn. Weeping may endure for the night, but joy cometh in the morning. Hang on to those promises; we are approaching the glorious provision of God the Father.

REMEMBER THIS TRUTH...

The daily application of God's Word through praise, proclamation, and prayer is the direct pathway to success and prosperity.

Chapter 9

BECOMING THE YOU GOD SEES

WHO ARE YOU? WHO DO YOU WISH TO BECOME? WOULD YOU PREFER to be someone else? Do you like your job? Do you like your spouse? Do you like your relatives? Do you like anyone? Most importantly, do you like yourself?

After fifty years of counseling, I have concluded that many people would prefer to be someone else or at least to lead very different lives than what they live. So I ask you: Who do you wish to become?

Evidence that we have difficulty being ourselves comes from several sources. Consider the medical magic of plastic surgery. Plastic surgeons are expected to repair self-esteem by correcting physical features with which people are unhappy.

Plastic surgery is essential sometimes to correct severe burns or critical health conditions, but the majority of elective plastic surgery is performed because we dislike what we see in the mirror. Mirrors don't lie—thank God, they don't laugh!

The fact that we don't like ourselves is evidenced in the millions of self-help books sold every year in America's bookstores. In addition to the tsunami of self-help books, there are the self-help seminars where disillusioned attendees who are deeply unhappy with their lives and unhappy with their future expect to find a miracle. The sad conclusion is that their deep-rooted, lifelong emotional and spiritual problems are not going to be resolved in a "Hip-Hip-Hooray" weekend seminar.

God is your Creator!

He made you an original masterpiece; stop trying to become a cheap copy of someone you were never intended to be. If you masterfully copy someone else with the help of the finest plastic surgeons on Earth, after

187

spending a fortune you will still be a second-rate substitute for the original masterpiece God intended.

A Greek poet who lived about four hundred years before Christ scripted this thought-provoking concept: "As within—so without."[1] No matter what physical changes you make on the outside, there will be no positive change on the inside without a change in your attitude.

Saint Paul puts his pen to parchment and writes a concept in Romans 5:2 (TLB) that every person on earth should commit to memory: "For because of our faith, he has brought us into this place of highest privilege where we now stand, and we confidently and joyfully look forward to actually becoming all that God has had in mind for us to be."

Read that verse again! God has something specific in mind for you. He has a divine design for your life—something unique, something super special, something above and beyond your ability to think or imagine. Paul is saying that we have *an assignment*—we are to "joyfully and confidently" look forward to "becoming all that God has in *mind*"!

BEING YOU IS NOT ...

Being you does not mean surrendering to self-indulgence.

Self-indulgence through gambling, excessive spending, lust, drugs, and alcohol has drained more blood, foreclosed more homes, plunged more people into bankruptcy, crushed the dreams of more children, cut off more wedding rings, filled more divorce courts and mental hospitals, defiled more innocence, blinded more eyes, twisted more limbs, dishonored more women, broken more hearts, and dug more graves through suicide than the winds of war have ever wounded or killed.

> Woe to you, scribes and Pharisees, hypocrites! For you cleanse the outside of the cup and dish, but inside they are full of extortion and self-indulgence.
>
> —MATTHEW 23:25

Knowing who you are in Christ conquers all forms of self-indulgence.

Being you is not a license to retreat apathetically from life. Apathy is a manifestation of moral and spiritual cowardice that can utterly destroy your life. The more technology dependent we become as a people, the more we attempt to escape life and refuse to acknowledge the problem. The more we withdraw from God's people, the more we move away from God Himself. "For the turning away of the simple will slay them, and the complacency of fools will destroy them" (Prov. 1:32).

A Call to Action

If Christianity is anything, it's a call to action! A Christian never falls asleep in the fire or in the fight, but he can grow lethargic in the sunshine.

REMEMBER THIS TRUTH...

In the moment of decision, the best thing you can do is the right thing, the next thing you can do is the wrong thing, and the worst thing you can do is nothing!

Christianity teaches us to put our hand to the plow and not look back. It talks about climbing mountains of impossibility and conquering the giants that seize your possessions. It talks about being salt and light, and it warns that if the salt has lost its saltiness, it is worthless and good for nothing but to be trodden underfoot.

Through the centuries, some English words have lost their meaning; *virtue* is one of them. To the Romans of the first century, the word *virtus* meant a great deal more than morality or chastity. It characterized the very finest of Roman manhood: strength, valor, courage, and excellence.[2]

Courage means you are willing to stand and confront the culture in which you live. Courage means you are willing to be what Christ called you to be—salt and light to your generation.

Salt was valuable in biblical times. It was often used as currency. Men worked in a *salarium*, from which we get the word *salary*. When someone failed to do his fair share of the work, it was said of him, "He's not worth his salt." Salt was also used as a preservative and used to prevent decomposition.

Jesus said concerning salt: "Salt is good, but if it loses its saltiness, how can it be made salty again? It is fit neither for the soil nor for the manure pile; it is thrown out" (Luke 14:34–35, NIV).

The message? The pastor, evangelist, or Christian who will not fight the moral corruption of his culture, in God's opinion, is worthless. The Christian who professes devotion to Christ and claims redemption through His blood but will not speak out against abortion, same-sex marriage, and the assault on the American family is worthless. Have you lost your saltiness?

REMEMBER THIS TRUTH...

A person who sleeps in the lap of apathy becomes a contributor to evil when they should have been a disturber of its conscience.

Some are calling for Christians to stop speaking out concerning the current culture war. Their answer to the conflict is appeasement, not being salt and light. Appeasement is surrender on the installment plan—we are surrendering to the gods of this world one appeasement at a time. This is exactly the opposite of what Jesus taught. He confronted His culture. He looked at His audience one day and said, "You are of your father the devil" (John 8:44).

Saint Paul was beaten, falsely accused, slandered, stoned, and left for dead. He spent years in prisons. Why? He confronted his culture. He was salt and light. He didn't become a religious lapdog for Caesar and his politically correct prophets.

Being salt and light requires action, and action may bring trouble, but God promises to deliver us from *all* our troubles.

We are always in the fire or on the anvil. Through fiery trials, God is shaping us for high flight and greater victory as we struggle through the problem toward the provision.

The work of God is held back, not by the evil and the wicked, but by those who think of themselves as being good but yet refuse to get involved. Moses had a comfortable, quiet, and peaceful life on the backside of the wilderness, but God told him of the oppression of the Jewish people in Egypt, and Moses got involved.

David heard the bellowing challenge of Goliath every morning just like the other forty thousand cautious cowards in the army of Israel. David grabbed his slingshot, selected five smooth stones, and got involved.

Jesus Christ looked from the balconies of heaven and saw humanity bound by the chains of slavery to sin and Satan; He got involved and gave His life as a ransom for our redemption.

REMEMBER THIS TRUTH...

You can be so heavenly minded that you become no earthly good!

Too many people who think of themselves as *good people* are on the sidelines a safe distance from the battle. They are content to watch others run the risk, take the losses, and sustain the injuries. Your faith is an action faith, it is an exciting faith; don't waste it by not participating in it! So many Christians are thinking about the next world that they have ceased to be effective in this world.

OVERCOME NEGATIVE THINKING

Viktor Frankl's book, *Man's Search for Meaning*, records the account of Dr. Frankl's experience as a courageous Jew who became a prisoner during the Holocaust.[3]

He describes this horrible time in his life in vivid detail. His family was taken away. He was stripped of all his belongings. His home, possessions, watch, and even his wedding ring were confiscated from him. His head was shaven, and all of his clothes were torn from his body. He was left with nothing.

Frankl was marched into a Gestapo courtroom falsely accused and interrogated and found guilty by the German high command. Years of indignity and humiliation followed in the concentration camp. No hope. No anticipation of a future, only certain death. Most of us would have given up, but Dr. Frankl chose not to.

Even though he experienced devastating brutality, he realized he had the power to choose one thing—his mind-set. No matter what the future had in store for him, he could choose his state of mind. He asked himself these questions: "Do I give up or persevere? Do I hate the Gestapo or forgive them? Do I exist in a world of deprivation and self-pity or endure the hardships?"

Dr. Frankl had justifiable reasons to give up, to hate, and to feel sorry for himself, but he chose otherwise. He chose to exist in a world he created in his mind, a mind where hope thrived and expectation flourished. He survived and was finally liberated. However, his spirit was liberated from captivity long before his physical body, because his beliefs in those painful years sustained him. Dr. Frankl believed that what happens to us makes up 10 percent of our life, and how we respond determines the other 90 percent![4]

Viktor Frankl overcame negative thinking, and so must you. Negative thinking has no redeeming purpose. Negative thinking overpowers the believer before he can take hold of his promise. If you expect nothing, you will obtain nothing. Don't give in to thoughts that conquer your hope in what God has planned for you.

Paul teaches the believer to avoid negative thinking:

> Finally, brethren, whatever things are true, whatever things are noble, whatever things are just, whatever things are pure, whatever things are lovely, whatever things are of good report, if there is any virtue and if there is anything praiseworthy—meditate on these things.
>
> —PHILIPPIANS 4:8

Character, conduct, and success are molded within our thoughts and attitudes. We will act on the things we think about. It is imperative to approach your problem with a positive outlook. Dwight D. Eisenhower said, "No one can defeat us unless we first defeat ourselves."[5]

Don't be afraid of failure when confronted with a problem. Set your mind on the fact that you will do the best you can to overcome the challenge you are faced with, and leave the rest to God. The great inventor Charles F. Kettering said, "Once you have failed, analyze the problem and find out why, because each failure is one more step leading up to the cathedral of success. The only time you don't want to fail is the last time you try."[6]

Automobile tires, in the early years, were hard and inflexible. An American inventor searched for a way to make rubber soft and flexible. It was a problem everyone recognized, yet only one man solved—Charles Goodyear.

He had no formal education, and in 1821 he went into partnership with his father in a hardware business that later failed. Goodyear experimented for many years, with no success, to find some means of improving the quality of natural rubber so that it would not become brittle when cold or soft and sticky when hot.

He purchased from a rival inventor the patent rights to a process for impregnating rubber with sulfur, although this treatment had not been particularly successful.

But in 1839, after years of failing to find a solution to the problem, Goodyear discovered a process called *vulcanization*. Charles accidentally dropped a piece of rubber that had been treated with sulfur on a hot stove. The results? He discovered that when rubber and sulfur are heated together at a high temperature, the rubber adopts the desired properties he was looking for.[7] Vulcanization is still the basis of the rubber manufacturing industry.

The next time you drive down a bumpy highway, and your tires absorb the shock without cracking the enamel on your teeth, you can thank a problem solver named Charles Goodyear.

Don't be afraid of trouble. Train yourself to see a problem as an opportunity for triumph. Strive for success in spite of the problem. Have the courage to live your dream no matter what the obstacles! Booker T. Washington said, "Success is to be measured not so much by the position that one has reached in life as by the obstacles which he has overcome while trying to succeed."[8]

Overcome negative thinking, take hold of your promise, and learn to recognize the opportunity with the problem.

REMEMBER THIS TRUTH...

Trouble is not a sign that God doesn't love you. Trouble is a sign that you are a card-carrying member of the human race.

THE JOURNEY OF BECOMING

When I attended Trinity University, I took an educational psychology course using a text called, *Perceiving, Behaving, and Becoming*. I am going to focus on the last word—becoming.

You are forever in the process of becoming the person you will be. The word *becoming* implies the direction you are taking in your personal spiritual, physical, emotional, and intellectual growth and development. Life is a journey; it's not a destination. Every ending is a new beginning to your future, and every beginning is an ending to your past.

Let me illustrate this concept in the process of becoming a spouse. When you get married, it is the end of your single life. When you stand before your pastor, priest, or rabbi and exchange your marriage vows before God, it's a new beginning. Who you used to be is forever over, and who you are going to be is just beginning. Just how radically your life has changed you won't fully comprehend for at least six months. Marriage is not a picnic; it's a testing ground for your character, your courage, and your integrity.

Bill Cosby believes that for two people in a marriage to live together day after day is unquestionably the one miracle the Vatican has overlooked.[9]

Falling in love is easy; living together happily ever after requires a great deal of work and personal sacrifice. I have married hundreds of couples, and each of them stands before me beaming with hope and happiness. I speak the marriage vows that say, "I take you *for better or for worse, for richer or for poorer, in sickness and in health,*" and have them repeated after me, I know the two people before me are totally ignorant of the sacrifices it will take to make their marriage successful.

I'm sure they hear the words "…for better, for richer, and in health," but the words, "…for worse, for poorer, and in sickness," seem foreign to the new couple.

I repeat, in life and in marriage, you never arrive; you are always on the road toward your destiny. Let me say it in one simple sentence; a good marriage is hard work!

Happy marriages begin when we marry the ones we love, and they blossom when we love the ones we marry.[10]

Having a good marriage is harder today because the new morality of our society endorses cohabitation without the covenant of marriage. Living together without a covenant is no more like marriage than taking a warm shower is like standing under Niagara Falls!

Every Christian marriage is built on covenant. A marriage covenant is the death of two individual wills and the birth of a new, unified will. After you exchange your vows with one another, God sees both of you or He sees neither of you. The crisis exists when two self-centered people get married and neither is willing to crucify that self-absorbed self-will for the betterment of the marriage.

If wives and husbands would practice giving love instead of waiting to receive it, the divorce courts would be empty. I've heard angry wives shout in rage during a marriage counseling session, "He doesn't deserve my love."

My response? "Give it to him on credit; God knows you do everything else on credit."

I have heard husbands yell, "She wants me to tell her I love her. Why do I have to tell her that all the time? She knows I do!"

My response? "You should tell her you love her because she needs to hear it! Did you ever hear of the man who refused to kiss his wife and then killed the man who did?"

The process of "becoming" in the marriage relationship reaches the pinnacle of perfection when the wife makes the husband glad to come home and he makes her sorry to see him leave.

REMEMBER THIS TRUTH...

The process of becoming in marriage is more than finding the right person; it's being the right person.

When you get married, your union will, in the fullness of time, produce a beautiful baby. Again, this is the end of who you were and the beginning of who you will become. You are now parents.

Before the baby was born, you and your spouse could jump in the car and take a trip to anywhere with minimal planning. That's over forever! When you take a trip with your new baby, your sports car looks like a moving van loaded with *things for the baby*. You sell your sports coupe and buy a minivan even though you swore you would never own one. You sell your love-nest bungalow and buy a bigger house, and realize that who you used to be is gone with the wind. You are in the process of becoming.

The day will come when your last baby will grow up and leave the house for college, the military, or perhaps marriage. It's a sad day as you see your pride and joy wave good-bye with that heart-gripping smile and know that they will never come home again just like they left.

You are living a day of change and transition; it's called *becoming*. In a short time your baby girl will come home for a visit with some hairy-chested, hormone hurricane who says, "I love her," and you will resist the violent urge to vomit on the floor. The words, "Touch her and you'll die," get strangled in your throat as your wife stares holes in your head, and you hear yourself saying something mechanical like, "Come in, we're glad to have you!"

In spite of all you do or say, they get married, and you realize you are becoming something you have never been—an in-law. As time passes, you begin receiving mail from AARP, Social Security, and coupons from Luby's Cafeteria advertising discount meals for seniors. Your back goes out more often than you do. All the names in your little black book now belong to doctors. In the evening, you sit on the back porch and watch the sunset—if you can stay awake that long. At night you turn the lights off for economic reasons, not romance. You are *becoming* a senior citizen.

Then it happens; your journey of *becoming* presents you with one of the absolute joys of life—you're a grandparent. In the process of *becoming*, I am now a senior citizen with eight beautiful grandchildren who are the joy of my life. I am the founder and senior pastor of Cornerstone Church, which, thankfully, is packed to the walls for multiple services every Sunday morning with nineteen thousand plus active members. God has blessed me with a loving and beautiful wife, Diana, who makes every day an adventure and a joy.

Life could not be better!

But I want you to know it is the end result of hard work, many trials and tribulations, and, of course, triumph and victories. Wherever you are in the journey of *becoming*, enjoy every day as a gift from God. You will never live this day again. When the sun sets, it is gone forever. You are in the process of *becoming* every day of your life. Look forward with confidence and joy for this priceless gift; you only have but one life to live.

> To everything there is a season, a time for every purpose under heaven: A time to be born, and a time to die; a time to plant, and a time to pluck what is planted; a time to kill, and a time to heal; a time to break down, and a time to build up; a time to weep, and a time to laugh; a time to mourn, and a time to dance; a time to cast

away stones, and a time to gather stones; a time to embrace, and a time to refrain from embracing; a time to gain, and a time to lose; a time to keep, and a time to throw away; a time to tear, and a time to sew; a time to keep silence, and a time to speak; a time to love, and a time to hate; a time of war, and a time of peace.

—Ecclesiastes 3:1–8

And this, my friend, is the journey of *becoming*…

Expect a Miracle

The next step toward your provision is to expect a miracle! As a pastor I have the honor of witnessing many miracles. Most of them are preceded by what seems to be an insurmountable problem. Allow me to share Robby McGee's inspirational testimony.

In August of 1988, it seemed as if everything I had worked for and dreamed of was coming true. I was newly married and traveling throughout the United States singing and playing in a Christian band. I was also beginning to have some success as a songwriter, and our band had just been offered our first major recording contract with Word Records.

I had been on the road traveling for three straight weeks and decided to take a small vacation between road dates. We were scheduled to sing in Panama City, Florida, on Labor Day weekend, so I thought it would be great to spend a few days relaxing on the beach. I had grown up in Texas enjoying the sport of scuba diving and was excited about trying out some of my new diving equipment. As the dive boat pulled away from the dock, I had no idea that this would be the day that my life would change forever.

Aside from the strong current and rough seas, the dive that day was fairly normal until I tried to get back in the boat and began having trouble trying to get my fins off my feet. The crew noticed I was having trouble and helped pull me into the boat.

Upon entering the boat, my body became completely paralyzed and I collapsed on the deck. I was in and out of consciousness on the hour-long trip back to the dock where I was met by an ambulance and rushed to Bay Medical. At first, they thought that I was suffering from a mild case of the bends and would be fine in a few days. However, as they further examined me in the emergency room, I was diagnosed with an air embolism that had caused swelling in my spinal cord and brain.

They immediately decided to begin treatment in their hyperbaric chamber, which resembled a small submarine about five feet in diameter and approximately ten feet long. I remained in the chamber for seventy-two hours, with a respiratory therapist who would constantly administer oxygen to me in an attempt to heal the nerve damage that had been caused by the swelling.

Over the next few weeks, they continued daily treatment in the chamber with little or no results. During that time, the doctors determined I had a C7 spinal cord injury and decided to have me flown back home and admitted into the Little Rock Rehab Institute.

My pastor and his family welcomed my wife, Vanessa, and me at the airport and took us to their home to stay for the weekend before checking into the rehab center. I remember how helpless it felt not being able to sit up on my own or bathe or feed myself. I literally had to be picked up and carried everywhere I needed to go.

The following Monday, after checking into the facility, as the pastor was helping transfer me from the wheelchair to the bed, the nurse stopped him and told him that I was going to have to learn to do it for myself. My pastor insisted that I couldn't do it, and her reply was, "He will either learn to do it, or it won't get done."

As I began the therapy process, I realized their goal was to teach me how to get around and function in a wheelchair. However, my desire was to walk again. Even though I could not sit up or do anything other than wiggle one big toe, I wanted to walk.

What followed was months of learning and relearning how to do the simple things. The first few days and weeks I remember being full of faith and believing God that everything was going to be all right. However, as more and more time passed by with little progress, I got to the point where I wanted to quit. I felt like everything I had worked for up to that point in my life had been taken away.

I began to struggle with feeling like less of a man and started to pull away from my wife, my friends, and anyone who knew me before my accident. I remember thinking that everyone would be better off without me and that it would be best if I started a new life with people who did not know the "Robby" before the accident.

I began to lie in the hospital bed late at night questioning God, questioning my faith, and struggling with the thoughts of not being able to walk again or sing again or play piano again or for my wife and me to be able to have children. The irony was I had traveled all over the country and prayed and seen God do incredible miracles in other people's lives. However, I found out that it's different when you're the one who is lying in the hospital bed. Not different to God, just different to you.

One night after having been in the hospital about four months, I remember coming to a point of hopelessness. I didn't want another hospital visit, I didn't want to hear another scripture, I didn't want another encouraging word—I wanted and needed God to make Himself real.

I remember crying out to God in prayer, and as I began to pray, God began to speak peace to my heart. He let me know that regardless of whether or not I ever walked again, sang again, played the piano again, or was able to have children, He loved me, and He had a purpose and a plan for my life.

Although nothing physically changed, I felt my mind and spirit totally transformed through the power and comfort of the Holy Spirit. I didn't get up and start running, singing, or playing, but I knew at that moment that everything was going to be all right.

Over the next few months I began the gradual process of walking. I started with a walker, graduated to forearm crutches, then to two canes, then one. I also went back on the road with my band, began to sing and play, and Vanessa and I had our first child, a little boy named Tyler. All the impossibilities became possible with God.

It has been twenty years since my accident, and I am in awe of the purpose and plan that has unfolded since that night God spoke to me in the hospital. I currently serve as president of an international ministry whose goal is to win two million people to Christ every year for twenty years!

Robby expected a miracle and received one! He became the person God destined him to be. What about you? Do you need to adjust your vision to the promises that are available to you? If you don't make this crucial adjustment to the way you look at the challenges you face, recognizing them as opportunities to receive God's provision, you won't be prepared to receive your miracle. In the next chapter you will hear more about God's miraculous provisions. Are you ready to receive your miracle?

Chapter 10

THE MIRACLE PROVISION

MARCHING FROM THE SLAVERY OF EGYPT THROUGH THE BLAZING inferno of the wilderness for forty years, without one person becoming sick or feeble, into a land flowing with milk and honey was a major-league miracle.

Do you need a miracle?

Sooner or later, it will happen to you. The phone will ring, and your calm, tranquil, and well-ordered life will enter into a raging storm. Sooner or later, you will face a crisis that you cannot manage with your resources alone, and you will need a miracle from God to survive.

Your crisis may come when you hear the voice of your doctor robotically report, "You have cancer!" The doctor declares your death sentence, saying, "It's incurable, it's untreatable, and it's inoperable." Fear will seize you by the throat with an iron grip. You must have a miracle from God, or you will die.

Your crisis hour may come when the policeman calls and the voice on the other end of the phone says, "Your child has been seriously injured in a major car accident. Please hurry to the hospital emergency room." When you arrive at the emergency room, you see the blood-spattered gurneys lining the hall echoing the deep-throated moans coming from those whose agony is beyond the expression of words.

Then you see your child's bleeding and broken body. Your child left your home less than an hour ago, a beautiful and healthy teenager without a care in the world. You examine the twisted body and instantly realize that you need a miracle from God to save your child's life.

Your crisis may come when your husband or wife walks into the den and makes a declaration that sucks the oxygen out of the room: "I want a divorce. I never loved you. Our marriage is over."

You didn't even know you had a marriage problem! You thought you were living in Shangri La. Shangri La just became Dante's *Inferno*! You need a miracle from God to bring healing to a wounded marriage that appears to be in its death throes.

I have Good News that can transform your life, your health, your marriage, your failing business career, or any health crisis you may be facing. My life-changing declaration is that our God is a miracle-working God! He is an awesome God, and absolutely nothing is impossible with Him.

In the genesis of time, He breathed into a handful of dirt, and man became a living soul. That's a mighty miracle scientific minds can't grasp or explain thousands of years after the fact. He separated the day from the night and flung the glittering stars against the blue velvet of the night. He set the sun ablaze, His version of the eternal flame.

He holds the seven seas in the palm of His hand. He is the shepherd of the stars, for He calls them by name. He measures space with the span of His hands, and the blast of His nostrils can split the cedars of Lebanon.

He is the God of might and miracles. He is the God of grace and glory. He is the God of power and patience, and He is waiting to help you.

He breathed life into the ninety-year-old dead womb of Sarah and gave her reproductive power so that she could produce Isaac. Her husband, Abraham, was one hundred years of age. Abraham went home and told Sarah, "I've had a visit with the Lord, and we're going to have a son this time next year."

Sarah laughed! I think she laughed to keep from crying.

When you're ninety years of age, having a bald-headed baby with a megaphone mouth and bionic lungs is not number one on your "to do" list! When you spell "diaper" backward, you spell "repaid." Think about it!

Nevertheless, when God says it's going to happen—get ready! It may not be in your timetable, but it will be in God's perfect moment.

That night in Abraham's tent, passion and vitality exploded in two sterile bodies, and nine months later, Isaac, the son of laughter was born. That's a miracle!

The God we serve parted the Red Sea for Moses and the children of Israel, and they walked across the seabed on dry ground. He rained manna from the heavens for forty years for their provision.

He caused sufficient water to gush from a rock in the barren wilderness to refresh the children of Israel and all of their livestock. He held the sun still for Joshua as Israel fought to achieve a military victory in the valley.

He muzzled the mouths of lions for Daniel. He walked in the fiery furnace with the three Hebrew children who would not bend, bow, or burn to the idols of their world. His son, Jesus Christ of Nazareth, was born in the womb of a virgin, defying medical science and agnostics. It was a miracle for the ages.

That Son became the healing Jesus, the miracle-working Son of the living God. He healed the lame, the deaf, and the blind. He healed blood diseases and leprosy. He healed paralytics with nerve disorders. He healed one on one, and He healed the masses.

He healed long distance when He healed the Centurion's son, because there is no distance in prayer. The Bible says, "Jesus is the same yesterday, today, and forever." What He did on the shores of the Sea of Galilee in Israel, He can do for YOU today at this very moment. He CAN do it; He WANTS to do it for YOU right NOW!

Jesus Christ said to His church, "Greater works than these he [believers] will do!" The era of miracles is not over. Peter walked down the street, and the sick were instantly healed by the supernatural power of God Almighty in his shadow. That's miracle-working power.

The Bible says, "And these signs will follow those who believe: In My name they will...lay hands on the sick, and they will recover" (Mark 16:17–18).

Our Father, which art in heaven, is still *Jehovah Rophe*. That means He is the God who heals all of our diseases. His Son Jesus is still the Great Physician. He is still the balm of Gilead that takes the pain and suffering from every disease. He is still the conqueror of death, hell, and the grave.

You don't have to understand miracles to have one.

I don't understand how a black cow eats green grass and gives white milk and produces yellow butter...but it happens every day.

Can you explain electricity? Few know exactly what makes electricity work, yet we do not hesitate to use it even though we cannot explain it.

Would you rather sit in darkness until you can understand the mystery of electricity?

Do you understand how food is converted to energy when you eat it? Do you understand how that greasy cheeseburger you just ate, chased down with a chocolate shake and two portions of french fries, is converted into fuel to drive your body? No one understands it, but you don't stop eating cheeseburgers until you do understand it.

Look at the miracle of a newborn baby. Nine months earlier, that baby didn't exist. Now the baby has perfectly shaped ears, nose, mouth, hands, feet, and knows exactly how and when to cry to get your attention.

Minutes after the baby's birth, the baby is feeding at his mother's breast. Science did not give babies a learning manual giving them instructions on *where* and *how* to find lunch. The baby understands nothing, but masterfully obtains nourishment for months.

The point is this: if we are willing to experience only what our minds can understand, we will in turn live very shallow and empty lives. We will never experience the supernatural, because the supernatural will never be received logically.

Do you need a miracle?

When you want what you've never had, you need to do what you've never done.

You need to have faith in God, because nothing is impossible to those who believe in a God who never fails.

REMEMBER THIS TRUTH...

Faith starts out before you know how it's going to turn out.

Faith is the victory that overcomes the world. By faith, Noah built an ark that saved his household. By faith, Abraham looked for a city whose builder and maker was God. By faith, Sarah conceived at the age of ninety to produce Isaac, the son of laughter. Have faith in God because God never fails. But above all else, remember that without faith it is impossible to please God.

Allow me to give you the scriptural foundation for miracles.

Man has a twofold nature. He is both physical and spiritual. Both natures have been equally addressed in Scripture. The God of the natural is the God of the supernatural. The God who enforces the laws of gravity and physics enforces the laws of the supernatural.

Your physical body is exposed to disease, and your soul is corrupted by sin. The plan of redemption has made it possible for your sins to be forgiven and for your body to be healed.

Psalm 103:2–3 states, "Bless the LORD, O my soul, and forget not all His benefits: who forgives all your iniquities, who heals all your diseases." Notice the connection made between the spiritual and the physical. Note that all sin is forgiven first, and *then* all diseases are healed. Not some, but *all* are healed.

I have established that the first promise of healing found in the Bible is in Exodus 15:26, where God made a promise to the children of Israel after they came through the Red Sea:

> If you diligently heed the voice of the LORD your God and do what is right in His sight, give ear to His commandments and keep all His statutes, I will put none of the diseases on you which I have brought on the Egyptians. For I am the LORD who heals you.

Just how successful was God's Medicare program for the children of Israel for the forty years they wandered in the wilderness? King David answers that question in Psalm 105:37, saying, "He also brought them out with silver and gold, and there was none feeble among His tribes." Think of that. The children of Israel were two million strong as they left Egypt, and God kept every one of them in perfect health throughout their wilderness walk.

Isaiah 53:4–5 says, "Surely He has borne our griefs and carried our sorrows…and by His stripes we are healed." The words *borne* and *carried* denote more than sympathy. They represent actual substitution. They represent the absolute removal of our travails.

The point is this: Jesus Christ has carried our sins and our sicknesses away. He is our burden bearer, and He was God's scapegoat at Calvary. When Jesus screamed in agony as He hung on the blood-soaked Roman cross, "It is finished," it was in that moment death died, diseases were conquered, and our sicknesses were forever destroyed.

Matthew 8:16–17 states:

> He...healed all who were sick, that it might be fulfilled which was
> spoken by Isaiah the prophet, saying: "He Himself took our infir-
> mities and bore our sicknesses."

Ancient Israel celebrated five biblical holidays or festivals, which include
Passover, Pentecost, Tabernacles, Rosh Hashanah, and Yom Kippur. Yom
Kippur was a time of fasting and atonement.

During this feast, two goats were brought into the temple by the high
priest.

The priest placed his forefinger and thumb in the blood of the first goat
and placed it on the second goat, casting the sins and sicknesses of Israel
upon it. The second goat was called the scapegoat. After this substitution,
the scapegoat would be released into the wilderness as a symbol that the
sins of the people had been carried away.

Jesus Christ is the portrait of both goats. First, He was slaughtered
straightaway when He went to the cross. Second, God the Father, our
High Priest, dipped His thumb and forefinger in the blood of Jesus Christ
and cast them upon Him, for He bore our griefs and carried our sorrows,
and with His stripes we are healed.

Those two words, *borne* and *carried*, denote more than sympathy. They
denote the fact that God has taken care of the problem so that we don't
have to carry it anymore. What a miracle! We should rejoice in the victory
daily for that provision.

The healings by Jesus were not occasional; they were continuous. They
were not exceptional; they were universal. Jesus never turned the sick away.
The Bible says, "He...healed all who were sick," and "As many as touched
him were made well" (Matt. 8:16; Mark 6:56).

John 14:12 (KJV) says:

> Verily, verily, I say unto you, He that believeth on me, the works
> that I do shall he do also; and greater works than these shall he do;
> because I go unto my Father.

Note the phrase, "the works that I do shall he do also..." It is God's intention for you to expect healing as a part of the New Testament church.

The Bible says in Mark 16:17–18, "And these signs shall follow them that believe; in my name shall they cast out devils; they shall speak with new tongues...they shall lay hands on the sick, and they shall recover" (KJV).

James 5:14–15 says, "Is anyone among you sick? Let him call for the elders of the church, and let them pray over him, anointing him with oil in the name of the Lord. And the prayer of faith will save the sick, and the Lord will raise him up. And if he has committed sins, he will be forgiven."

There is a distinct relationship between sin being confessed and forgiven and bodies being healed.

Ask the question, "To whom is this power committed?" Not to the apostles who are passing away, but to the elders of the church, who are within easy reach of every suffering soul the length and breadth of the New Testament church.

Note the time in which this commission was given. Not at the beginning of the apostolic age, but at the end. The meaning was very clear. Miracles were not to cease with the death of the apostles. Miracles are to continue in every Bible-believing church where there are elders who pray the prayer of faith and anoint the sick with oil in the name of Jesus.

I want you to recognize that the prayer for the sick is a command. It is intentional and part of God's plan for us. The prayer of healing is God's perfect prescription for disease.

Romans 8:11 states, "But if the Spirit of him that raised Jesus from the dead dwell in you, he that raised up Christ from the dead shall also quicken your mortal bodies by his Spirit that dwelleth in you" (KJV). The phrase "quicken your mortal bodies" means that the power of the Holy Spirit will overcome the physical sickness in your body and heal you.

Finally, as a voice that was speaking for eighteen centuries, let us hear the sweet words of Hebrews 13:8: "Jesus Christ is the same yesterday, today, and forever." This is an echo of the voice of Jesus, which said, "Lo, I am with you always even to the ends of the earth."

His presence has never been withdrawn from the earth. God's love has never been removed. His power to set the captive free, to redeem, to deliver, and to heal has never been diminished. He is the same, the same, the same...yesterday, today, and forever.

The Word of God is the source of all miracles, which includes divine healing.

> My son, forget not my law [Word]...for length of days, and long life, and peace, shall they add to thee.... It shall be health to thy navel [source], and marrow [restoration] to thy bones.
> —PROVERBS 3:1–2, 8, KJV

> For they [the Word of God] are life unto those that find them, and health to all their flesh.
> —PROVERBS 4:22, KJV

> He sent his word, and healed them.
> —PSALM 107:20, KJV

The facts are in, and the evidence is very clear! Jesus Christ of Nazareth is still the Great Physician. There is no sickness, there is no disease, there is no affliction, and there is no problem that He cannot solve or heal.

REMEMBER THIS TRUTH...

As we search for miracles, we come back again to this word, obedience. Miracles are the only thing that can happen when you obey the Word of God and meet God's conditions.

Consider the simple illustration of the ice tray. When you take an ice tray, fill it with water, and place the tray in the freezer compartment of your refrigerator where the temperature is below 32 degrees, you don't close the door and start pleading for the water in the ice tray to become ice.

You don't stand in front of the refrigerator, wring your hands, and dance in a circle crying out, "Oh, please turn to ice." The fact is, you have followed the laws of science; the water can't do anything but turn to ice. When you obey the law of God, you don't have to stand and say, "I've tithed. I've gone to church on Sunday when I wanted to watch the Super Bowl, and, in fact, I've served You all the days of my life. I have obeyed Your voice. Please heal me!"

When you put you faith in our infallible God and obey His voice, then healing is the only thing that can happen. I repeat, when you meet God's conditions for miracles, miracles are the only thing that can happen.

Ask yourself this question: Am I meeting God's spiritual conditions for healing?

Seven Bible Conditions for Healing

1. Confession of known sin

The first condition for healing is the confession of all known sin. Sin can bring sickness. Please understand that *not* all sickness is the result of sin. (See John 9:1–3.) But according to the Word of God, some is.

In the New Testament, Saint Paul chastised those who were taking communion unworthily (in sin) within the Corinthian church, saying, "Many among you are weak and sick, and a number of you have fallen asleep [death]" (1 Cor. 11:30, niv). Some Paul admonished for taking communion in spite of the fact that they were engaging in sexual activity with their own family members (1 Cor. 5:1). Their sinful lifestyle made them unworthy.

Psalm 103:2–3 presents the sequence for receiving healing:

> Bless the Lord, O my soul, and forget not all His benefits: who forgives all your iniquities, who heals all your diseases.

The sequence indicates that *first* your sin is forgiven, and, *second*, then your body is healed.

The Bible indicates several ways sickness may enter into the body of believers:

- Resentment (Job 36:13)
- Bitterness (Lam. 3:5–6)
- The refusal to forgive others (Matt. 6:14–15)
- Rebellion against spiritual authority (Isa. 1:4–5)
- Lying (Ezek. 13:19)
- Tale bearing (Jer. 6:28)
- Accusing the brethren (Rev. 12:10)
- A critical spirit (Matt. 7:1)
- Murmuring (Num. 16:41)

When I ask a person to tell me what they are looking for in life, some will say they are searching for God as if He could get lost; when we lose God, it is not God who is lost. He will become real when we confess our sins, accept Christ as Savior, and release the bondage of the past.

Are any of these gateways to sickness present in your mind and spirit? If they are, you are literally inviting sickness into your body. God is able and ready to forgive you of all of your sin. Simply repent and ask God to forgive you, and you will begin your journey to your miracle provision.

2. Believe your healing is God's will.

You must believe that it's God's will to heal you. You must expect a miracle. The Bible says, "Beloved, I pray that in all respects you may prosper and be in good health, just as your soul prospers" (3 John 2, NAS).

In Exodus 15:26, God declares to His children, "For I, the LORD, am your healer" (NAS). When was this promise given? Right after the children of Israel crossed the Red Sea. There is important symbolism within the story of the children of Israel in Egypt. As slaves, the Jewish people were actually *owned* by Pharaoh, who is the type or foreshadow of Satan. Egypt is the type of bondage in sin, and the deliverance of the people from slavery in Egypt is the type of salvation. Moses is the type of the deliverer (Jesus Christ), and the Red Sea is the type of water baptism.

The first promise that God gave to the children of Israel after they passed through the Red Sea (water baptism) was that every person in Israel had the right to be healed. Therefore, *you* have the right to be healed.

We read in Mark 16:17: "And these signs will follow those who believe: In My name they will cast out demons; they will speak with new tongues; they will take up serpents; and if they drink anything deadly, it will by no means hurt them; they will lay hands on the sick, and they will recover."

Some Christians believe that the day of miracles is over. According to the Word of God, that's absolutely wrong. Jesus Christ has not changed— He "is the same yesterday, today, and forever."

To the historic church, Jesus is the great "I Was." To the futuristic church, Jesus is the great "I Will Be." To the Bible-believing church, He is the great "I Am." He is the God of the now. He is the bread of life now. He is living water now. He is the Lion of the tribe of Judah now. He is the Great Physician *right now*.

3. The Word of God

Healing is activated by the Word of God.

> My son, do not forget my law...For length of days and long life and peace they will add to you....It will be health to your flesh, and strength to your bones.
> —PROVERBS 3:1–2, 8

> He sent His word and healed them.
> —PSALM 107:20

> My son, give attention to my words...For they are life to those who find them, and health to all their flesh.
> —PROVERBS 4:20, 22

The Word promises never to return void. It is the source of our healing. We must proclaim it over our lives. If a physician instructs us to take a little blue pill every day without fail, promising it would heal our affliction, we would do it immediately and methodically. We would not ask questions, because we trust the knowledge of the physician. Jesus Christ is our Healer; His Word declares it! God our Father promises that His Word will bring healing to our bodies; therefore, we should *take it* faithfully, *ingest it*, and *proclaim it*, trusting that it will bring our healing.

THE PROCLAMATION OF HEALING

Lord Jesus Christ, You were wounded for my transgressions, bruised for my guilt, and by Your stripes I am healed and made whole. I have died to sin and live to righteousness because of the cross of Christ.

I confess my sins before You that they be forgiven, and I release the prayer of faith that will save me from my sickness. I have confidence that Your loving hand will restore me. I will obey Your command and ask the elders to anoint me with oil and have them pray with me for my healing.

Jesus, I know You have heard my prayer and forgiven all of my iniquities and healed me of all my diseases.

Father God, You sent Your Word to heal and rescue me from the grave. As I seek a right relationship with You, Your light breaks forth like the morning and brings forth in me restoration and the power of new life.

As I revere Your name, You will arise with healing in Your wings, and I will go forth and leap with joy.

As I walk in the good news of the gospel, I will be healed of every disease, weakness, and infirmity. I am made whole by the power of Your Word. I will arise and go forth.

I release the faith that I have in You to heal me of all my diseases, for Your Word is life to those who find it and health to all our flesh.

Your favor surrounds me as a shield, for I know that no weapon—or disease—formed against me will prevail, for this is my inheritance as Your child. Anything that has not been planted by You shall be torn up by the roots.

I thank You because what the enemy has hidden in darkness You have exposed and covered with Your precious blood. The blood of the spotless Lamb is on the doorpost of my soul, and the death angel cannot penetrate it.

You have come that I might have abundant life, and Your grace and mercy sustain, refresh, and strengthen me in my time of suffering. Jesus, You are the Lord of my life, and You have promised to bind my wounds and heal my afflictions. According to Your Word, You have taken my sin, disease, and afflictions to the cross; therefore, no disease has authority over my body.

Father God, You have set before me life and death. I choose life. You have set before me blessing and cursing. I choose the blessing. Any generational curses that have tormented my family will be destroyed by the power of Your Word.

I reject any infirmity and every form of witchcraft and every type of warfare that have come against my body.

Lord, I thank You that through the sacrifice of Jesus on the cross, I have passed out from under the curse and entered into the blessings of Abraham whom You blessed in all things—I am blessed with good health and favor.

I will not fear for You are with me—You are my God. You promised *to strengthen, help, and uphold me with Your righteous right hand. When I hear Your voice and obey Your commandments, none of the diseases of Egypt will come upon me, for You are the Lord who heals me. You laid Your hands on the sick, and they were healed.*

I was bought with a price, and I will glorify the Lord with my body, for my body is a temple of the Holy Spirit. I am not my own. I will talk of Your wondrous works. I will give You thanks for You are good. I will declare Your greatness and bless Your name forever and ever.

(For additional scriptures, see Psalm 105:2; 145:1; Isaiah 41:10; 53:5; 54:17; 58:8; Malachi 4:2; Matthew 4:23; 15:13; Acts 9:34; 14:9; James 6:15; Exodus 12:7; 13; 15:26; Galatians 3:13–14; 1 Corinthians 6:19; Luke 4:40.)[1]

4. Healing cannot be earned.

It is important to recognize that we cannot earn our healing. Jesus Christ purchased our healing at the cross. We can't do anything to earn our healing. There is no amount of money that will buy healing, and no form of legalism from any denomination will guarantee our healing.

Isaiah proclaimed, "By His stripes we are healed"—and that means right now (Isa. 53:5). Our sickness is gone! Our Savior took it from us and carried it away. One very dark day in Jerusalem, there was a supernatural exchange, and Calvary became the place of our miraculous provision.

All of God's promises took form at the cross with this Great Exchange:

- God took our poverty and gave us wealth.
- He took our sickness and gave us divine healing.
- He took our guilt and gave us forgiveness.
- He took our rejection and gave us acceptance.
- He took our death and gave us everlasting life.

I thank God for the Great Exchange!

5. Acting on faith

You must act upon your faith. Jesus said to the man by the pool of Bethesda, "Rise, take up your bed and walk" (John 5:8). The message? "I want you to act upon your faith." Jesus gave the man three action points in one short command: rise, take, and walk. He wanted him to act on his faith.

Jesus told the man with the withered hand, "Step forward.... Stretch out your hand" (Mark 3:3, 5). What happened? The man's "hand was restored as whole as the other"; he was healed! Message? "I want you to do something. I want you to exercise your faith by taking action." You must do your part first before God does His.

Moses put his foot in the Red Sea and started walking out into the water in faith *before* God parted the sea. Elijah poured twelve barrels of water on the sacrifice *before* God sent the fire. Elijah had faith that God would do His part, but he knew he must do his part *first*.

> LORD God of Abraham, Isaac, and Israel, let it be known this day that You are God in Israel and I am Your servant, and that I have done all these things at Your word.
>
> —1 KINGS 18:36

The disciples were told to, "Launch out into the deep and let down your nets for a catch" (Luke 5:4) *before* the Lord provided the catch of fish they had been toiling for.

When four men took their diseased friend to where Jesus was holding a healing service, they were turned away because the house was full. Those with little faith might have said, "This is not your day," or, "The door of opportunity is closed." But is that how these four friends responded? No. These were men of action...men of faith. They climbed up on the roof, tore into the ceiling, and lowered their friend into the place where healing triumphed. They took action on their faith!

The woman with the issue of blood woke up one morning and decided that she was sick and tired of being sick and tired. She heard there was a healer in town by the name of Jesus of Nazareth. Because of her condition, she was forbidden to interact with men, especially a rabbi. But today was her day—the day she would risk it all and act on her faith.

She traveled into town and pressed against the crowd until she touched the hem of Jesus's garment. Suddenly, after all those years of affliction, she felt the healing power of her Creator flow through her body. She was healed! Had she not acted on her faith, she would have stayed home alone without hope for tomorrow and died.

In all of these illustrations the Lord is demanding that we do something to act upon our faith.

The Bible says, "Faith without works is dead" (James 2:26). We must learn to act on our faith. Jesus asked the man at the pool of Bethesda, "Wilt thou be made whole?" (John 5:6, KJV). Why? Because some people don't want to be healed. They have learned to manipulate their friends and loved ones through their condition. Being able to command people to go there and come here to gain attention gives these poor souls a sense of power. These people need spiritual deliverance before they are able to take action for their healing.

Perhaps you've given up all hope that you can be healed.

REMEMBER THIS TRUTH...

When you want what you've never had, you
have to do what you've never done.

Think of Naaman, the valiant commander of Aram's army, who had leprosy. He was referred to the prophet Elisha for healing. Naaman believed that there would be some sort of *healing protocol*, but instead of meeting face-to-face, the prophet sent a messenger to him with strange instructions: "Go and wash in the Jordan seven times, and your flesh shall be restored to you, and you shall be clean" (2 Kings 5:10).

Naaman was upset, saying, "Indeed, I said to myself, 'He will surely come out to me, and stand and call on the name of the LORD his God, and wave his hand over the place, and heal the leprosy'" (v. 11). I fully understand Naaman's angry response to such bizarre demands. I can just hear Naaman's mind spinning in anger and doubt: "Dip in the dirty Jordan! Why not one of the cleaner rivers? What will my men think of me? This is ridiculous!"

However, after listening to the wise counsel of his servants, Naaman did as Elisha had instructed, and, as promised, healing came to him.

Sometimes God will ask you to do something you have never done to attain something you have never had. Believe! All things are possible to those who believe.

6. Denounce the kingdom of darkness.

Matthew 8:16 reads: "When evening had come, they brought to Him many who were demon-possessed. And He cast out the spirits with a word, and healed all who were sick."

REMEMBER THIS TRUTH...

There is power in the name and the blood of Jesus.

Notice that Jesus cast evil spirits out "with a word." He did not interview demons; He cast them out. Deliverance from evil spirits and healing go hand in hand like spring and sunshine, but you must first denounce the kingdom of darkness.

Does this frighten you? Never fear what Jesus taught (Ps. 56:11). His teaching is the gateway to deliverance (v. 13), and it may be the answer to the problem in which you now find yourself.

There are ten steps toward deliverance.

1. Personally affirm your faith in Christ (Gal 2:16).
2. Humble yourself before the Lord (2 Chron. 34:27).
3. Confess any known sin (Ps. 32:5).
4. Repent of that sin (Acts 3:19).
5. Forgive all (Mark 11:25).
6. Break your ties with the kingdom of darkness (Isa. 55:7).
7. Denounce generational curses (Exod. 20:5–6).
8. Cast demons from your life (Matt. 12:28).
9. Believe that God desires you to be free from bondage (2 Cor. 1:9–10).
10. Finally, take your stand with God through His Word (2 Thess. 2:15).

Derek Prince was a master teacher of God's Word, and he led several deliverance services in my church, much to the benefit of my congregation. He also firmly believed in using God's Word to proclaim our deliverance. The following proclamation is taken from his book *Prayers and Proclamation*:

PROCLAMATION OF DELIVERANCE

- *We overcome Satan when we testify personally to what the Word of God says the blood of Jesus does for us (Rev. 12:11).*
- *Through the blood of Jesus I am redeemed out of the hand of the devil (Eph 1:7).*
- *Through the blood of Jesus all my sins are forgiven (1 John 1:9).*
- *Through the blood of Jesus I am continually being cleansed of all sin (1 John 1:7).*
- *Through the blood of Jesus I am justified, made righteous, just as if I'd never sinned (Rom. 5:9).*
- *Through the blood of Jesus I am sanctified, made holy, set apart to God (Heb. 13:12).*
- *Through the blood of Jesus I have boldness to enter the presence of God (Heb. 10:19).*
- *The blood of Jesus Christ cries out continually to God in heaven on my behalf (Heb. 12:14).*[2]

7. *Healing comes from the Holy Spirit.*

Healing comes on the wings of the Holy Spirit.

The fact is that God the Father desires our healing. Jesus Christ, God's Son, paid for our healing at the cross. God the Holy Spirit brings the healing to us. Romans 8:11 states, "But if the Spirit of Him who raised Jesus from the dead dwells in you, He who raised Christ from the dead will also give life to your mortal bodies through His Spirit who dwells in you."

The Holy Spirit abides in an atmosphere of praise and worship. Once His power is released, supernatural miracles happen.

Believe that He, whose name is Love, will send the best. When God makes a promise, faith believes it, hope anticipates it, and patience quietly awaits it. And just like the children of Israel, we too are the heirs of the promise that God will heal all of our diseases.

In an earlier chapter, I told of the supernatural healing of my sixty-nine-year-old mother from *terminal cancer*. I shared the miracle of my uncle,

Rev. Joel Lavon Hagee, when the hand of God healed him from blood poisoning. Another healing miracle in the Hagee family is of our daughter Tish. Her testimony is intended to bring hope to those in need of a miracle. Remember, nothing is impossible to God!

Two years ago, a major health crisis in the person of my daughter walked through my front door. That particular Sunday seemed like all the rest. My office was filled with the sounds and laughter of my five children, their spouses, and a quiver full of grandchildren. As always, I asked my children how they are in the midst of my kissing and hugging the grandkids.

Tish, the oldest of my five children, showed me a pea-sized knot on her right ankle that had suddenly appeared the week before. She said it was painless and of no bother to her, but she had made a doctor's appointment for early the next week to have it examined. Earlier in the week, Tish had made an appointment with the doctor to treat her acute bronchitis. During this appointment, the doctor tried to drain what he thought was a ganglion cyst, but to no avail. He referred her to a local podiatrist for further observation.

Four days later, Tish was in the podiatrist's office where the doctor examined her ankle and agreed with the previous diagnosis. He also tried to drain the cyst, but the bruised mass was not moving or yielding any fluid.

X-rays and MRIs were taken, and even though they showed no ganglion characteristics, the podiatrist still believed it to be ganglion in nature. So he decided to remove the cyst and have it tested. The next day Tish went in for routine outpatient surgery, scheduled to last no more than one hour. It was to be a non-event.

The surgery lasted longer than anticipated. Over the next few days, her foot and ankle were swollen, numb, and packed with ice. As she later recollected, "Even though it was painful, it was a nice break from housework, laundry, running after kids, and life in general. My husband was waiting on me hand and foot, taking the kids back and forth to school, doing the dishes and laundry, and feeding the dogs. Church members and friends were bringing over an overabundance of food. Life was good."

Five days later, her cell phone rang. On the other end of the phone was the podiatrist. "I know you are coming in for a follow-up tomorrow," he said, "but I wanted to inform you now that the tests results came back from pathology, and you have leiomyosarcoma. You need an appointment with an oncologist immediately." That was the last thing Tish heard him say.

She said of this horrible moment:

"Did he just say I have a sarcoma? Sarcoma is cancer. And what was the first part he said? What kind of sarcoma? Did they mix up the test results? Surely this can't be right. I better write it down. Maybe the pathologist got it wrong. People that get cancer DIE! My dog just died of cancer. Was he really talking to ME? Did he read the wrong chart? Did he dial the wrong number? He's not an oncologist. I'm not a smoker. How could I have cancer? I might eat too many candy bars, but that wouldn't give me cancer. Would it? Maybe I should start jogging. Did he just tell ME I have cancer? There is no way I could have cancer. A month ago this bump wasn't even on my leg, and I'm not in any pain. Everyone said it was a ganglion cyst. It can't be cancer! He can't be talking about me. I'm only 37! Maybe he missed that day in cancer school. I'm healthy. I look great. I feel great. I'm really young and very active. I don't have time for this. I have a ganglion cyst. They are looking at the wrong medical chart. I can't possibly have cancer. I don't feel sick. I'm just too young to have cancer. This can't be happening to ME!"

The disjointed conversation inside my head was endless and chaotic. There was no point where it became logical or where any questions were answered. It was all very surreal as I tried to wrap my mind around the fact that I had just been diagnosed with cancer. I, Tish Hagee-Tucker, a 37-year-old woman with an unscathed health record and two young girls, had just been diagnosed with cancer, a terminal disease, over the phone. Thank God I wasn't driving!

The next thing I knew, the podiatrist was asking me, "Are you sure you're OK?" I said yes and hung up. I was in total shock. The doctor had informed me that the pathologist who diagnosed the growth was trained at M. D. Anderson in Houston, Texas, a hospital that is world renowned for its research and treatments of all types of cancers. There was no mistake in my diagnosis. They were reading the right chart. I had cancer.

Tish was in the middle of a life-threatening problem. She called home and spoke to Diana and simply stated, "The doctor called, and the results are back, and I have cancer." Stunned, Diana told her to come over immediately. She then called me into our home office where she was looking for details on the Internet about the dreaded enemy that had suddenly invaded our family. She looked at me with tears in her eyes and said, "Tish just called, and her doctor said she has cancer. It is a sarcoma, and I am trying to find it on the Internet to see what we're up against."

Tish had never had surgery before, and her first trip to the outpatient clinic determined that she had cancer. What were the odds of that? The cancer she had been diagnosed with affects one in every four million sarcoma patients. It is so rare that very little research is done on this specific type of cancer. It does not respond to conventional treatments like chemotherapy and usually has to be cut out after lengthy radiation treatments. There are few survivors.

Reality was stabbing my daughter and the rest of the family like a knife in the chest. There was no escaping the new turn our lives were taking after just one phone call. Suddenly and without warning, she was up close and personal with death. Nothing would ever be the same.

I was numb. Cancer? This is my daughter. It can't be true. I am the pastor of thousands. This is usually a phone call I receive about some other family, not my own! Diana and I stared in silence at the screen trying to wade through words like "amputation," "no response to conventional treatment," "lethal," and "nine months to five-year survival rate." It was enough! I told Diana to press the "delete" button on the computer. "We are never going there again! We will not speak of death. We are choosing life!" We held each other and prayed for our daughter.

In the Hagee family, when someone has a problem, we "circle the wagons." We surround the one in the problem with prayer and offer every means of physical, emotional, and spiritual support possible until their problem is resolved. In 2 Corinthians 10:3–4 it says, "For though we walk in the flesh, we do not war according to the flesh. For the weapons of our warfare are not carnal but mighty in God for pulling down strongholds." This battle would have to be won in the heavens.

I knew Tish was relying on her family to engulf her in prayer, and that we would do. She arrived at the house to find me standing on the front porch.

My children believe that when you hand me a million-dollar problem, I can resolve it in ten seconds with a two-million-dollar answer. It is overwhelming to think of the kind of trust and confidence they have in me. They usually hear me say something like, "The price of gas is a problem. The federal deficit is a problem. The war in Israel is a problem. What you have is not a problem. All you need to do is…" This time I had no quick answer.

Tish got out of the car and hobbled into my arms, and I tightly embraced my baby girl as she wept. The look on my face was the look of shock. Very few things take me by total surprise—this was certainly uncharted territory for me, and for the whole family. I am all about getting to the source of any problem as soon as possible, and this was no exception. We went into the house and called the doctor to hear the news firsthand and to ask many, many questions.

The podiatrist advised us once again to see a sarcoma specialist immediately. While he was talking to us on the speakerphone, I felt like we were having a conversation about a church member—someone else's mother, sister, wife, co-worker, anybody else but my daughter. The reality is that as a pastor I consistently receive calls that someone is sick or dying. No matter who it is, you never get used to the word *cancer*. You never want to hear that someone has a terminal disease. You never want to hear that someone's child is dying. Now it was my child! We heard the facts, and now we needed a plan.

Before Tish left the house that night, I announced in my familiar tone of absolute confidence, "We have to turn to the Bible. It has been a good book for us, and God will not fail us now." I said what I said in pure faith because we were faced with what seemed an insurmountable problem.

Tish later wrote in her testimony:

> And that was it. It was like a switch had turned on inside of me and my boxing gloves were on. I was down, but not out (Psalm 37:23–24). It was time to shake the dust off of my shoes and put the smile back on my face.
>
> I could no longer think of my two beautiful, blonde-haired, blue-eyed daughters wearing black dresses and waving good-bye as my coffin was lowered into the ground. I could no longer think of how my husband would be affected by losing another family member to

cancer in such a short period of time. I couldn't lament the things I hadn't done or places I hadn't visited. I had to focus 100 percent of my energy on God's Word and how much had been planted in my soul over the past thirty-seven years (Isaiah 40:8). I needed to personify the attitude of gratitude, for I had truly been given far more than I ever deserved.

I was about to watch the seeds that had been planted over almost four decades come into full bloom almost overnight. We had all been knocked down by the news, but staying down was not an option (Joshua 23:10). As the old saying goes, "Quitters never win and winners never quit."

By the time I arrived at my house, exhaustion had taken its toll. I said a very quick and simple prayer before going to bed. When I talk to God I keep it simple and I keep it real. I don't try to pretend like I'm Shakespeare or that God doesn't already know my circumstances. God knows that I am educated and I don't have to speak in Elizabethan English to prove it (Matthew 14:12–14). Matthew 7:7–8 says, "Ask, and it will be given to you; seek, and you will find; knock, and it will be opened to you. For everyone who asks receives, and he who seeks finds, and to him who knocks it will be opened." I wanted to knock very, very loudly tonight so God would know He had my full attention.

I got down on my knees, with my head and ankle throbbing, and said, "God, thank You for this opportunity. I don't know what You want me to do right now or how this will turn out, but I know that You knew the answer before I knew there was a problem. Thank You for trusting me with this cancer. Thank You for allowing me to grow in You. I know You must trust me a lot, to give me such a great assignment, so I want You to know that I am listening. I want to hear You the very first time. I don't know how long or difficult this road will be, but I ask that You give me strength for the journey. I'm not asking You to make my journey easier or the road shorter; I'm just asking for You to be with me, to guide me, and to give me Your strength because I simply cannot do this on my own. And I am begging You to please let me live, if this be Your will, because I would love to be able to spend the rest of my long life with my two precious little girls that You gave me. Please don't let them watch their Mommy die. In Jesus' name, amen."

I was so physically and emotionally exhausted that I immediately fell into a deep sleep. When I woke up, I knew that God's Word would be my seat belt for the rough road that was surely ahead of me. I knew that He would cover me with His wings and no harm would come to me as long as I looked to Him for the answer. I knew His promises of healing would not return void.

For the next several days I found myself walking around in a dense fog. People would ask me how I was doing, and I would smile and give my usual, "Fine, thanks. How are you?"

I had to keep reminding myself that I was the one who had cancer this time. It wasn't a church member or friend; it was ME. When I looked in the mirror I saw the same thirty-seven-year-old woman who had been there the day before. It's like on your birthday when people ask if you feel older; I didn't feel like I had cancer.

Life to date had been pretty great, but I had not been very grateful. Now I was the cancer girl, the one whom people didn't know what to say to when she passed by. I was *that* girl. I was the one whom everyone looked at with pity in their eyes. It was very disconcerting, as if I was having an out-of-body experience.

The following Sunday morning, my dad gathered the elders of our church in his office, and each one laid hands on me as they began to collectively pray 1 Timothy 4:14–15 over me: "Do not neglect the gift that is in you, which was given to you by prophecy with the laying on of the hands of the eldership. Meditate on these things; give yourself entirely to them, that your progress may be evident to all."

I had known these people for most of my life. As a family, we had prayed when their kids were sick or when they had been to the hospital (some with cancer), but never in my wildest dreams had I expected to be the one being prayed over because of a terminal disease. It was a tremendous honor to have these prayer warriors, these men of faith, surrounding me, and I knew we would be celebrating my healing in due time.

That morning Dad preached a sermon that he composed after learning of my diagnosis. I have heard hundreds of sermons in my life, but this particular one will always be my favorite. It was my sermon. It was about healing. *He is the Master of the impossible. He is at His best when we are at our worst. He had not been surprised by my diagnosis. He knew the beginning and the end.*

The fog started to dissipate, and I began to expect great things as we searched for further diagnosis and treatment options. We still knew very little about my disease, how much cancer was inside my body, or if I could even begin treatments. Fear is an amazing thing. It can grip you like an invisible, choking hand and suffocate you. Yet, God's promises are even more amazing. I found much comfort in Psalm 56:3–4, which says, "Whenever I am afraid, I will trust in You. In God (I will praise His word), in God I have put my trust; I will not fear. What can flesh do to me?"

Make no mistake. Satan plays mind games when doctors inform you that you have a terminal disease. Denial is not a way to defeat cancer. I wanted to acknowledge the problem and then give it to God. It was too heavy for me to carry alone, so I laid it at His feet and asked to be carried for a while, because my body and mind were both exhausted and bruised.

When I started to think about Jesus carrying me, I started to think about the cross and what it really meant to my life. I had heard this story a million times and could recite it in my sleep. But now more than ever, the story of the cross was very real and meaningful to me. Jesus could have said one word and saved Himself when faced with death. He could have said one word, and I would have no hope of surviving cancer. But He chose to die so that I would not have to. Isaiah 53:5 foretold of my redemption: "But He was wounded for our transgressions, He was bruised for our iniquities; the chastisement for our peace was upon Him, and by His stripes we are healed."

He took my cancer to the cross. He, who was without sin, took MY cancer and my shame and my sin, and died. He died in my place. He died so that I could continue to live with my girls. He died for ME. And by His stripes I was healed. I had my promise! Now I was in the problem and had to press through to the provision.

When someone says you have a terminal disease for which there is no cure and very few survivors, it gets your attention.

The more I thought about the cross, the more unworthy I felt. What had I done with my life to deserve that kind of love? What had I done to deserve that kind of mercy? Nothing, yet Jesus allowed His body to be nailed to the cross so that He could hold the keys to death, hell, and the grave. He did this for me so that when the doctor called to tell me, "You have cancer," I could quote Psalm 118:17–18, which promises: "I shall not die, but live, and declare the works of the LORD. The LORD has chastened me severely, but He has not given me over to death."

I began to rejoice by choice as my dad had instructed us through the tough times of our lives. I memorized my biblical promises and spoke them every day. E-mails started pouring in from people I didn't know in places I didn't know existed. Preachers, bishops, rabbis, military personnel, government agents, janitors, cafeteria workers, teachers, day-care workers, bankers, governors, powerful businessmen, and even children began to e-mail and send cards.

I received many flowers and gifts, and I felt like God was pouring out His overwhelming mercy and love on my life. My father's dear friend Rabbi Scheinberg called to tell me that he had been praying for me in Jerusalem at the Prayer Wall, and his congregation was praying for me daily at his synagogue in San Antonio. He said, "We are praying for you in stereo."

What Satan had meant for evil, God was using for my good. As the news began to spread and people continued to call from all over the world, I began to feel God's total peace wrap around me like a warm blanket. I had done nothing to deserve this measure of grace and was only beginning to understand the depth of God's love for me.

God's mercy was raining down on me like a refreshing spring shower. The name of my cancer was leiomyosarcoma, but I knew the name that was above all other names, and it was His name that would be my salvation.

Psalm 61 was the Scripture God gave me, and Psalm 91 was the passage my dad's mom, Grandma Hagee, had read when she over-came cancer. I read both psalms every day. I memorized them for days until my head throbbed and my eyes burned. Psalm 61 begins: "Hear my cry, O God; attend to my prayer. From the end of the earth I will cry to You, when my heart is overwhelmed; lead me to the rock that is higher than I" (vv. 1–2).

God heard my cry, and soon I was on a miracle journey toward my provision. Through research from a family friend, it was determined that one of the foremost sarcoma specialists in the country practiced at M. D. Anderson. My father made a phone call on my behalf, and I was on my way to Houston, just seven days after my diagnosis.

As Diana and I were driving to Houston for the very first time, she was conducting business on the phone as usual and I was leisurely flipping through the pages of the latest gossip magazine. I was lost in my magazine when Diana hung up her phone and looked directly at me and said, "I want you to please forgive me for anything that I have ever done to offend you. At a time like this you need to get everything in your life in order and make sure you have forgiven everyone for whatever they may have done to you." Getting things right with God and man was an easy task at this point.

In short order, we arrived at the hotel. I fell into deep slumber the second my head met the oversized down pillow, but not for long. For the first time since I heard the word *leiomyosarcoma*, fear gripped me like a wounded animal shredding its prey. I was being hunted, and Satan was doing his best to destroy me. I woke up in a cold sweat with the deafening sound of my own heartbeat ringing loudly in my ears. I felt powerless against the raging sea of fear inside me. Very few things in life had ever scared me, but I was now meeting a new enemy I had not truly been confronted by before…raw and relentless fear.

The surgical bandages on my foot and leg were wrapped so tightly they felt as if my circulation was being cut off and at any point my bandages would explode in all directions much like the Incredible Hulk's t-shirt when he gets angry. As I reached down to rip the bandage from my foot I very clearly heard God tell me, "Don't touch a thing. I am healing you from the top of your head to the soles of your feet."

A few hours later I awoke with a smile on my face and a sense of renewed purpose. My focus was back on the Word of God, exactly where it needed to be. "This is the day the Lord has made and I will rejoice and be glad in it" (Psalm 118:24).

When Diana woke up I told her with absolute certainty and a smile on my face, "This is going to be a good day." Before we left for M. D. Anderson to meet with the doctors for the very first time, we read Psalm 61 and Psalm 91. Diana prayed for God's favor, that the doctors would relay any news in a positive way, no matter how grave the reality. God had promised me He was healing me from the top of my head to the tips of my toes, so Diana prayed that God would assign the Generals here on earth to help form an army to defeat this disease encapsulated within my body.

My mind is a very colorful place, and I had envisioned a hospital something like the one my girls were born in. I never imagined anything of this magnitude. It took my breath away as we began to drive up the long street that houses the many buildings encompassed by M. D. Anderson. It was a medical metropolis like nothing I had seen before.

Nothing in my life had ever prepared me for the gut-wrenching reality I was now facing as I sat in the sarcoma wing. I started to take a closer look at my surroundings and found huge pictures of people all over the walls. Who were these people? I had plenty of time on my hands before they would inevitably call my name, so I started wandering the halls, looking at these pictures.

Each picture was dedicated to a survivor. The picture showed the survivor, usually enjoying their favorite hobby wearing an enormous smile from ear to ear, with a caption underneath telling about the type of cancer they survived and how their positive attitude helped them stay alive. Between the picture and the description was the type of cancer they had with a huge red line through it. They had won! They had defeated the cancer and wanted to tell others their story.

My name was called, and I was finally entering the exam room and asked to tell about my short cancer history. Finally my oncologist entered the room and my expectations went through the roof. I was finally going to get some long-awaited answers from an actual, bona fide sarcoma doctor.

My diagnosis was uneventful, and boring at best. It was not going to be the next Sunday night movie on prime-time television. I wanted some clear answers from someone who treated sarcoma and didn't get their medical knowledge from prime-time television. My dream was about to come true.

In one of the greatest art masterpieces I have ever seen, my oncologist began to sketch the details of my case on the crisp white paper lining covering the exam table. "There are three things that we look for when evaluating cancer. First we look for depth. The depth of your tumor was not deep by our standards. The fact that you could see it with your naked eye tells us that it was superficial by our standards. It is rare to have this type of cancer in the extremities and even more rare to be able to see it so clearly with the naked eye.

"The second thing we look for is size. The size of your tumor is three centimeters. If it was five centimeters or more, we would have to start chemotherapy immediately." I looked at my doctor and said, "Yeah me!" He said, "Yes, that's great. And you even get to keep your hair." We both laughed.

"The third thing we look for is the grade. On a scale of 1 to 4, yours is a 4, meaning it is the most aggressive, most likely to recur and most likely to move to another part of the body. But you have two of the three things going for you." I laughed when I told him that rare and aggressive were both character traits I understood very well.

I was so relieved to know what I was up against. I was grinning from ear to ear, knowing that even in the worst of circumstances God had stood by me.

Tish had five weeks of radiation on her ankle. She completed her treatments with a great attitude and without any side effects. After a two-month rest from treatment, she endured an eleven-and-a-half-hour surgery. The surgery included removing the rest of the tissue from the tumor bed, transplanting muscle and tissue from her inner right thigh into the ankle, and grafting skin from her outer right thigh onto the surface of the ankle.

Every subsequent test for the last two years has confirmed that my daughter is cancer free! Healed! Tish was in a problem bigger than most could handle. She went to the Promise Book—the Word of God. There was nowhere else to go. From that fountain drawn from Emmanuel's veins, Tish received hope, she built up her faith by proclaiming its promises, she gained courage, and, most importantly, she received her miracle healing.

If you ask Tish how she feels, she will tell you, "I feel like celebrating, because God used me as a testimony of His amazing grace and perfect love. I celebrate because I am still here and I still have my leg. I celebrate my new and improved life, for I am blessed and highly favored. I celebrate for I have been promised a long and satisfied life. I celebrate because my daughters will watch me grow old in good health. My story is simple. I claimed the promise, sailed through the problem, and received the miracle provision. Our God is an awesome God!"

THE MIRACLE PROVISION IS FAVOR
Favor is the unmerited grace of God.

> Now therefore, listen to me, my children, for blessed are those who keep my ways. Hear instruction and be wise, do not disdain it. Blessed is the man who listens to me, watching daily at my gates, waiting at the posts of my doors. For whoever finds me finds life, and obtains favor from the LORD.
> —PROVERBS 8:32–35

If you have received Christ, then you have received everlasting life and therefore have inherited God's favor.

No matter what the problem, the promise of favor brings the provision. Psalm 106:4–5 declares that you are to "rejoice in the glory of your inheritance."

The following proclamation is taken from God's Word. It is filled with promises for His children. They are real. They are for you. They are for today. They will take you through the problem and into your miraculous provision. Declare them, believe them, and watch the fulfillment of them in your life!

PROCLAMATION OF THE
MIRACLE PROVISION: FAVOR

In the name of Jesus, I am the righteousness of God; therefore, I am entitled to covenant kindness and favor. The favor of God is among the righteous. His favor surrounds the righteous; therefore, it surrounds me. I expect the favor of God to be in manifestation everywhere I go and in everything I do. Never again will I be without the favor of God. Satan, my days in Lodebar cease today. I am leaving that place of lack and want. I am going from the pit to the palace because the favor of God rests richly on me and profusely abounds in me. I am part of the generation that will experience the immeasurable, limitless, and unsurpassed favor of God. This will produce in my life supernatural increase, promotion, prominence, preferential treatment, restoration, honor, increased assets, great victories, recognition, petitions granted, policies and rules changed on my behalf, and battles won that I don't have to fight. The favor of God is upon me; it goes before me, and, therefore, my life will never be the same.

(For additional scriptures, see 1 Corinthians 1:30; Acts 3:25; Psalms 5:12; 44:3; 84:11–12; 97:11; 112:1–4; 1 Timothy 1:14; Colossians 2:15; John 10:10; Deuteronomy 28:1–13; 33:23; Genesis 39:21; Exodus 2:17; 3:21; 5:8; 8:5, 8; 11:3; 2 Chronicles 20:15; 29; 1 Samuel 16:22.)[3]

Conclusion

DIAMONDS IN THE DUST

Let's examine the diamonds (promises) in the dust (problems) we have discovered in the pages of *Life's Challenges—Your Opportunities*.

1. Everything God offers man on Earth comes to him in the form of a promise. There are more than three thousand sacred promises that open the golden gates of the treasury of heaven for you and those you love. As you walk through these gates, you will be blessed exceedingly and abundantly above and beyond anything that you can ask or imagine.

REMEMBER THIS TRUTH...
The provision is in the promise.

2. After you receive a promise, a loving God takes you into a tailor-made problem, revealing to you the spiritual, emotional, moral, and financial imperfections in your life. Problems will make you neither *weak* nor *strong*, but they will reveal what you are. The prophet Isaiah wrote, "And though the Lord gives you the bread of adversity and the water of affliction..." The brightest crowns that are worn in heaven have been tried, smelted, polished, and glorified through the furnace of a great problem.

    Gold is tried in fire, and God's children are purified in the furnace of adversity.

231

REMEMBER THIS TRUTH...

A man on his knees can see more and farther into the future than a man on a mountaintop. Problems force us to pray with an intensity that causes God to incline His ear toward our cry.

3. How you conduct yourself in the problem will determine how long you stay in the problem. It took God one day to get the children of Israel out of Egypt; it took Him forty years to get Egypt out of them.

   Murmuring, complaining, rebelling against spiritual authority, refusing to forgive another, and disobedience to the known will of God can keep you in the problem for the rest of your life. Stop it!

   In an act of spiritual discipline, raise your hands in the darkest night of your life and praise God in heaven for the victory that you can only see through the eyes of faith. Then and only then will you will see the miracle of God's provision.

REMEMBER THIS TRUTH...

The person who accepts responsibility for his or her problem is the person who will overcome it.

4. The greater the promise, the greater the problem. If God gives you a million-dollar promise, you can count on a million-dollar problem. Moses spent forty years on the backside of the wilderness in God's boot camp for leaders before God sent him to challenge Pharaoh. The wilderness comes before the rod turning to a serpent, before the water being turned to blood, before cobra fights before royalty, and before Israel's enemies being drowned in the Red Sea.

REMEMBER THIS TRUTH...

Trial comes before triumph. The cross comes before the crown. Darkness comes before the dawning. Promises come before problems, and problems come before provision.

5. You can conquer the problem through divine discipline or temperance. Discipline is not punishment. Discipline proves you are a member of the family of God. Anyone who rejects the discipline of God is considered *illegitimate* by God Himself (Heb. 12:8–9).

    Jesus was the Son of God, but did nothing He was not instructed to do by His Father in heaven. Jesus suffered in God's boot camp: "Though He was a Son, yet He learned obedience by the things which He suffered" (Heb. 5:8).

REMEMBER THIS TRUTH...

Your success in life is ultimately measured by the problems you create or the problems you solve.

6. Experts have calculated that the Israelites could have walked across the wilderness in ninety days—*but it took forty years.* Why? Because the children of Israel made careers of their problems. Are you?

    Jesus went through His time in the wilderness where He was tempted of the devil in forty days. Why? Because He went straight through the problem, using the Word of God as His compass. Determine to be a problem solver—go straight through your problem to God's glorious provision for your life.

REMEMBER THIS TRUTH...

The quickest way out of the problem is straight through.

7. God has signposts to guide you through the problem to
your promised land. These signposts are to be honored and
obeyed. Remove them, ignore them, or try to take short
cuts, and you will die in your problem.

REMEMBER THIS TRUTH...

*God has given us a Road Map: His Word. Within
this supernatural Guide are many "signposts" out
of our wilderness. Among them are faith, diligence,
excellence, knowledge, patience, and integrity.*

8. Your vision determines your provision. *Jehovah Jireh* means
literally "God sees!" The theological implication is that if
God sees your need, He will meet your need.

God has given to you the ability via the Word of God
to establish a specific vision for your life, your marriage,
your family, your business, your ministry, and your financial success. Your vision is focused by the Word of God on
a daily basis. Keep your eyes on the prize, go for the gold,
and confess daily that it's now your time to stand in the
winner's circle!

REMEMBER THIS TRUTH...

A good attitude is more important than good aptitude.

9. We all have a divine destiny. We must choose to become
all that God has purposed us to become. True Christianity
requires action.

REMEMBER THIS TRUTH...

Your future is just as bright as the promises of God.

10. Reach for the grand prize—the favor of God. It's better than riches. It's better than apples of gold in pitchers of silver. It's better than bushels of priceless diamonds and goblets of precious rubies. The favor of God is the golden key to the gates of heaven. It is given only to the obedient, to the disciplined, and to those who endure their problem to reach the promised land. The favor of God is the Miracle Provision.

Now therefore, listen to me, my children, for blessed are those who keep my ways. Hear instruction and be wise, and do not disdain it. Blessed is the man who listens to me, watching daily at my gates, waiting at the posts of my doors. For whoever finds me finds life, and obtains favor from the LORD.

—PROVERBS 8:32–35

Notes

CHAPTER 1
WHY DO I HAVE ALL THESE PROBLEMS?

1. Jack Hayford, general editor, *Spirit-Filled Life Bible* (Nashville: Thomas Nelson, 1991), 105.

2. Rebbetzin Esther Jungreis, *Life Is a Test* (New York: Shaar Press, 2006), 65.

3. As quoted in Richard Farson and Ralph Keyes, *Whoever Makes the Most Mistakes Wins* (n.p.: Free Press, 2002), 32.

4. Alistair Begg, "Morning and Evening," *Truth for Life* daily broadcast, March 4, 2008.

5. As quoted in *The Impossible Takes Longer*, David Pratt, compiler (New York: Walker and Company, 2007), 169.

6. Ibid., 61.

7. James S. Hewett, ed., *Illustrations Unlimited* (Wheaton, IL: Tyndale House, 1988), 272.

8. Ibid., 19–20.

CHAPTER 2
EVERY PROBLEM HAS A PURPOSE

1. As quoted in Cliff Carlson, "Summary Notes: *Knocking on Heaven's Gates: Discovering the Appointed Time of Prayer,*" http://www.yourlivingwaters.com/pdf_files/knocking_on_heavens_gates_notes.pdf (accessed November 5, 2008).

2. "Truth-in-Action Through Esther," *Spirit-Filled Life Bible*, 706.

3. Hewett, *Illustrations Unlimited*, 272.

4. Rabbi Moshe of Sambur, *A Chassidic Master*, quoted in Rabbi Abraham J. Twerski, *Twerski on Prayer* (n.p.: Shaar Press, 2004).

5. Jungreis, *Life Is a Test*.

6. Ibid., 93.

7. Hewett, *Illustrations Unlimited*, 17–18.

CHAPTER 3
EVERY PROBLEM HAS A PROMISE

1. Clovis G. Chappell, *Questions Jesus Asked* (Nashville: Abingdon, 1948).

2. Hewett, *Illustrations Unlimited*.

3. This paragraph has been adapted from "The Promises of God," a sermon preached on Friday evening, May 17, 1850, by Reverend C. G. Finney at the Tabernacle Moorfields.

4. Hewett, *Illustrations Unlimited*, 189.

5. Derek Prince, *The Power of Proclamation* (London: DPM-UK, n.d.), 6.

6. M. G. Plantz, "The Soul's Sincere Desire," as quoted in Hewett, *Illustrations Unlimited*, 417.

7. The following section is adapted from Derek Prince, "Appropriating All of God's Promises," *Foundational Truths for Christian Living* (Lake Mary, IL: Charisma House, 1993, 2006), 100–102.

8. End of adapted section.

9. Prince, *The Power of Proclamation*, 111.

CHAPTER 4
DON'T GET TRAPPED IN THE PROBLEM

1. Glenn Van Ekeren, *Speaker's Sourcebook II* (New York: Prentice Hall Press, 2002), 148.

2. Ibid.

3. Ibid.

4. Eric Fromm, *Escape From Freedom* (New York: Holt Paperbacks, 1994).

5. Charles M. Schultz, *The Complete Peanuts, 1963–1964* (n.p.: Fantagraphics Books, 2007), 25.

6. Van Ekeren, *Speaker's Sourcebook II*, 303.

7. NotableQuotes.com, "Helen Keller Quotes," http://www.notable-quotes.com/k/keller_helen.html (accessed November 4, 2008).

8. M. Scott Peck, MD, *The Road Less Traveled* (New York: Simon & Schuster, 1978).

9. Information from Paul K. Conkin, MA, PhD, professor of history, Vanderbilt University, and author of *Puritans and Pragmatists, Eight Eminent American Thinkers*, and *The Southern Agrarians*.

10. This quote is widely attributed to Alexander Fraser Tytler, Lord Woodhouselee, but is unverified. See Suzy Platt, *Respectfully Quoted* (n.p.: Barnes & Noble Publishing, 1993), 84, http://books.google.com/books?hl=en&id=2Tu3bScwKKAC&dq=library+of+congress+respectfully+quoted&printsec=frontcover&source=web&ots=xtNXyFMX-p&sig=M9MutcGgPmQtrO6AHHVgF-uk9Dw&sa=X&oi=book_result&resnum=1&ct=result#PPT109,M1 (accessed August 20, 2008).

11. The impact of increasing the lenience and generosity of welfare in undermining work and prolonging dependence has been confirmed by controlled scientific experiment. During the late 1960s and early 1970s, social scientists at the Office of Economic Opportunity (OEO) conducted a series of controlled experiments to examine the effect of welfare benefits on work effort. The longest running and most comprehensive of these experiments was conducted between 1971 and 1978 in Seattle and Denver and became known as the Seattle/Denver Income Maintenance Experiment, or "SIME/DIME." Advocates of expanding welfare had hoped that SIME/DIME and similar experiments conducted in other cities would prove that generous welfare benefits did not affect "work effort" adversely. Instead, the SIME/DIME experiment found that each $1.00 of extra welfare given to low-income persons reduced labor and earnings by an average of $0.80. The significant anti-work effects of welfare benefits were shown in all social groups, including married women, single mothers, and husbands. The results of the SIME/DIME study are directly applicable to existing welfare programs: Nearly all have strong anti-work effects like those studied in the SIME/DIME experiment. See: Gregory B. Christiansen and Walter E. Williams, "Welfare Family Cohesiveness and Out of Wedlock Births," in Joseph Peden and Fred Glahe, *The American Family and the State* (San Francisco: Pacific Institute for Public Policy Research, 1986), 398.

12. Taken from Van Ekeren, *Speaker's Sourcebook II*, 392–394.

13. Ibid.

14. Ibid.

15. Ibid.

16. Ibid., 354.

17. John Cook, ed., *The Book of Positive Quotations* (New York: Gramercy, 1999), 561.

18. M. Scott Peck, MD, *People of the Lie* (New York: Touchstone, 1998), 75.

19. Charles R. Swindoll, *Improving Your Serve* (Nashville: Thomas Nelson, 2002), 45.

20. Adapted from Hewett, *Illustrations Unlimited*, 221.

21. ThinkExist.com, "Mark Twain Quotes," http://en.thinkexist.com/quotation/forgiveness_is_the_fragrance_that_the_violet/215234.html (accessed September 2, 2008).

22. *Homiletics*, January 2005, as quoted in Lectionary.org, "The Short List," http://www.lectionary.org/Sermons/Stray/OT/Micah%2006.01-08,%20ShortList.htm (accessed September 2, 2008).

23. ThinkExist.com, "Dr. Joyce Brothers' Quotes," http://en.thinkexist.com/quotation/an_ individual-s_self-concept_is_the_core_of_his/147493.html (accessed August 20, 2008).

24. Ray Burwick, *Self-Esteem: You're Better Than You Think* (Wheaton, IL: Tyndale House, 1993).

Chapter 5
How to Solve the Problem

1. As quoted in Donald DeMarco, *The Heart of Virtue* (San Francisco: Ignatius Press, 1996), 217.

2. "O to Be Like Thee" by Thomas O. Chisholm. Public domain.

3. Friedrich Nietzsche et al., *Human, All Too Human: A Book for Free Spirits* (New York: Cambridge University Press, 1996).

4. Respect for Life, "Respect Life Quotes," http://www.respectforlife.ca/resources/quotes.html (accessed November 5, 2008).

5. Associated Press, "Gov. Lamm Asserts Elderly, If Very Ill, Have 'Duty to Die,'" *New York Times*, March 29, 1984, http://query.nytimes.com/gst/fullpage.html?res=9E01E5D91E39F93A A15750C0A962948260&sec=health&spon=&pagewanted=1 (accessed August 20, 2008).

Chapter 6
The Quickest Way Through the Problem Is Straight Through

1. Hewett, *Illustrations Unlimited*, 417.

2. Steve Deger and Leslie Ann Gibson, eds., *The Book of Positive Quotations*, John Cook, compiler (Minneapolis, MN: Fairview Press, 2007), 180.

3. Ibid., 180.

4. Ibid., 177.

5. Ibid.

6. Adapted from quote by Maltbie D. Babcock, in Deger and Gibson, *The Book of Positive Quotations*, 67.

7. Deger and Gibson, *The Book of Positive Quotations*, 68.

8. Ibid., 69.

9. Ibid.

10. Derek Prince, *Thanksgiving, Praise and Worship* (Charlotte, NC: Derek Prince Ministries, 1996), 30.

11. John Bunyan, *Pilgrim's Progress*, Christian Classics Ethereal Library, http://www.ccel.org/ccel/bunyan/pilgrim.v.vii.html (accessed September 3, 2008).

12. Neil Cooper, "Interesting Facts About Israel, the 100th Smallest Country," *The Israel Report*, September 12, 2005, http://theisraelreport.com/commentary2005_interestingfacts.html (accessed September 3, 2008).

13. Ibid.

14. Ibid.

15. NewsoftheDay.com, "Facts About the 100th Smallest Country, With Less Than 1/1000th of the World's Population," Good News From Israel! http://www.newsoftheday.com/israel/old/2004_09_01_index.html (accessed September 3, 2008).

16. Vivienne Walt, "Unfriendly Skies No Match for El Al," *USA Today*, October 1, 2001, http://www.usatoday.com/news/sept11/2001/10/01/elal-usat.htm#more (accessed September 3, 2008).

17. DailyToursIsrael.com, "Israel: Diverse, Creative, and Free," http://dailytoursisrael.com/tag/tours-israel/ (accessed September 3, 2008).

18. Ibid.

240 LIFE'S CHALLENGES—YOUR OPPORTUNITIES

19. Mary Vanac, "Israeli Transplant MDG Medical Raises $14 Million," *The Plain Dealer*, February 28, 2008, http://blog.cleveland.com/medical/2008/02/israelicleveland_transplant_ md.html (accessed September 4, 2008).

20. Avi Machlis, "Camera-in-a-Pill Now Before Health Care Community," Israel21c.org, March 11, 2002, http://www.israel21c.org/bin/en.jsp?enPage=BlankPage&enDisplay=view &enDispWhat=object&enDispWho=Articles^l99&enZone=health (accessed September 4, 2008).

21. Neal Sandler, "High Tech Puts Israel in the Black," *BusinessWeek*, May 13, 2008, http:// www.businessweek.com/globalbiz/content/may2008/gb20080513_652625 .htm?chan=globalbiz_europe+index+page_top+stories (accessed September 4, 2008).

22. Jon Fedler, "Israel's Agriculture in the 21st Century," December 24, 2002, Israel Ministry of Foreign Affairs, http://www.israel-mfa.gov.il/MFA/Facts%20About%20Israel/ Economy/Focus%20on%20Israel-%20Israel-s%20Agriculture%20in%20the%2021st (accessed September 4, 2008).

23. Cooper, "Interesting Facts About Israel, the 100th Smallest Country."
24. Ibid.
25. Lionpac, "Fun Facts About Israel," http://sky.prohosting.com/lionpac/funfacts.shtml (accessed September 4, 2008).
26. Ibid.
27. Ibid.
28. Ibid.
29. Ibid.

30. Israel21c News Service, "Israeli Solar Energy Innovator Sees Multiple Ways to Serve U.S. Consumers," June 30, 2002, http://www.israel21c.org/bin/en.jsp?enPage=BlankPage& enDisplay=view&enDispWhat=object&enDispWho=Articles^l138&enZone=technology (accessed September 4, 2008).

31. Bob Blythe, "Haym Salomon," The American Revolution: Lighting Freedom's Flame, http://www.nps.gov/revwar/about_the_revolution/haym_salomom.html (accessed July 2, 2007).

32. Albert M. Wells, compiler, *Inspiring Quotations* (Nashville, TN: Thomas Nelson, 1988), 143.

33. "Turn Your Eyes Upon Jesus" by Helen H. Lemmel. Public domain.

34. National Association of Educators, "Comprehensive Biography of Theodor Seuss Geisel," http://www.nea.org/readacross/resources/seussbiocomp.html (accessed September 4, 2008).

35. Don Pierson, "Ask the NFL Expert: Age Matters, Especially With Head Coaches," NBC Sports, May 23, 2007, http://www.msnbc.msn.com/id/18820990/displaymode/1098/ (accessed September 4, 2008).

36. Coca-Cola Company, "The Chronicle of Coca-Cola: Birth of a Refreshing Idea," http:// www.thecoca-colacompany.com/heritage/chronicle_birth_refreshing_idea.html (accessed September 4, 2008).

37. Steve Strauss, "Ask an Expert: An End, Then a Beginning," USAToday.com, May 16, 2005, http://www.usatoday.com/money/smallbusiness/columnist/strauss/2005-05-16-end -beginning_x.htm (accessed September 4, 2008).

38. Jamie Sue Austin, "Michelangelo, Leonardo, and Raphael: The Premier Artists of the Italian High Renaissance," LifeinItaly.com, http://www.lifeinitaly.com/art/renaissance.asp (accessed September 4, 2008).

39. Christopher Lawlor, "Q&A: Michael Jordan on High School and the Jordan Classic," USAToday.com, April 14, 2005, http://www.usatoday.com/sports/basketball/draft/2005-04 -14-jordan-qa_x.htm (accessed September 4, 2008).

40. Hewett, *Illustrations Unlimited*, 155.

41. Edward Wagenknecht, *American Profile: 1900–1909* (Amherst, MA: University of Massachusetts Press, 1982), 217.

42. Essortment.com, "Frank W. Woolworth, Pioneer of the Five and Dime Stores," http://www.essortment.com/all/woolworthfw_ramc.htm (accessed September 4, 2008).

43. Jack Canfield and Mark Victor Hansen, *Chicken Soup for the Soul: Living Your Dreams*, 10th anniversary edition (Deerfield Beach, FL: HCI Books, 2003), 322.

44. Norman Vincent Peale, *You Can If You Think You Can* (New York: Simon and Schuster, 1987), 117.

45. BrainyQuote.com, "Harriet Beecher Stowe Quotes," http://www.brainyquote.com/quotes/authors/h/harriet_beecher_stowe.html (accessed August 21, 2008).

CHAPTER 7
SIGNPOSTS TO THE PROMISED LAND

1. Microsoft Encarta Online Encyclopedia, "D-Day Invasion," http://encarta.msn.com/encyclopedia_701702421/D-Day.html (accessed September 5, 2008).

2. Ibid.

3. Jena Pincott, ed., *Success* (New York: Random House, 2005), 205–212.

4. Deger and Gibson, *The Book of Positive Quotations*, 161.

5. Van Ekeren, *Speaker's Sourcebook II*, 326.

6. DivineViewpoint.com, "Words of Wisdom by Theodore Roosevelt," http://www.divineviewpoint.com/TR_words_of_wisdom.htm (accessed August 22, 2008).

7. Van Ekeren, *Speaker's Sourcebook II*, 139–140.

8. J. Vernon McGee, *Thru the Bible*, volume 5 (Nashville: Thomas Nelson, 1990), 722.

9. Ibid.

10. Hayford, *The Spirit-Filled Life Bible*, 1736.

11. The Churchill Centre, "Churchill Facts," http://www.winstonchurchill.org/i4a/pages/index.cfm?pageid=435 (accessed August 22, 2008).

12. John Bartlett, *Familiar Quotations*, 10th edition, 1919, viewed at Bartleby.com, http://www.bartleby.com/100/498.3.html (accessed November 6, 2008).

CHAPTER 8
YOUR VISION DETERMINES YOUR PROVISION

1. Van Ekeren, *Speaker's Sourcebook II*, 60.

2. Ibid., 47–48.

3. The Quotations Page, "William James (1842–1910)," http://www.quotationspage.com/quotes/William_James/ (accessed November 7, 2008).

4. James Allen, *As a Man Thinketh* (n.p.: Kessinger Publishing, 2004), 52.

5. Van Ekeren, *Speaker's Sourcebook II*, 45.

6. Ibid., 47.

7. Ibid.

8. David Schwartz, *The Magic of Thinking Big* (n.p.: Fireside, 1987), 133.

9. Hewett, *Illustrations Unlimited*, 41.

10. J. Sidlow Baxter, *Awake, My Heart* (n.p.: Kregel Classics, 1994).

11. Van Ekeren, *Speaker's Sourcebook II*, 48.

CHAPTER 9
BECOMING THE YOU GOD SEES

1. Van Ekeren, *Speaker's Sourcebook II*, 58.

2. McGee, *Thru the Bible*, 722.

3. Viktor E. Frankl, *Man's Search for Meaning* (Boston, MA: Beacon Press, 2006).

4. Adapted from Van Ekeren, *Speaker's Sourcebook II*, 59.

5. Deger and Gibson, *The Book of Positive Quotations*, 349.

6. Van Ekeren, *Speaker's Sourcebook II*, 157.

7. Jason Zasky, "Rubber Stamp: How Charles Goodyear Became the First Name in Rubber," FailureMag.com, http://www.failuremag.com/arch_history_charles_goodyear.html (accessed September 11, 2008).

8. National Parks Service, "Booker T. Washington National Monument Home Page," http://www.nps.gov/archive/bowa/home.htm (accessed September 11, 2008).

9. Bill Cosby, *Love and Marriage* (New York: Bantam Books, 1990), 205.

10. Van Ekeren, *Speaker's Sourcebook II*, 249.

CHAPTER 10
THE MIRACLE PROVISION

1. John Hagee, *Man of God 18 Days of Promise—Proclamations Releasing the Power of God's Word* (n.p.: n.d.), 51–52.

2. Prince, *The Power of Proclamation*.

3. Hagee, *Man of God 18 Days of Promise—Proclamations Releasing the Power of God's Word*, 51–51.

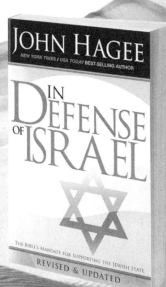